MW01038681

An Outline Study of Romans

by Dr. Wesley L. Gerig

1

Table of Contents

Foreword

Someone has observed that there are three stages of Bible study that many students of the Bible pass through. The first is the "cod-liver" oil stage where they treat the study of the Bible like taking medicine. Although it tastes terrible, they swallow it anyway because they know it is good for them. The second phase has been called the "shredded-wheat biscuit" stage, dry but nourishing. And the third is the "peaches-and-cream" category, where reading and studying the Bible is eagerly anticipated and sincerely enjoyed.

To be honest with you, I cannot remember having gone through stages one and two at any time in my Christian life. Actually, as far back as I can remember, the study of the Bible for me has been "peaches and cream." As a result, for many years my aim has been to whet the spiritual appetites of college students, Sunday School classes and entire congregations for intensive study of God's Word and for the practical application of its truths to their personal living. To this point in my ministry, I have attempted to do this mostly by word of mouth rather than by the printed page. However, former students of mine have often asked me when I planned to put some of my biblical exegetical notes into print. For that reason I have decided to prepare for publication my outline study of Paul's epistle to the Romans. It is my hope that this will bring to light for them some scriptural truths that they may have overlooked in their previous study or may have forgotten from their earlier exegetical work in the letter to the Romans.

Of all the 66 books in our Bible, Romans is probably one of the most important to master. It presents systematically and completely God's program of justification by faith, proceeding all the way from why we need it to how, via sanctification, it should affect practically our living in various areas. In addition, Paul in Romans deals with most of the major expressions related in one way or another to the Christian faith. Note the following as they appear in Romans:

Sin	3:9; 4:7, 8; 5:12; 6:1ff.; 8:3; 14:23 and many other references
Condemnation	5:16, 18; 8:2
Works	2:6; 3:20, 27, 28
Repentance	2:4
Salvation	1:16; 10:19; 11:11; 13:11
Justification	4:25; 5:18
Faith	1:17; 3:22, 25, 27, 28; 16:26 and many other references
Redemption	3:24; 8:23
Propitiation	3:25
Sanctification	15:16 (a verb)
Obedience	1:5; 16:26
Glorification	8:17 (a verb)

The content of my exegetical work in this volume is not a verse-by-verse commentary of Romans but an outline study of the book, attempting to uncover for the reader Paul's methodical and progressive treatment of the doctrine of justification by faith. The epistle can be divided into the following major sections.

I.   SALUTATION: (1:1-7) in which Paul introduces himself, his gospel, the Christ of his gospel, his addressees (the Roman Christians); and his desires for his readers (grace and peace);

II. INFORMATION: (1:8-15) in which Paul praises their faith, mentions his unceasing prayers for them, and states his six purposes in desiring to visit them;

III. SUMMARIZATION: (1:16, 17) in which he describes the gospel he has been preaching and will bring with him when he comes to Rome, a gospel based on faith; (This is the summary of the epistle and should keep the reader reading through the next section in which Paul plans to condemn all on the basis of their own personal works.)

IV. CONDEMNATION: (1:18-3:20) in which Paul aims to get everyone under God's condemnation and wrath who are depending on their own works for their justification; (It is interesting and purposeful that the word "faith" does not occur but once in this section (3:3) and there it does not mean "faith" or trust but "faithfulness.")

V.   JUSTIFICATION: (3:21-5:11) in which Paul presents an available justification which God has provided for all on the basis of faith or believing; (In this section he describes justification by faith, illustrates it from the Old Testament, and then states the blessings from it for those who receive it.)

VI. IMPUTATION: (5:12-21) in which Paul speaks about the imputation of Adam's sin to the accounts of all people in Adam and the removal of that sin from the accounts of all believers in Christ; (What he means is that we become Christians in the same way we become sinners in the first place, by imputation. The imputed sin of Adam is removed from the believer's record and the righteousness of Christ is reckoned to his account.)

VII. SANCTIFICATION: (chapters 6-8) in which Paul deals with the absurdity of continuing on in sin that grace may become greater, once we have been justified or declared righteous by faith. Since we have died with Christ to sinning of all kinds we ought to be living for righteousness and holy living;

VIII.   RENUNCIATION BUT SALVATION: (chapters 9-11) in which Paul deals parenthetically with physical Israel's relation to justification by faith, including a strong emphasis on God's sovereignty, on Israel's free will and her rejection of justification by faith, and then Israel's resultant salvation by faith at the return of Christ, her Messiah;

IX.   CONVERSATION (conduct): (12:1-15:5) in which Paul presents how the Christian who is totally presented to God for His use will live in various relationships;

X.   TERMINATION: (15:6-16:27) in which Paul deals with terminal matters: his past service, his future plans, his request for their prayers, his greetings to people in Rome, and his closing commands and benedictions (5 of them).

Along with my comments on the text of Romans, I have included my personal translation of the epistle. My personal addition to the modem translations which have been produced is an attempt to indicate in English for the non-Greek reader the tenses of the Greek verbs used throughout the epistle. These are particularly important since the present subjunctives, imperatives and infinitives generally emphasize action that is continuous or repetitive, while the aorist of the same verbal moods refers to actions without any emphasis on continuousness or repetition. To summarize, often the present tense is progressive in its context while the aorist tense indicates punctiliar or point activity.

At the close of this volume, I have also included a series of factual and discussion projects based on the text. I have found that my most helpful Bible study regularly has been done with pencil and paper in hand. As I look for things to record, I find my mind wandering less and my notes becoming valuable assets for future study and meditation.

Introduction to the Epistle to the Romans

I. The City of Rome at the time of the writing of this epistle
   A. The Political Scene
   1. The emperor at the time: Nero (A.D. 54-68)
   2. Nero's advisors early in his reign:
      a. Burrhus, the head of the Praetorian Guard, the emperor's personal bodyguard
      b. Seneca, a very respected Stoic philosopher
      c. Agrippina (the younger), Nero's mother, who was a wicked woman who had designs to secure his power (Nero finally succeeded in having her killed).
   3. Nero's career: He became unpopular because of the following:
      a. The fear which everyone had of him, including his family, the senators and their families (Many of these he had slain.)
      b. The fire in A.D. 64 in which 10 wards of 14 in the city burned to the ground (Nero blamed the Christians for this; and it may have been as a result of this that Peter and Paul later lost their lives.)
      c. The revolt in the provinces, particularly in Egypt and Judea
      d. The murders by Nero of his wives, his brother, his mother and many others. He divorced and then killed Octavia, his one wife, and then killed her successor, Poppaea, with a hasty kick to the stomach when she was pregnant.
      e. The public display which Nero made of himself on the stage. (This was bad enough for any Roman, let alone the Roman emperor.)
      f. The proscriptions, which were published names of persons condemned to death by the government, whose property was then taken by the state. (These resulted in many conspiracies and caused many people to commit suicide.)
      g. The neglect of the army by Nero, which was most dangerous since an emperor's ultimate basis of power was the strength of his army. (He was too concerned with the arts to keep in regular touch with the Roman legions.)
      h. Appendix: The result was a major revolt in Gaul, which he was able to suppress, and then a revolt of the Praetorian Guard, which forced him to flee for his life and ultimately to commit suicide in A.D. 68. He died at 32.
   B. The Cultural Scene at the time of the writing of this epistle
   1. Nero's domination of the arts in a very un-Roman-like way
   2. Nero's music involving his singing and his playing of the lyre, an ancient stringed instrument. (He would accompany his own singing and reciting.)
   3. His competing in the Greek games, particularly the chariot races.

   "While he [Nero] was singing no one was allowed to leave the theater even for the most urgent reasons. And so it is said that some women gave birth to children there, while many who were worn out with listening and applauding, secretly leaped from the wall since the gates at the entrance were closed, or feigned death and were carried out as if for burial. The trepidation and anxiety with which he took part in the contests, his keen rivalry of his opponents and his awe of the judges, can hardly be credited. As if his rivals were of quite the same station as himself, he used to show respect to them and try to gain their favor, while he slandered them behind their backs, sometimes assailed them with abuse when he met them, and even bribed those who were especially proficient." (*Seutonius*. J.C. Rolfe (tr.) Vol. 11 Cambridge, Mass.: Harvard University Press, 1959. p. 123)

"... he [Nero] little by little began to practice himself, neglecting none of the exercises which artists of that kind are in the habit of following, to preserve or strengthen their voices. For he used to lie upon his back and hold a leaden plate on his chest, purge himself by the syringe and by vomiting, and deny himself fruits and all foods injurious to the voice. Finally encouraged by his progress, although his voice was weak and husky, he began to long to appear on the stage, and every now and then in the presence of his intimate friends he would quote a Greek proverb meaning 'Hidden music counts for nothing.' And he made his debut at Naples, where he did not cease singing until he had finished the number which he had begun, even though the theater was shaken by a sudden earthquake shock. In the same city he sang frequently and for several successive days." (*Seutonius*. J.C. Rolfe (tr.) Vol. 11 Cambridge, Mass.: Harvard University Press, 1959. pp. 115,116)

(Seutonius' dates were A.D. 69-121. He was a Roman writer of history, about whom we have relatively little information. He was a writer of The Lives of Caesars, the only one of his works that has come down to us in its entirety.)

"... Nero appeared himself in public, and sang and played and acted for the prize, and sought the plaudits of the crowd. He did not take it up as the mere pastime of an idle day, but practiced and studied in real earnest, showed feverish jealousy of rival actors, and humbly bowed before the judges, as if the contest was a real one. No one might leave the theater while he played; Vespasian was seen to nod, and sunk at once in his good graces. Five thousand sturdy youths were trained to sit in companies among the audience and give the signal for applause." (Capes, W.W. Roman History: The Early Empire. New York: Charles Scribner's Sons, 1901. pp. 111,112)

4. His recitals: disgusting to everyone
5. Appendix: He was an "artist" who had the misfortune to have to serve his country as emperor.

C. The Financial Scene at the time of the writing of this epistle. Nero bankrupted the treasury of the Roman Empire.

D. The Social Scene at the time of the writing of this epistle as characterized by the following:
   1. Frivolity on the surface with much discontent underneath
   2. Dominion of the nobility, the Senators and others, by Nero
   3. Slaves who constituted two thirds of the population of the city of Rome, over one and a half million in number (Many of these were the victims of war and were many times better educated than their Roman masters. They were a threat to peace.)
   4. Sports to occupy the time of the lower classes ("Bread" and the "circus" were attempts to keep the lower classes contented. These involved chariot racing, wild beast hunts, and gladiatorial exhibitions to the death.)
   5. Communal baths, the social centers of the day, sometimes covering whole city blocks. (In addition to the baths, these buildings also contained libraries and all sorts of games for the patrons.
   6. Special treatment for the Jews of the empire. (This included exemption from military service, permission to send collections of money to Jerusalem for support of the temple, and the establishment of their own courts of justice.
E. The Religious Scene at the time of this epistle
   1. State religion: The Emperor, Augustus, began a revival of the worship of the old Roman gods, involving the repair of the temples and the reinstitution of the old sacrifices. This was continued under the succeeding emperors.
   2. Emperor worship: Also practiced was the worship of the deceased emperors and the genius of the reigning one.
   3. Stoicism: The philosophy of the day was Stoicism, its motto being, "Grin and bear it." And when you could bear it no longer, suicide was the honorable way out. e.g. Seneca slit his wrists and bled to death in a bath house.
   4. Oriental Religions: The religions from the East, such as the mystery cults, along with Judaism and Christianity, were coming into the West. Many of the mystery cults were fertility cults and were very immoral. People were reaching out for some way of salvation.

II. The Cause of the Roman Church: no direct evidence for its founding
   A. A positive answer: The Roman church was not founded by either Peter or Paul. although it is rather certain that both of them were in Rome before they died.
      1. Introductory remark from Sanday and Headlam, International Critical Commentary, Romans, p. xxv. The Roman church probably owed its organized existence to Peter and Paul but it did not originate with either of them. Note that the epistle is addressed to the saints in Rome, not to the church in Rome.
      2. Peter (I Pet. 5:13) wrote from Babylon, which was probably a covert name for Rome. However, it is certain that he did not found the church there.

11

        a.   Paul would have mentioned this somewhere in the epistle to the Romans, (an argument from silence, however)

        b.   Paul would have stayed away from his (Peter's) territory. In Romans 15:20 he writes that he liked to preach Christ where He was not already known. He does not want to build on another person's foundation. He was a church planter.

        c.   Peter was not in Rome until the end of his life, according to many witnesses.

        d.   The church of Matthew 16:18, which Jesus Christ promised to build, was not the Roman church. Jesus said, "I will build my church…"

    3.   Paul (Acts 28) could not have founded the Roman church for the following reasons.

        a.   The church congregation, a group of believers, came out to meet Paul as he was coming into Rome the first time. This was not true in other cities where he preached the gospel. See Acts 28:15.

        b.   The letter to the believers in Rome assumes a church of some sort there, before his arrival, to receive it.

B.   Possible answers as to origin of the Roman church

    1.   Jews from Rome in Jerusalem on the day of Pentecost who returned. (They would probably have needed more teaching to be competent missionaries to found a church. Anyway they were sojourners in Jerusalem, not pilgrims.)

    2.   Early Christians from Jerusalem scattered after the death of Stephen Acts 8:4. (There was great movement in the empire.)

    3.   Early converts of Paul's from others of his churches. (This would explain another reason why Paul wanted to go there. These Christians were not his spiritual children but his spiritual grandchildren. Also he had many friends there. See Rom. 16

    4.   Appendix: The Roman church did not begin in the Jewish synagogues because the leaders either knew nothing about the Christian teaching or they were pretending to know nothing about Christianity. See Acts 28:17-22.

III.The Congregation at Rome
  A.   A predominance of Gentile Christians, according to the
       traditional and probably the correct view (Paul seems to
       recognize this church as coming under his jurisdiction as
       apostle to the Gentiles. See. Rom. 1:5,6,14).
  B.   A predominance of Jewish Christians. This view is based on
       Romans 9-11, which however, seems to be a parenthesis in the
       thought development of the book.
  C.   Conclusion: Undoubtedly, there were a number of Jewish
       believers in the Roman congregation; however, the majority
       seem to have been Gentile.
       1.   Rom 1:5-7 In these verses Paul numbers his Roman readers
            among the Gentile churches.
       2.   Rom 1:13-15 Paul includes them among the "Greeks and
            barbarians" to whom he considers himself a debtor.
       3.   Rom 11:13 Paul addresses them as "you Gentiles."
       4.   Rom 15:14-26 Paul implies that they are among the
            Gentiles whom he is offering as a sacrificial offering to God.
       5.   Rom 16 Paul sends greetings to people in Rome whom he
            names; and over one half of the names are either Latin or
            Greek names.
IV. The Correspondence with Rome
  A.   Reasons for Paul's having written a letter to the Roman Church
       1.   An introductory matter: Paul does not state any definite
            purpose in the letter itself.
       2.   Paul did have a very definite personal interest in the
            church.
       3.   Paul had a definite plan to visit Rome in the near future
            and wrote the letter to prepare the way for his visit. Rom
            1:13; 15:22-24:28,29; Acts 19:21
       4.   Paul had a personal desire for their prayer support for
            his mission to Jerusalem with the money for the poor of
            Jerusalem from Macedonia and Achaia. Rom 15:31
       5.   Paul wanted to commend Phoebe, the possible carrier of
            the letter, to the church. Rom 16:1,2
  B.   Reasons for Paul's having written this kind of a letter to the
       Roman Church
       1.   A polemical purpose: an attack on a Judaistic heresy or
            some Jewish Christians with wrong ideas (critique: The
            tone of the epistle is certainly not polemical and warlike,
            like Galatians.)
       2.   An apologetic purpose: an attempt at appeasing certain
            factions in the church hostile to him so that they would
            give him a favorable reception when he came (critique:
            There is no indication of this in the letter either.)
       3.   An instructive purpose: Paul wanted to give them
            a systematic exposition of Christian truth aimed at
            enlightening them and stimulating their faith. (a doctrinal
            or dogmatic purpose)

4. An introductory purpose: Paul wanted to inform the church regarding himself, his plans and his message of justification by faith. (In this way he could insure himself of a sympathetic church in Rome when he arrived.)

F. Time and Place of writing: approximately A.D. 57 from Corinth, probably on the third missionary journey. (At this time he spent 3 months in Greece before sailing for Jerusalem with an offering from Macedonia and Achaia for the poor in the Jerusalem church. See Acts 20:3)

V. Some Characteristics of the Epistle (peculiarities)
   A. Characteristic #1: It was written to a church which Paul had not founded.
   B. Characteristic #2: It was written to a church which Paul had not visited yet.
   C. Characteristic #3: It was written in the nature of a logical treatise rather than a letter. It presents Paul's own theological viewpoint.
   D. Characteristic #4: It was apparently written to meet no emergency in the church situation of the time. In other words, it was not occasioned by any problem in the Roman group of believers which we can ascertain.

A Survey of the Epistles to the Romans

I. A bird's eye view of each chapter
   A. Chapter 1: Salutation, information regarding Paul's praise for the Roman Christians, his prayers for them, and his purposes in wanting to come to see them; the key verses of the book; Paul's condemnation of the Gentile world on the basis of their listed evil works.
   B. Chapter 2: Principles of God's judgment to fall on the Gentiles Paul has just condemned and the Jews he is about to condemn; the condemnation of the Jews on the basis of their evil works and false trust in their name "Jew," their having the law, and their physical circumcision.
   C. Chapter 3: Questions which the Jews might raise; Paul's condemnation of everyone on the basis of their evil works; the characteristics of justification by faith now available.
   D. Chapter 4: Two Old Testament illustrations of justification by faith: Abraham and David; the characteristics of Abraham's faith which was reckoned for righteousness.
   E. Chapter 5: The blessings of justification by faith; the comparison and contrast of Adam and Christ in connection with condemnation and justification.
   F. Chapter 6: The Christian's death to sin and living to God and righteousness; freedom from a life of sin and occasional acts of sinning; the use of the analogies of baptism and also of the bond-servant.
   G. Chapter 7: The Christian's death to law as a legalistic means of holiness; the use of the bond of marriage; the good character of law: the description of the carnal Christian who has not died to law and a description of his wretched condition.
   H. Chapter 8: Paul's listing of the blessings of the Spirit-led life. the one being lived in the Spirit and in accordance with the Spirit's leading.
   I. Chapter 9: Israel's relation to the program of justification by faith; Paul's sorrow for Israel; a stress on the sovereignty of God in relation to Israel.
   J. Chapter 10: Israel's rejection of justification by faith; a stress on the free-will of man in relation to justification by faith; a good balance for Romans 9, the chapter on sovereignty
   K. Chapter 11: Israel's rejection not total or permanent; the olive tree analogy; Israel's ultimate salvation at the return of the Lord from heaven.
   L. Chapter 12: The beginning of the practical section of the book; the command for totally presenting oneself to God as a living sacrifice; how such a person will live in regard to various relationships; his partners in the church, people in general and persecutors in particular.
   M. Chapter 13: His relation to the powers that be. God's prescriptions, and to the present period or age.

N. Chapter 14: His relation to his partners in the church, those that are weaker than he is and those who are stronger than he is.

O. Chapter 15: Paul's past ministry, his present plans, and his desire for their prayer support for his future ministry in Jerusalem.

P. Chapter 16: Paul's greetings to friends in Rome; his conveying of greetings from those with him; his closing exhortations; his final benediction.

II. A general outline of the entire book
A. Salutation: introduction of Paul, his gospel, his Christ, his readers, and his desires for them (1:1-7)
B. Information: regarding his praise for their faith, his prayers for them, and his purposes in wanting to come and to see them (1:8-15)
C. Summarization: the key verses of the book (1:16-17)
D. Condemnation of the Gentiles on a works' basis, the principles of God's judgment, the condemnation of the Jews and the condemnation of everyone on a works basis (1:18-3:20)
E. Justification: its characterization, two illustrations of it from the Old Testament, Paul's characterization of Abraham's faith and the results of justification by faith (3:21-5:11)
F. Imputation: the comparison and contrast of Adam and Christ (5:12-21)
G. Sanctification: death to sinning of all kinds and the law, a picture of the carnal Christian and the picture of the Spirit-led person and his blessings (6-8)
H. Renunciation but ultimate salvation: for Israel (9-11)
I. Conversation (or walk): how a totally presented Christian will live in various relationships (12:1-15:4)
J. Termination: the final matters Paul gives to wrap up the letter (15:5-16:27)

III. Some suggested reasons why Paul was chosen as the author of Romans
He was...
A. A Pharisee of the Pharisees with a great knowledge of the Old Testament.
B. A theologian and a philosopher with an ability to think keenly and clearly.
C. A student of pagan philosophy and ways.
D. An apostle to the Gentiles.
E. A missionary of reputation throughout the Roman Empire.
F. A friend of many people in Rome.
G. A recipient of divine revelation so he had a correct concept of the Gospel.
H. A man with time in Corinth: Acts 20:3 He had a three month layover in Greece.
I. A man with a messenger in Phoebe (Rom. 16:1,2).
K. An administrator with an ability to help churches get established.
J. A Roman citizen.

16

CHAPTER ONE

The Salutation of the Epistle to the Romans

Romans 1:1-7

¹Paul, a bond-servant belonging to Christ Jesus, a called apostle, who has been set apart for the gospel of God, ²which was promised beforehand through His prophets in the holy Scriptures ³concerning His Son, the One who came into being from the seed of David according to the flesh, ⁴the One who has been marked out the Son of God with power according to the spirit of holiness by the resurrection from the dead, Jesus Christ, our Lord, ⁵through whom we received grace and apostleship for obedience [stemming] from faith among all the Gentiles on behalf of His name, ⁶among whom you yourselves also are called ones belonging to Jesus Christ, ⁷to all the ones being in Rome, beloved ones of God, called saints: Grace be to you and peace from God our Father and the Lord Jesus Christ.

I.   Paul's Introduction of Himself
    A.   A serving one: Paul calls himself a bondservant belonging to Christ. He stresses the relationship of the bondservant to his master or owner. The owner is in undisputed possession of his servant. The stress is on the obedience, loyalty and humility of a bondservant.
    B.   A sent one: Paul calls himself a called apostle, an apostle by calling. He was not an apostle by an act of his own. He was thinking in terms of what God wanted him to do, not what he wanted to do.
    C.   A separated one: Paul calls himself "a saint," one separated unto the gospel of God to receive it and to preach it. This is our insurance that what follows is not his invention but God's message to us. See also Gal. 1:15 and Acts 13:2.
    D.   A securing one: Paul claims that he is a receiver of grace (undeserved favor) and apostleship. Along with the grace he was shown came a task or special responsibility involving toil and suffering.

II. Paul's Introduction of the Gospel
    A.   The instrumentation: The Gospel was promised beforehand through God's prophets. The term "prophets" includes all the sections of the Hebrew Old Testament. Moses was a prophet (Deut. 18:18); the former and latter prophets were undoubtedly such; and David, who penned many of the Psalms (or writings) was a prophet (Acts 2:30).
    B.   The location: The Gospel was promised beforehand in the Holy Scriptures. An outstanding characteristic of the book of Romans is the many quotations from the Old Testament, which

17

Paul held in high esteem. The Gospel has its roots in a body of writings unique and separated from all others. The Gospel is in the Old Testament.

C. The summarization: The Gospel has as its core God's Son, Jesus Christ. He is the contents of the Gospel in a nutshell.

D. The characterization: The Gospel, or in the Greek euangelion (euangelion), is the good news that Jesus Christ died to save us from our sins, from the penalty of our sins, and unto eternal life now and forever.

III. Paul's Introduction of Christ
   A. Christ's humanity: He came into being from the seed of David according to the flesh.
      1. Christ has a complete human nature. As Adam and Eve before they fell, there was nothing missing in Jesus Christ which was essential to human nature. Remember that sin is not a DEMAND of human nature but a DAMAGING of it. Paul's emphasis here is on the incarnation of Christ.
      2. Christ belongs to history. The word "became" ties Him to the world of sense and change. In eternity things do not become, they are.
      3. Christ belongs historically to the seed of David according to the flesh.
   B. Christ's divinity: He was marked out the Son of God with power according to the spirit of holiness by the resurrection from the dead.
      1. His person: "Marked out as being the son of God with power." This happened at his resurrection. "Marked out" is the best translation for the Greek word used here. "Predestined" is too strong and "declared" is too weak.
         a. The manner of His being marked out: with power or powerfully His state before the resurrection was one of humiliation while after it was one of exaltation.
         b. The manner of His being marked out: according to the spirit of holiness.
            This is probably a reference to Christ's holy human nature. Death could not hold him prey because he was sinless. Others have taken this spirit of holiness to be a reference to Jesus Christ's divine nature or the Holy Spirit, in which case the word "Spirit" is capitalized.
         c. The means of His being marked out: by the resurrection from the dead.
            This was the official setting forth of Christ as the divine Son and authenticated all He had said before He died. He was the divine Son of God before He was resurrected but not with power as He was afterward. This did not involve a change in His relation with the Father, only as He was visible to mankind.

2. His presents to Paul: grace and apostleship
   a. The end for which this grace and apostleship was given: OBEDIENCE
      This was the object of Paul's ministry, more obedience on the part of Christians.
   b. The source of this obedience: FAITH
      This obedience was to stem from their faith.
   c. The location of this obedience: AMONG ALL THE NATIONS (GENTILES)
      Paul was the apostle to the Gentiles, although he never refused to preach the gospel to Jews when the occasion presented itself.
   d. The interest of this preaching of obedience: ON BEHALF OF CHRIST'S NAME or for His glory
      This was not for his own advantage or for the advantage of the Gentiles but for the advantage of Christ and His cause.
C. Christ's names: His names used by Paul indicate a great deal about Him.
   1. Jesus (Savior)
      This name stresses his historical identity and work and was the name given to Him by Joseph and Mary. He was to save His people from their sins.
   2. Christ (the Anointed One, or in Hebrew, the Messiah)
      In the gospels this name is most often a title, whereas in Paul's writings it is his preferred proper name for Jesus. This name stresses his official position.
   3. God's Son
      Paul's use of this name refers to Jesus Christ's divinity as the second Person of the Godhead. "The Son of Man" is the main theme for divinity in the gospels and is used almost exclusively by Jesus of Himself.
   4. Our Lord
      This name suggests supreme rule and sovereignty. It is an exalted name for Jesus Christ as used here.
D. Appendix: an oddity
   The emphasis in this salutation to an epistle stressing the great work of justification by faith is not on the work done but on the Doer of the work. There is nothing here about justification. Actually it is not odd because it is logical to want to know who Christ is before one studies what He has done.

IV. Paul's Identification of His Addressees
   A. Their position in general: among the Gentiles or the nations
   B. Their position relative to Christ: called ones belonging to Jesus Christ
      As Paul was an apostle by calling, they were Christians by calling.
   C. Their place of residence: Rome

Note that the epistle is addressed specifically to "all the saints in Rome," not to the church in Rome. It may well be that the formal establishment of the group of believers as a church came with the arrival of Paul and Peter in Rome later on.

D. Their position relative to God: beloved by God
With this beautiful title for Christians, Paul stresses God's love for them. Our love for God is stressed in Romans 8:28. See also Rom. 8:35, 38 and 39 for another emphasis on God's love for Christians.

E. Their position relative to holiness: saints by calling
A saint is one who is separated from sin and unto God and holy living. Remember that sainthood is both a GIFT (positional holiness) and an ACHIEVEMENT (experiential holiness). All Christians have Christ's righteousness put their accounts; but then the life of growth in obedience and Christlikeness should begin.

V. Paul's Invocation (Prayer) for the Roman Christians: Grace to you and peace from God our Father and the Lord Jesus Christ.
A. Grace equals undeserved kindness and favor from God. This is a Greek term.
B. Peace or shalom equals well-being and prosperity of every kind from God. This is a Hebrew term of greeting.

Conclusion
Why is this introduction necessary to the whole Roman epistle? Paul was unknown by face to many in Rome. This epistle was to prepare the way for his first visit.

CHAPTER TWO

Information Paul Gives By Way of Preface

Romans 1:8-15

⁸First of all, I continue giving thanks to my God through Jesus Christ concerning all of you [pl] because your [pl] faith is being proclaimed in the whole world. ⁹For God is my witness, whom I continue serving with my spirit in the gospel of His Son, that unceasingly I continue making mention of you [pl] always in my prayers, ¹⁰praying if somehow now at last I shall succeed in the will of God to come to you [pl]. ¹¹For I am fervently longing to see you [pl] in order that I may impart some spiritual gift to you [pl] in order that you [pl] may be established, ¹²that is [in order that I] may receive encouragement among you through [our] mutual faith, both yours and mine. ¹³And I am not wanting you [pl] to continue being ignorant, brothers, that many times I determined to come to you, but I was prevented until now, in order that I might have some fruit also among you [pl], just as also among the remaining Gentiles. ¹⁴For both to the Greeks and to the barbarians, both to wise ones and to foolish ones, I am a debtor; ¹⁵thus my eagerness is to preach the gospel also to you [pl], the ones who are in Rome.

I. Paul's Praise for the Roman Christians 1:8 "I continue giving thanks to my God through Jesus Christ... because your faith is being proclaimed in the whole world."
   A. A tactful commencement for a letter to a church he had not founded. Paul's usual way of beginning an epistle is to praise when he can do it sincerely.
   B. A sincere compliment. Paul is not soft-soaping the congregation or polishing the apple insincerely.
   C. An inclusive confession concerning their faith. This "faith" may refer to their trust in God or their Christianity. Their "faith" is continuing to be declared everywhere he goes in the Roman Empire. This may be a hint that this church had been here for some time.
   D. A continuous custom on Paul's part.
       He continually gives thanks for the Roman believers when he hears others talking about their "faith."

II. Paul's Prayers for Them 1:9,10 "Unceasingly I continue making mention of you always in my prayers, praying if somehow now at last I shall succeed in the will of God to come to you."
   A. The cause for the oath: It was improbable that a person would pray in this way for a church he had never seen. Consequently, he puts himself under oath in the normal way a Jew of that day would do it. Paul did not want them to think he was exaggerating or using hyperbole.

B. The character of his praying:
1. Character #1: inwardness, emphasizing his sincerity
    This was stressing the inward side of his service while his
    preaching was the outward.
2. Character #2: continuousness
    He speaks as follows: "unceasingly I continue making
    mention of you always in my prayers." He meant that he
    prayed without intermission, constantly, incessantly for
    them. See I Thess. 5:17 where the same Greek word for
    "incessantly" is used.
3. Character #3: definiteness
    He claims to make mention of them. This could have been
    the way he remembered the names of many of them. He
    prayed for them.
4. Character #4: purposefulness
    He prayed that it might be God's will NOW that he come to
    see them.
5. Character #5: submissiveness
    Note that even this pet project of Paul's is on the altar.
    Paul's great desire was to preach the gospel in Rome;
    however, he will not come if God is not willing at this time.
    His cherished plan was on the altar.
6. Character #6: mediateness or intercession.
    Intercession is praying or entreating on behalf of someone
    else. Note Paul is interceding here on behalf of them,
    fellow-believers in Christ.

III. Paul's Purposes in Wanting to Visit Them 1:11-15
    A. His reasons for wanting to visit them
        1. Reason #1: to impart to them some spiritual gift, a purpose
            which implies a lack on their part.
            a. Probably not a gift of the Spirit, as listed twice in I Cor.
                12, since "gift" is singular here
            b. Probably not a gift listed as fruit of the Spirit in Gal.
                5:22,23
            c. Probably the gift of spiritual edification and growth
                from instruction from an apostle. Note the importance
                of going ahead and growing as a Christian, not staying
                where we are in the spiritual life.
        2. Reason #2: to help in their establishment as Christians and
            as a church
        3. Reason #3: to gain encouragement for himself from their
            fellowship
            He sincerely hopes to gain from them for his own spiritual
            life. They will help him too.
        4. Reason #4: to secure some fruit among them as among the
            other Gentiles
            a. Possibly converts
            b. Possibly growth in their spiritual lives
            c. Possibly both of the above

5. Reason #5: to pay off his debt to them
    He considered himself a debtor to both the cultured
    Gentiles and the uncultured Gentiles, the wise and the
    simple.
    a. Not a legal debt
        He had not received anything from them which put
        him in their debt.
    b. A moral debt
        He had found something good which they needed,
        salvationor justification by faith, which they needed
        desperately and to which they had a moral right.
6. Reason #6: to preach the gospel in Rome also

B. His possible hindrances to visiting them
    What may have hindered him from coming to them sooner?
    There is no indication made here.
    1. Possible evangelistic trips elsewhere: There were too many
        open doors and/or too many places where a beginning with
        the gospel had not yet been made.
    2. Possible persecution and attempts to get away from it so as
        to give his baby churches time and occasion to put down
        roots
    3. Possible illness in body: Note that Doctor Luke is with Paul
        at the time of the writing of this epistle: Acts 20:1-6. This is
        one of the "we" sections in Acts.
    4. Appendix: Notice that Paul is now willing to come to
        Rome, if God is willing.

CHAPTER THREE

A Summarization of the Message of the Epistle

Romans 1:16, 17

16For I am not being ashamed of the gospel. For it is power from God for salvation for every one who is believing, for the Jew first and for the Greek. 17For a righteousness from God in it is being revealed by faith unto faith, just as it stands written, "But the one who is righteous by faith will live."

I. **The Confidence of Paul in the Gospel**
"I am not being ashamed of the Gospel" Even though Paul was aware that the gospel was "a stumbling block to Jews and foolishness to Gentiles," he was not ashamed to preach Jesus Christ crucified as the hope of the world. Note his use of a litotes, an understatement in which an affirmative is expressed by the negative of the contrary. "I am not being ashamed" means that he was proud of it.

II. **The Characterization of the Gospel — "the power of God"**
   A. The power of God
   Rome was interested in power and consequently Paul stresses the greatest power of all. The greatest argument for the gospel is its power demonstrated in action.
   B. The medicine of God
   The Greek word dunamis (dunamis) used here was used by the Old Greek doctor, Hippocrates, in the 5th century B.C. for "medicine." The Gospel is God's cure for the world's ills, both spiritual and otherwise.

III. **The Concern of the Gospel — "salvation for everyone"**
   A. Salvation from sin; from a life of sin and individual acts of sinning
   B. Salvation from the punishment of sin, called "the wrath of God" in Rom. 1:18
   C. Salvation unto eternal life and blessedness, both now and forever
   See John 10:10 where Jesus claimed to have come that they might continue having life (now) and might continue having it more abundantly.
   D. Salvation which is potentially universal, i.e., for everyone
   It is a salvation that can be received by everyone without distinction or discrimination. It is for those of any color of skin, any race, or any culture.

IV. **The Condition for Receiving the Gospel** "everyone who is believing"
"Faith" and "believing" are cognate or related words in the Greek language. The condition for salvation is not baptism or church membership or circumcision or obedience to the law.
A. Saving faith involves PERCEPTION, a knowledge of the message and the Person of the message. You cannot believe in Someone or something you have not heard about. See Rom. 10:13-15.
B. Saving faith involves RECEPTION of the message as true. The demons can go this far. They believe that there is one God. James 2:19
C. Saving faith involves SUBMISSION to the Person of the message. It involves a total trust and committal of oneself and one's life to the Person and the promises of God's Word. It involves a staking of one's life, present and future, on the truthfulness of the Gospel found in the Bible. Anything short of this is not saving faith.

V. **The Consecution in Preaching the Gospel** "to the Jew first, and also to the Greek" This was the temporal order followed by Paul. If there was a synagogue in the town, Paul went there first.
A. Not a special privilege for the Jews: All are on the same footing with respect to the Gospel.
B. A historical priority: Historically this was the order in which Paul preached. It was the easiest way then to get an intelligent hearing in a hurry. The Jews in the synagogues knew their Old Testament; and there were also God-fearers (Gentiles) associated with the synagogues who were prepared to hear and to respond favorably to the Gospel.

VI. **The Contents of the Gospel** "a revelation of a righteousness from God, a revelation by faith unto faith" Here is the theme of the book of Romans.
A. An identification of this righteousness
1. Not an attribute of God
There is no definite article in front of "righteousness" in the Greek. His righteousness remains the same, whether we believe or not. His righteousness, (the attribute) is bad news for the sinner as it leads to condemnation of the sinner, not his pardon.
2. Not something God gives to us
In justification. God does not make us righteous. Note that the text says that a righteousness is revealed to us, not given to us. At the present time. God makes us new creations in Christ Jesus (II Cor. 5:17) but He does not make us righteous creations.
3. Something imputed to us or put to our account by God
The verb "to justify" means to pronounce or declare righteous, as a verdict from a judge. It is a forensic term, having to do with the court room. Christ's human

righteousness is put to the account of every believer in Christ. This is not something done by us or in us but for us. God treats the sinner just as if he had never sinned on the basis of what Christ has done for him. Reaping may remain however.

  B. **The relation of this righteousness to faith**

      The various possibilities are as follows:

      1. not "from Old Testament faith to New Testament faith"

      2. not "from weak faith to strong faith"

      3. not "from a little faith to a larger quantity of faith"

      4. not "out of faith (rather than works) unto (those who have) faith"

      5. possibly "entirely of faith from start to finish"

   * 6. revealed by faith (the receiving instrument) unto faith (the end for which it was revealed) Note that the Greek text positions "by faith unto faith" immediately after the verb "is being revealed." Faith is the instrument of the revelation to the end that faith may increase.

      7. not "a righteousness by faith unto faith" but "a revelation by faith unto faith"

VII. The Confirmation of this Gospel from the Old Testament

  A. Translation #1: King James' Authorized Version A.D. 1611
      ". . . but the just shall live by faith."

  B. Translation #2: American Standard Version A.D. 1901
      ". . . but the righteous shall live by faith."

  C. Translation #3: The New American Standard A.D. 1963
      "But the righteous man shall live by faith."

  D. Translation #4: The New International Version A.D. 1973
      "The righteous will live by faith."

  E. Translation #5: The Greek word order
      "... but the one who is righteous (or just) by faith (i.e., on the basis of his faith) will live." The fact stressed here is not living by faith but being justified or declared righteous by faith. The context of the book is the determining factor. Hab. 2:4, Gal. 2:20 and Heb. 10:38 stress "living by faith."

Appendix: The possible reasons for Romans 1:16,17 being here

  A. These key verses of the book of Romans introduce the main theme of the letter, which is justification by faith.

  B. These key verses also should keep the reader reading through the "condemnation" section of the book, viz., 1:18-3:20. Paul is going to condemn everyone in this section on the basis of their sinful works and faith will not be seen again until 3:21 and following. He apparently wanted to make sure that his readers knew that there would be hope at the end of his condemnation of everyone on the basis of works. There is "a light at the end of the tunnel" to keep them reading.

CHAPTER FOUR

Paul's Condemnation of the Whole World on the Basis of Personal Works

Romans 1:18-3:20

The Condition of the Gentile World ~ Romans 1:18-32

¹⁸For wrath from God is going to be revealed from heaven against all ungodliness and unrighteousness of mankind, those who continue holding down the truth in unrighteousness; ¹⁹because that which is known concerning God is clear among them; for God has made it known to them. ²⁰For His invisible [attributes] from the [time of] the creation of the world by means of [His] created things being perceived, are being clearly seen, namely His eternal power and godhead, so that they are without excuse; ²¹because although they had known God, as God they did not glorify [Him] nor did they give thanks, but they were given over to worthless things in their thoughts and their foolish heart was darkened. ²²Although they were claiming to be wise ones, they became fools; ²³and they exchanged the glory of the immortal God for the likeness of an image of mortal man and of birds and of four-footed animals and of creeping things. ²⁴Wherefore <u>God delivered them over</u> in the lusts of their hearts unto uncleanness in order to continue dishonoring their bodies among them, ²⁵since indeed they exchanged the truth of God for the lie, and they worshipped and served the creature rather than the One who created [it], who is blessed forever. Amen.

²⁶Because of this <u>God delivered them over</u> unto dishonorable emotions; for, on the one hand, their females exchanged the natural [sexual] use for that contrary to nature; ²⁷and likewise, on the other hand, the males, because they had left the natural [sexual] use of the female, burned with their lust for one another, males with males continuing to commit this shameful act and continuing to receive back in themselves the penalty of their error which was unavoidable.

²⁸And just as they did not approve of having God in their knowledge, <u>God delivered them over</u> to an unapproved mind, to continue practicing the things not proper, ²⁹[those] who are filled with all unrighteousness, maliciousness, covetousness, badness; full of envy, murder, strife, deceit, depravity; tale-bearers, ³⁰slanderers, haters of God, insolent persons, proud, boasters, inventors of evil things, to parents disobedient, ³¹without understanding, covenant-breaking, without natural affection, merciless; ³²who, although the righteous requirement of God they have fully known, that those who

are practicing such things are worthy of death, not only continue practicing them but also continue giving approval to those who are practicing [them].

I. **The Sins of the Gentile World:** The Gentile world needs the gospel because of their terrible sinfulness.
   A. General Sinfulness
      The following are the general words for sin which appear in Paul's list of Gentile sins.
      1. ungodliness 1:18 a lack of reverence for God, no attention given God although such a person may be a good moral individual
      2. unrighteousness 1:18, 29 a departure from a righteous and true standard
      3. wickedness 1:29 an evil that is active and delights in harming others
      4. covetousness 1:29 an illicit desire for more of anything, not just money
      5. evil 1:29 an inherent, innate, resident evil which makes a person destitute of every quality which would make them good
   B. **Specific Sins**
      The following are specific sins of which the Gentile world then was guilty. Note the length and the variety of sins; and still it is only a sampling.
      1. suppression of the truth -1:18 holding down the truth, the right, in their living unrighteously - All of their sinning is in spite of knowledge.
      2. refusal to glorify God as God - 1:21 Each individual is doing what is right in his own eyes and becomes his own god.
      3. unthankfulness 1:21
         (The three sins above head the worst list of sins in the entire Bible. The following come from them.)
      4. vain reasoning which honors the creature rather than the Creator 1:21
      5. vain profession of wisdom, when actually they are fools 1:22
      6. idolatry in which they worship and serve the creature, passing God by altogether 1:23, 25
      7. immorality as they dishonor their bodies "Sex has become an entertainment today."
      8. homosexuality, which is not just a sickness but a sin
         (Note Paul's distinction in this paragraph between homosexual tendencies and homosexual actions. The former cannot be helped; the latter can.)
      9. envy 1:29
      10. murder, which Jesus widened to hatred 1:29 See Matt. 5:21, 22.
      11. strife, which is born out of envy and jealousy 1:29
      12. deceit 1:29

28

13. malignity, which is malicious craftiness that manifests an evil disposition towards others
14. whispering, which refers to secret slander to hurt another's reputation 1:29
15. backbiting, which refers to open spreading of slander 1:30
16. hatred toward God, which exhibits itself in gladly eliminating God if they can 1:30
17. insolence and pride, leading to the insulting of other people 1:30
18. pride and haughtiness, which leads to despising others and delighting to make others feel small 1:30
19. boasting (bragging) 1:30
20. invention of evil things 1:30 Not content with ordinary ways of sinning, they are "always thinking of new ways of sinning." See the Living Bible.
21. disobedience to parents 1:30 How terrible a sin this must be to appear here!
22. lack in understanding 1:31
23. covenant breaking and breaking of promises This is seen in covenants broken between nations and marriage partners. Note the contemporary divorce rate.
24. unnatural affections without love for kindred This shows itself in divorces, wife and child abuse, adultery and fornication, infanticide, abortions, euthanasia, etc.
25. mercilessness 1:31 For example, a slave was then a thing to be tortured or even killed.
26. support and encouragement of evil doers 1:31 They not only do these things but applaud others who do them, thus leading others astray.
27. Appendix: This is probably the worst list of sins in the Bible and describes rather accurately the current scene as well. See also II Tim. 3:1-7.

II. **The Situation of the Gentile World** "without excuse" 1:19-21
   A. Question #1: Why are they? God, according to Paul here, has revealed Himself to all mankind.
      1. Rom. 1:18 All mankind possess the truth in some way but they are suppressing it.
      2. Rom. 1:21 All mankind have the possibility of knowing God but they have rejected Him. Hence their ignorance and lostness is without excuse.
   B. Question #2: How can they know? Their revelation about God comes from the following three sources:
      1. Rom. 1:19 creation or nature 1:19 Creation shows us a Creator to be reverenced. See also Acts 14:17 and 17:27ff. This is outward revelation.
      2. Rom. 2:13-15 conscience or the law of God written on each person's heart—this is inward revelation. Every person knows enough to be living better than he is in worship and morals. Conscience shows us a Law-giver go be obeyed.

29

3. Rom. 2:4 circumstances, otherwise known as the providential goodness of God shown each person - These are the good things of God intended to lead us to repentance. Circumstances of this kind show us a Provider to be thanked.
        4. Appendix: But only the canon of the Scriptures, the Bible, shows us a Savior to be received.
    C. Question #3: What can be known about God from the above three sources?
        1. Rom. 1:20 His eternal power and divinity. As you can tell something about a homemaker from the way she keeps her house and a student by the way he keeps his room, you can tell much about God by the way He keeps His universe.
        2. Rom. 2:13-15 His laws regarding right and wrong. We do not know all about good and bad, but enough to know that some things are taboo. For example, if a person is honest with himself, he will have to admit that the things forbidden in the 10 commandments are wrong, even apart from written revelation.
        3. Rom. 2:4 (Cf. Acts 14:17) His goodness, kindly care, interest in people. His providential blessings
        4. Appendix: God's plan of salvation is not revealed outside the Scriptures. There is light from the above three sources but it is not enough light to save a person. The light is sufficient to render one inexcusable, even though he needs more light to be saved. It is because of the various amounts of light available to us that God has ordained degrees of punishment in hell. The verses to support this doctrine will be given later. See page 32, Appendix.
    D. Question #4: If God has revealed himself so plainly through the world, why do men not see?
        1. First of all, there is blindness on the part of mankind generally.
        2. Secondly, people do not take the time and effort to see. It demands becoming quiet and still with time for meditation.
        3. Thirdly, what little light does get through to him from nature, his conscience, and providential happenings is suppressed so that he can go on living an unrighteous and ungodly life without his conscience bothering him. See Rom. 1:18.

The following quotations from three secular magazines indicate that there is within each of us a moral guide of some kind, call it what you will: "something inside us," "19th century morality," "a nagging thing from one's parents," "the pangs of old-fashioned conscience," or "the internal government that will not let us violate it without some kind of internal pain and guilt." A way of knowing that even people with seared consciences (I Tim. 4:2) still have the law of God written on their hearts is to observe how they dislike unjust things being done to them. As one person put it, how do we know, for example, that cannibalism is wrong? We know it because cannibals do not like to be eaten.

30

For most of the college coeds, "sex is full of anxiety." This anxiety creeps into the confidence of even the most seemingly emancipated college girls. Few of the sexually freer girls seemed to be enjoying their freedom. "Something inside just doesn't let us," a Barnard junior complained. "We think we're so casual, but we aren't really—if we were, why would we make ourselves suffer so, and why would we be always vowing to reform?" See McCall's Magazine. September, 1963.

Harvard College's Dean John U. Monro, who has two daughters himself, warns there is a shock in store for young women. "They go along in 20th century attitudes until the girl gets pregnant and 19th century morality comes back into play." See Look Magazine. September, 1963.

Admits Ellen Sims, a girl... of 15 who says she has turned celibate after sleeping with three boys when she was in the eighth grade: "I was ashamed of myself. Sometimes I wish I didn't even know what I've done." Similarly, University of Pittsburgh Junior Kathy Farnsworth confesses, "I know sex isn't dirty. It's fun. But I always have this nagging thing from my parents in my head. They'd kill me if they knew ... Occasionally the pangs of old-fashioned conscience are so strong that a student drops out of school and requires months of therapy before he is able to resolve the conflict between his "liberated" behavior and the standards acquired from his parents, that he still unconsciously accepts. See Time Magazine. August, 1972.

III. **The Sentence upon the Gentile World**
    A.   The withdrawal of God's hand 1:24,26,28
         God let them go ahead with their sinning.
    B.   The permission of sin to run its course
    C.   The abandonment of mankind as punishment for his abandonment of God first; God never gives up on a person until they have given up on Him. See 1:23,25, and 28a.
    D.   The deliverance of man over to the following: as punishments for sin:
         "God punishes sin with sin." Stifler, Romans, p.24
        1.   Uncleanness in the area of his lusts: sexual license
        2.   Shameful passions: unnatural appetites, corrupt affections, viz., homosexuality and lesbianism
        3.   A reprobate mind: a mind that is morally corrupt, that is unable to tell the difference between good and evil
    E.   Appendix: God's reason for doing this: His respect for the free will of man which He has given him. God could violate mankind's free will but He doesn't, especially as it relates to his salvation.
IV. **The Summary of This Section:** Mankind is guilty of the following:
    A.   A sinning against God
    B.   A sinning against light
    C.   A sinning against nature
    D.   A sinning against their fellowmen

E. A sinning against themselves
F. Appendix: The result is that the wrath of God is revealed from heaven against them. Rom. 1:18 This wrath is not an emotion but the following:
   1. an impersonal force
   2. an inevitable punishment that comes from sinning and breaking the laws of God
      It is like the punishment that comes from the breaking of the laws of gravity or electricity. Break them and one suffers the consequences.
   3. an unavoidable reaction that comes from the clash of God's utter holiness with sin
      It is "the reaction of the Divine righteousness when it comes into collision with sin." Sanday and Headlam, I.C.C. on Romans, p. 35
   4. an automatic consequence of our rebellion against God's moral order reflected in His laws
   5. directed wrath against all ungodliness and unrighteousness of mankind.

V. **Appendix:** The subject for which one must have an answer: Is God unjust to punish with hell a heathen man who dies, having never heard of Jesus Christ?

Answer: God has given all mankind light from three sources: creation, conscience, and providential circumstances. Let a person walk in the little light which he has from these sources, and God will get him the additional light he needs about Jesus Christ in order to be saved, (eg. Acts 8 and the Ethiopian eunuch and Acts 10 and Cornelius) Neither of these men were saved until God's witness got to them. If these people do not get the additional light they need, it is their own fault, not God's. See Rom. 1:20.

The Judgment of God ~ Romans 2:1-16

¹Therefore you [s] are without excuse, every man who is judging; for wherein you [s] are judging the other [person] you yourself are condemning; for the same things you [s] who are judging are practicing. ²But we know that the judgment of God is according to truth against the ones practicing such things. ³And are you [s] thinking this, O man who is judging the ones practicing such things and doing [the] same things, that you yourself will escape the judgment of God? ⁴Or the riches of His goodness and forbearance and longsuffering are you [s] despising, being ignorant that the goodness of God is bringing you [s] to repentance? ⁵But according to your [s] hardness and impenitent heart you [s] are continuing to treasure up for yourself wrath on the day of wrath and revelation of the righteous judgment of God, ⁶who will pay back to each one according to his works; ⁷on the one hand, to the ones who continue seeking for glory and honor and immortality on the basis of endurance in good work, [He will pay back] eternal life; ⁸but, on the other hand, to those who both continue disobeying the truth out of selfishness and who continue obeying unrighteousness [will be] wrath and anger--⁹tribulation and anguish against every soul of man who continues working evil, both of [the] Jew first and [the] Greek; ¹⁰but glory and honor and peace [will be given] to every one continuing to work goodness, both to [the] Jew first and to [the] Greek. ¹¹For there is no respect of persons with God.

¹²For as many as sinned without law, without law also will perish; and as many as sinned with law, by means of law will be judged, ¹³for the hearers of law are not just before God, but the doers of law will be justified; ¹⁴(for whenever Gentiles, those not having the law, by nature continue practicing the things of the law, these, although they are not having the law, are for themselves a law ¹⁵because they are showing the work of the law written on their hearts, while their conscience is bearing witness in support [of the fact] and their thoughts among themselves are repeatedly condemning or even defending [them]) ¹⁶on the day when God is going to judge the hidden things of men according to my gospel by means of Jesus Christ.

Introduction

Note how in Rom. 2:1-16 Paul begins generally to get the Jews' attention. Then in 2:17ff. He goes on to apply condemnation and judgment to the Jews specifically.

I. **The Principles of Divine Judgment which will fall on the Gentiles Paul has just condemned in 1:18-32 and the Jews whom he plans to condemn in 2:17ff.**

GOD'S JUDGMENT WILL BE:
A. Individual: a judgment according to individual, personal responsibility Since some are judging others, they should apply the same principles to themselves 2:1
B. Truthful: a judgment according to truth at which time it will be impossible to deceive God 2:2
C. Inescapable: a judgment that cannot be bypassed 2:3
D. Accumulative: a judgment according to accumulated guilt 2:5, 8,9

33

E.   Wrath-full: a judgment that has to be different from the judgment seat of Christ in 2 Corinthians 5:10. (These people are treasuring up wrath for themselves.) 2:5

F.   Legalistic: a judgment according to works or deeds 2:6
The righteous before God at this judgment will be those who have obeyed the law perfectly. On this basis, no one can be justified before God. See Revelation 20:12,13.

G.   Revelatory: a judgment which will reveal the righteous character of God 2:5

H.   Universal: a judgment which will affect everyone, Jew and Gentile 2:6

I.   Earned: a judgment according to accumulated goodness 2:7,10

J.   Impartial: a judgment without regard for persons 2:11

K.   Proportionate: a judgment according to light received, and everyone has some 2:12

L.   Relative: a judgment according to one's obedience to the light given to them 2:13
"If his deeds are right, his being a Gentile will be no detriment; if they are wrong, his being a Jew will be no excuse." Stifler, Romans, p. 41.

M.   Fair: a judgment only according to light possessed 2:12, 14, 15

N.   Penetrating: a judgment of the secrets of people: hidden sins and motives 2:16

O.   Standardized: a judgment according to Paul's gospel, the one he preaches 2:16   Note: Judgment is a part of the gospel message.

P.   Performed by Christ: a judgment by Jesus Christ, since all judgment has been committed to the Son 2:16 See John 5:22.

II. **The Place of This Divine Judgment in Relation to the Christian:**
(The problem is that it looks like Paul is teaching justification by works in 2:7,10,13). How has this seeming inconsistency with his teaching elsewhere been explained?

A.   Some say Paul is speaking inconsistently. In other words, he speaks about justification by works here but elsewhere about a justification by faith.
1.   This view violates our view of inspiration and inerrancy.
2.   It fails to take into account the keen mentality of the Apostle Paul. If we can see the problem, he certainly could.
3.   It casts doubt on everything else Paul has written because, if he is wrong here, he could be wrong elsewhere.

B.   Some say Paul is speaking hypothetically. as if God were going to judge everyone apart from Christ, although we know He isn't. There is no indication of this here in Romans 2.

C.   Some say Paul is speaking generally, i.e., he is stating general principles of judgment here and not the method of justification. He is giving here a general description of God's action in judgment of the wicked. It is a judgment of every person according to his works, but not on account of his works. In the case of the wicked, it is also on account of their works.

34

Critique: It is hard to see the difference between "according to" and "on account of."

D. Some say Paul is speaking inclusively in one of two ways:
    1. Faith in Christ is included in Paul's theology as the highest work. See I Thessalonians 1:3.
        a. This contradicts Eph. 2:8,9.
        b. This view runs the risk of our meriting our justification by our working.
    2. OR Faith in Christ, if alive, includes within it good works. James 2:14-26. The works here spoken of are the lovely fruits of a living faith in Christ. "The deeds that gain a reward clearly imply faith in him who does them." Stifler, Romans, p.41.
        "Paul means here by 'good work' not their faith but their conduct as the expression of their faith." Cranfield, I.C.C. Romans, p. 151.

E. Some say Paul is speaking ideally here. If a person could earn his justification before God by doing his good works perfectly, then God would be obligated to give him eternal life as a wage. See 2:7,10. However, no one can earn his justification by good works and hence all are condemned on this basis and need another means to be justified before God. Compare 3:12,20. The reference here is to THE GREAT WHITE THRONE JUDGMENT of Rev. 20:11-14, where all mankind, apart from Christ and His cross, will have to appear and be condemned on the basis of their own works. The picture here is the picture of the condition of the world as if Christ had never come into it; and all Paul is trying to do in 1:18-3:20 is to get everyone condemned before God. Note the absence of the words "faith" and "believing" in 1:18-3:20 and their frequent appearance in 3:21-5:11. THIS VIEW SEEMS TO BE THE LOGICAL VIEW in the light of Paul's apparent method of presenting his material throughout Romans.

Note how he isolates one doctrine after another in the book. He starts in 1:18-3:20 by getting everyone condemned on the basis of a "WORKS" righteousness, finishing with the conclusion that on this basis there are "none righteous, not one." Then he discusses a justification that is available to us in 3:21-5:11, however totally based on FAITH alone. Then he talks about the imputation of Adam's sin to all in Adam and the imputation of Christ's righteousness to all in Christ (5:12-21), closing with a statement capable of being misunderstood. See 5:20: "but where sin became greater, grace became present in greater abundance." Then he does away with that misunderstanding by answering the question in everyone's mind, "Shall we continue remaining in sin in order that grace may become greater?" This he discusses in the SANCTIFICATION section of the book, chapters 6-8. Note also the isolation of God's sovereignty in Romans 9:1-29, of man's free will in 9:30-10:21 and his attempt to put the two ideas together in chapter 11.

An illustration of this found in Romans 2:6-11
Verse 6
God will pay back the wages to each one according to his works (the works)

Verse 7 GOOD
1. WORKS: continual seeking for glory, honor and immortality through endurance in good work
2. WAGES: eternal life

Verse 8 BAD
1. WORKS: continual disobeying of the truth out of selfishness and continued obeying of unrighteousness
2. WAGES: wrath and anger

Verse 9 BAD
1. WAGES: tribulation and anguish
2. WORKS: continued working of evil by both Jew and Greek

Verse 10 GOOD
1. WAGES: glory, honor, peace
2. WORKS: continued doing of the good by both Jew and Greek

Verse 11
FOR THERE IS NO RESPECT OF PERSONS WITH GOD

Our temptation is to read the end of the story into the beginning. We must put ourselves in the place of the Roman Christians who read this epistle for the first time. In man's present state of sinner, there is no hope in Romans 1:18-3:20 and all mankind is condemned.

III. **The Position of the Human Judge** (in direct contrast to the divine Judge)
Although Paul condemns in general terms here, he has the Jew in mind from 2:1. He becomes very specific in 2:17ff.   The Jew as...
A. Char. #1: inexcusable
B. Char. #2: critical
C. Char. #3: self-condemned
D. Char. #4: guilty of the same sins, specifically in terms of rejection of available light
E. Char. #5: under the judgment of God
F. Char. #6: self-righteous
G. Char. #7: hard and impenitent of heart
H. Char. #8: doomed

Summary

A. Conclusion #1: God is just and fair and will punish the sinner with death and reward the perfectly obedient with eternal life, whether Jew or Gentile. 2:7,10,13-15.
B. Conclusion #2: The doers of the law will be righteous in God's sight according to 2:6-10.
C. Conclusion #3: The mere possession of the law, as the Gentiles had it within their hearts and the Jews had it also written there and in the Mosaic Code, is not enough.
D. Conclusion #4: No man in his present state as sinner can (or will) earn his justification by obeying the law perfectly.
E. Conclusion #5: If any one desires a righteous standing before a righteous God, he must receive God's imputation of Christ's righteousness. However, this comes about on the basis of faith, not obedience or good works. Christ's perfect keeping of the law must be imputed to a person's account for him to be justified in God's sight. Note: This is not discussed in 1:18-3:20 but in 3:21-5:11.

Conclusion

Note that Paul begins here with condemnation and judgment. This is a necessary introduction to the gospel message. A person will only come to Christ when he is desperate and alarmed. In giving the gospel, we too must begin with why a person needs the Gospel; and wrath is the introduction to the good news. Often so few come to Christ for salvation because they have not heard the introduction.

Appendix

What would you say to an individual who asserted that Paul is teaching in Romans 2:1-16 that every man will be judged according to his works, and therefore, the apostle contradicts himself, having taught elsewhere justification by faith?

Answer: At this stage in the epistle, Paul is teaching a justification by good works, but only to get everyone under condemnation and miserable. He will introduce justification by faith in 3:21-5:11; and hence he is not contradicting himself. He is preparing the way for the good news of justification by faith by telling why the gospel message is needed. And that is all.

[17]But if [1st] you yourself continue bearing the name "Jew" and continue trusting in [the] law and continue glorying in God [18]and continue knowing [His] will and continue approving the things which are excellent because you [s] are being taught from the law, [19]and you [s] stand persuaded that you yourself are a guide of blind ones, a light of those in darkness, [20]an instructor of foolish ones, a teacher of babies, who is having the form of knowledge and of truth in the law-- [21]as for you [s], the one teaching another, you [s] are teaching yourself, are you [s] not? As for you [s], the one preaching not to be stealing, are you [s] stealing? [22]As for you [s], the one claiming not to be committing adultery, are you [s] committing adultery? As for you [s], the one detesting idols, are you [s] robbing temples? [23]You [s] who are boasting in the law, through the transgression of the law are you [s] continuing to dishonor God? [24]For the name of God because of you [pl] is continually being blasphemed among the Gentiles just as it stands written.

[25]For, on the one hand, circumcision is profitable if [3rd] you [s] are practicing the law; but if [3rd] a transgressor of the law you are, your [s] circumcision has become uncircumcision. [26]If [3rd] therefore the uncircumcision the righteous ordinances of the law continues keeping, his uncircumcision for circumcision will be reckoned, will it not? [27]And the uncircumcision by nature, if [partc.] it is fulfilling the law, will judge you [s], the transgressor of the law, by means of [your] written code and circumcision. [28]For the Jew who is one outwardly is not [the true Jew], nor is the circumcision which is outwardly in the flesh [true circumcision], [29]but the Jew who is one inwardly is [the true Jew] and circumcision of the heart, in [the] spirit, not in [the] letter [of the law], is [the true circumcision], whose praise is not from men but from God.

Romans 3
[1]What therefore is the advantage of the Jew, or what is the profit of circumcision? [2]Much in every way. For first, they were entrusted with the oracles of God. [3]For what if [1st] certain ones were not faithful, their unfaithfulness will not put the faithfulness of God out of business, will it? [4]May it not be so! But let God continue becoming true, and every man a liar, even as it stands written,

> *In order that you [s] may be justified by your [s] words*
> *And may win [the case] while you [s] are being judged.*

[5]But if [1st] our unrighteousness continues enhancing [the] righteousness of God, what shall we say? God, the One who is going to inflict wrath, is not unrighteous, is He? I am speaking according to men. [6]May it not be so! Since how [then] will God judge the world? [7]But if [1st] the truthfulness of God by means of my lie is made supremely great for His glory, why am I myself also still being judged as a sinner? [8][And why not] (even as we are being blasphemously reported and even as certain ones are saying that we are speaking) let us do evil things in order that good things may come? (whose condemnation is just). [9]What therefore? Are we being in a worse position [than they]? Not in every respect; for we previously brought a charge against both Jews and Greeks that all are under sin...

I.   **The Characterization of the Jew**
     The Jew was characterized by the following according to Paul here:
     A.   Char. #1   faith in the name "Jew"   2:17
     B.   Char. #2   trust merely in having the law   2:17

C. Char. #3 glorying in his knowing God   2:17
D. Char. #4 having a knowledge of God's will   2:18
    (in the Old Testament)
E. Char. #5 having a knowledge of the excellent   2:18
    way to live
F. Char. #6 having instruction out of the law, the Torah   2:18
G. Char. #7 having confidence in his leadership ability   2:19
    (actually false)
    1. leadership of the blind, the Gentiles
    2. leadership of those in darkness, the Gentiles
H. Char. #8 having confidence in his ability to correct   2:19
    others (actually false)
    1. Correction of the foolish, the Gentiles
    2. Correction of babies, the Gentiles
I. Char. #9 possessing the form of knowledge and   2:20
    truth in the law
J. Char. #10 refusing to teach himself   2:21
K. Char. #11 disobeying the law   2:21,22
    1. his stealing
    2. his committing adultery
    3. his temple robbing   See Acts 19:37.
L. Char. #12 trusting in his physical circumcision   2:25-29
M. Conclusion: Thus he also is guilty before God.
    1. His key sin: pride
    2. His key problem: himself

II. The Conclusion with References to the Jew 2:24
The name of God was blasphemed among the Gentiles because
of the Jews. The Jews outside Palestine were not missionaries but
stumbling blocks.

III. The Circumcision of the Jew
Paul's teaching here regarding physical circumcision can be
summarized as follows:
A. Statement #1: Physical circumcision is a profit, if one obeys the
    Law.
B. Statement #2: Physical circumcision becomes uncircumcision
    in God's sight, if you disobey the Law. There is, in other words,
    no profit in being a Jew or having the law or being physically
    circumcised if you disobey the law.
C. Statement #3: Spiritual circumcision is reckoned to those
    physically uncircumcised, if they obey the Law. However,
    the obedience must be a perfect obedience to be effective in
    salvation. See Gal. 5:3 and James 2:10.
D. Statement #4: Physical circumcision is no automatic guarantee
    one will escape judgment.
E. Statement #5: Physical circumcision has no ability to make
    one a true Jew but spiritual circumcision does; and spiritual
    circumcision is reflected in perfect keeping of the law. On this
    basis, only one true Jew ever lived, namely Jesus. Do not apply

Lev. 26:41, Deut. 30:6, Ezek. 44:7, Jer. 9:25, and Col. 2:11 here. Keep these verses in their context as we must keep these verses (2:25-27) in the context. Paul is only condemning all here.

F. Statement #6: Spiritual circumcision, that of the heart, is what counts before God, and that is demonstrated here by perfect obedience or law-keeping.

IV. **The Correction of Possible Misconceptions**   3:1-9

A. *Question #1:   If circumcision of the heart is what counts before God, what advantage does the Jew have?* What is the profit of physical circumcision? In other words, if circumcision of the heart or perfect obedience is what counts before God, what advantage does the Jew with his law and physical circumcision have? What about the privileges and superiority of the Jewish nation? Answer:

The benefit in being a Jew was and is that to the Jews were committed "the oracles of God." They had additional light while the Gentiles had to grope after God by means of the light in nature, their consciences, and the divine providences in their lives. Remember, however, that the more light one has, the more responsibility he has before God. "The oracles of God" refer to the spoken words of God in the Jewish Old Testament. For Paul the written Word in the Old Testament was "God's speech."

B. *Question #2: What if some were not faithful to their part of the covenant?* Shall their lack of faithfulness make of none effect the faithfulness of God? In other words, isn't the condemnation of the Jews inconsistent with the faithfulness of God and His promises to them? Rom. 3:3, 4
Answer:
1. Paul has not yet reached his discussion of the gospel message in Rom. 3:21-5:11.
2. He is still trying to condemn everyone, including the Jews, on a works basis. This is his main aim in Rom. 1:18-3:20.
3. He emphasizes here that the Jew cannot sin without punishment. He has no special advantage with his name "Jew," his having the Mosaic law, and his possession of physical circumcision.
4. He stresses here God's faithfulness to the Old Testament promises, even if the Jews are not.
5. He implies that God's faithfulness demands the condemnation of the Jews. Check the promises of God's blessing which are conditioned on their obedience. Deut. 30:15-20 and Josh. 23:14-16. In fact. God becomes unfaithful to his promises if he doesn't punish the Jews who do not meet His stated conditions.

6. Then Paul quotes Psalm 51:4 from the Old Testament to support his view. God is just in his punishment of sin. When God is brought to trial, the only verdict which can be brought against Him is innocent of any charge of unfaithfulness.

C. *Question #3: If our unrighteousness continues rendering conspicuous the righteousness of God, God is not unjust to punish us for something that advances Him and His glory, is He?* The verb used here means "to render conspicuous," "to set forth," "to enhance," or "to make to stand out," as a diamond stands out against a black velvet pillow. Rom. 3:5,8.
    Answer:
    1. He says the following explicitly: On this grounds. God can't judge anyone, Jew or Gentile sinner, because all could claim their sin enhances His righteousness. The Jews of that day would abhor that idea; for there was a saying going around that "God created the Gentiles to be fuel for hell." Some Jews at least seemed to be glad that the Gentiles were going to be punished.
    2. He implies the following: The end, namely, the enhancing of God's righteousness, can never justify the means, namely, man's sin. The good end does not make man's sin any less guilt-worthy, any more than the saving of a person's life justifies any lie told to accomplish it.

D. *Question #4: If the truth of God is advanced by the lie of man, why are men judged for that sin?* (This is the same question as #3 above, only stated a little differently.)
    Answer:
    The verb used here means "to make more conspicuous" and thereby to advance it or increase it.
    1. He says the following explicitly first: Taking this reasoning to its ultimate end, then the worse I am the better it is for God; for the more wicked I am, the more conspicuous will be the mercy of God in pardoning me. We should therefore do evil that good may come from it. And no good Jew would agree with this. In fact, they were criticizing Paul for teaching this.
    2. He implies the following: Again, the end never justifies the means to it.
    3. Appendix: Anyway, who ever said the glory of God is enhanced by the sins of mankind?

E. *Question #5: What then? Are we Jews in a worse position (than they, the Gentiles)?* The verb used here literally means "to have before" in the sense of surpassing to one's advantage or to one's disadvantage. Some suggest the former: "are we Jews better off than the Gentiles?" However, Paul has already answered this in Rom. 3:1,2. Rather here it should be translated "are we Jews worse off than the Gentiles?" Paul's answer clearly indicates the latter to be the better translation.

Answer: Paul answers, "Not in every respect," suggesting that they are worse off in one respect, namely, in the matter of having more light. The more light, the more responsibility one has. Note again that Paul does not answer "not at all", but "not altogether." However, in one sense, all mankind is under the same condemnation of sin. Paul affirms what he has been saying all along that all are under sin and therefore guilty before God. To repeat, the Jews are worse off only in the matter of having more light.

Conclusion: Paul proves in 2:17-3:8 that the Jew is also under condemnation, even though he is trusting in:
- A. His name "Jew,"
- B. His possession of the law and
- C. His physical circumcision
- D. Reasons: Because the things that matter before God for justification are
    1. Being a "true Jew," not one in name only,
    2. Obeying the law, not merely possessing it (an impossibility for all men in their present state) and
  Having a heart circumcision, not necessarily the physical one

Note on this "obedience" basis that the only true Jew that ever lived was Jesus Christ; for He alone kept the law perfectly, even to the very internal motives of the heart.

The Sinful Condition of the Whole World ~ Romans 3:9-20

⁹What therefore? Are we (Jews) being in a worse position [than they]? Not in every respect; for we previously brought a charge against both Jews and Greeks that all are under sin, ¹⁰even as it stands written,

> *There is none righteous, not even one;*
> *¹¹There is none who is understanding;*
> *There is none who is seeking God;*
> *¹²All have turned aside, together they have become unprofitable;*
> *There is none practicing goodness, there is not even one;*

> *¹³Their throat is a grave which has been opened;*
> *With their tongues they were deceiving;*
> *The poison of asps is under their lips,*
> *¹⁴Whose mouth is continually full of cursing and bitter hatred;*
> *¹⁵Their feet are quick to shed blood;*
> *¹⁶Destruction and misery are in their ways,*
> *¹⁷And the way of peace they have not known;*
> *¹⁸There is no fear of God before their eyes.*

¹⁹And we know that as many things as the law is speaking, it is speaking to those with the law, in order that every mouth may be put to silence and all the world may become liable to judgment with reference to God. ²⁰Wherefore by the works of law, no flesh will be justified before Him; for by means of law is the full knowledge of sin.

General remarks concerning the Old Testament quotations in Rom. 3:10-18

A.   Remark #1: Paul draws from various Old Testament books, such as one might do in creating a responsive reading in the back of one of our current hymnals.

B.   Remark #2: He gives no attention to the context of the verses.

C.   Remark #3: He does not rest his case for the sinfulness of all mankind on these Old Testament verses as he has already proved all mankind sinners by listing their actual sins. (1:18-3:8)

D.   Remark #4: He uses these only as an indication that the Old Testament Scriptures point in the direction of his view.

E.   Remark #5: He quotes from the Septuagint, generally speaking. On this matter we can trust the inspiration of the Holy Spirit.

I.   The Universality of Sin

A.   3:9   All are under sin.

B.   3:10   There is none righteous, not even one (because no one has kept the righteous standard of the law perfectly.)

C.   3:11   None is understanding, that is, having a right apprehension of divine truth.

D.   3:11   None is seeking God.

E.   3:12   All have turned aside.

F.   3:12   All are unprofitable, meaning all have gone bad or sour, like "sour milk."

G.   3:12   There is none doing good.

H.   3:19   Every mouth is stopped.

I.   3:19   All the world is under judgment.

J.   3:20   By the works of the law, none can be justified.

K. Appendix: cf. 3:21,22. "But now a righteousness apart from law (or obedience to law) has been manifested for all those who are believing." In other words, the salvation in the gospel is adequate for all those who have been condemned.

II. The Unsoundness of the Sinner, indicating the depth of his sinfulness
A. The infection of a person's words
1. His throat is an open tomb or sepulcher.
a. emphasis #1: the stench coming from a grave
b. emphasis #2: its desire to devour people
c. emphasis #3: its unloveliness
2. His tongue is characterized by deceitfulness.
3. His lips have underneath them the poison of snakes.
a. emphasis #1: the pain connected with a snakebite
b. emphasis #2: the death connected with it
c. emphasis #3: the poison connected with it. (The poison of the asp is hidden in a bag under the lips.)
4. His mouth is full of cursing and bitter hatred
B. The infection of a person's ways
1. His feet are swift to shed blood, meaning he thinks nothing of committing murder on the spur of the moment without any pangs of conscience.
2. In his ways are destruction and misery.
C. The infection of a person's thoughts
1. He has no knowledge of the way leading to peace. His mind is affected.
2. And there is no fear of God before his eyes.

III. The Uncoverer of His Sin: THE LAW with its purposes (This is Paul's conclusion to his section in which he condemns the entire world on the basis of works.
A. Purpose #1 for the law: To make the whole world blameworthy before God (Notice Paul's non-sequitur argument.) "What the law says, it says to those under the law that the whole world may be guilty before God." The argument does not follow. It is as if one argued, A=B and A=C and therefore X,Y, Z are letters.
1. Law = all law.
One way to get around the problem is to say that "law" in his argument is all law, including the law of God written on a person's heart. Rom. 2:14,15. The problem with this may be the fact that Paul as just quoted from the Old Testament which could mean that Paul means the Old Testament law, not all law.
2. Law = the Old Testament.
The argument then is that Gentile guilt before God is so self-evident that Paul only has to prove the Jews condemned to say then that all mankind is condemned.
*3. Law = the Mosaic Law.

44

The probable view is that the Mosaic law was given representatively to Israel and her failure to keep it equals the failure of all mankind to do so. It is like a person sampling a small portion of a field to see whether the whole field is good for growing potatoes. God cultivated carefully a small segment of mankind, the Jews, to see if it could obey his law. They couldn't so no one can. See Isa. 5:1-7.

B. Purpose #2 for the law: To give us a clear knowledge of sin
Note that Paul has a very high view of law.

C. Purpose #3 for the law: To demonstrate the futility of trying to achieve justification by obedience to the law
This is a side-effect and an after-effect of the giving of the law. As J. Gresham Machen writes, "A low view of law makes a man a legalist; a high view of law makes him a seeker."

Conclusion

Therefore, no one can be justified by his own righteousness or by his own keeping of the law. It is as if everyone in a room with no doors or windows is going to be condemned to suffer the wrath of God. It is obvious that we must do all we can to find a loose brick in the wall of the room to escape out of the enclosed room to safety. We cannot succeed in our escape any more than if we try by our own good works to save ourselves.

A. Only a fool keeps banging his head against the wall to escape from the condemned room when a door is open and available to him. Similarly, if the "door" of faith for justification is open to us, then only fools keep on trying to get their justification before God by the impossible route of personal lawkeeping.

B. The heathen man in many places is not even aware of the "door" of faith's existence.
The heathen in many places are not even aware of the fact that the path of justification by faith is available to them. This is where the job of the church and individual Christians comes in. We must tell them.

C. All a man has to do today to be lost is to do nothing with the light he has.
The reason for this is that we come into this life under the wrath of God. The decision to do nothing is a decision. Why don't people make the decision to accept Christ by faith? Some of them don't believe they have anything to fear from God in eternity; and others do believe it but are putting off making their decision, a dangerous option with all of the sudden ways today whereby a person may be ushered out into eternity.

Wrath and judgment are the introduction to any presentation of the gospel. Maybe more people are not accepting the gospel today because they have not heard why they need the gospel. Paul, in the first major section of Romans (condemnation: 1:18-3:20) is trying to get everyone miserable so that when he presents the Gospel in 3:21-5:11, his readers will want it.

CHAPTER FIVE

A Justification Available to Anyone Who Will Believe on Jesus for It

Romans 3:21-5:11

A Characterization of a Righteousness From God ~ Romans 3:21-31

21But now, apart from law a righteousness from God has been manifested, being witnessed by the law and the prophets, 22even a righteousness from God by means of faith in Jesus Christ, for all the ones believing, (for there is no distinction, 23for all have sinned and are continuing to come short of the glory of God), 24who are being justified as a gift by His grace by means of the redemption which is in Christ Jesus, 25whom God set forth [as] a propitiation, by means of faith, by His blood, for a manifestation of His righteousness, because of [His] passing over of the sins having happened before in the forbearance of God, 26for a manifestation, [I say,] of His righteousness in the present season in order that He may continue being just and justifying the one [who is having] faith in Jesus.

27Where therefore is the boasting? It has been excluded. By means of what sort of principle? Of works? No, by means of the principle of faith. 28For we continue reckoning that a man is being justified by means of faith apart from works of law. 29Or does God belong to Jews only? [He belongs] also to Gentiles, does He not? Yes, also to Gentiles, 30if [1st] indeed God is One who will justify [the] circumcision by faith and [the] uncircumcision by means of faith. 31Are we therefore putting law out of business by means of faith? May it not be so! but we are [really] establishing law.

Introductory matters
A. Note the emphasis on faith in this paragraph. This word did not appear at all in Rom. 1:18-3:20. (Note 3:3 where the word pistis means faithfulness.)
B. Note also the beautiful transition from the condemnation of everyone to justification by faith with the "But now ..."
C. Note the characteristics of a righteousness available for all receivers today:
   1. Its origination with God, and this is stressed three times in Rom. 3:21. This involves a status of righteousness which comes from God and was made available to us by God.
   2. Its separation from law Rom. 3:21. This means that it is apart from legal connections of any kind. It is apart from obedience to law of any kind. The definite article is omitted with "law" here.
   3. Its manifestation to the world 3:21. This means that this righteous standing before God has been brought to light. It is not hidden. A medicine which is under wraps and hidden will do very little good.
   4. Its proclamation by the law and the prophets 3:21.

Note the definite article with "law" here.

    a. The law: The gospel is proclaimed in the Old Testament law in the laws relating to the sacrifices and the priesthood.

    b. The prophets: The gospel appears in direct statement in the prophets. For an example, see Isaiah 53.

    c. The Old Testament generally: The gospel appears here through types and promises. (The Old Testament tells us what God will do and this demanded faith. The New Testament tells us what God has done and this also demands faith.)

5. Its foundation on faith in Jesus Christ 3:22.
Note that this is not a general faith in God but a specific faith in Jesus Christ and what He has done. This is the channel for our justification. It is through faith in Jesus Christ, our Savior.

6. Its congregation of all who believe 3:22 (This is a repetition of point 5).
The parenthesis (3:22b,23) indicates that there is no distinction in people but all have sinned, are continuing to fall short of God's glory, and hence need this salvation.

7. Its obligation for all. Every human being needs this salvation if he or she is to escape the wrath of God. The only other means of salvation, the "works" route, cannot be pursued successfully by sinners.

8. Its acceptation as a gift 3:24.
See John 15:25 where the same Greek word translated "as a gift" is translated "without a cause." "They hated me without a cause." Here our justification is "without any cause" or merit in us. Faith is the occasion or our justification, not the cause for it.

9. Its instrumentation by His grace 3:24.
The instrument or our justification is unmerited favor on the part of God. God does not give the sinner what he deserves.

10. Its initiation by God 3:24, 25. God set forth Christ as a propitiation for our sins so that he could provide a redemption in Christ Jesus.

    a. Expiation is not a good translation here as it puts too heavy an emphasis on man's payment and his making complete atonement for something. Expiation does not include any emphasis on the placating of the offended holiness of God by the sins of mankind.

    b. Propitiation equals the satisfaction of the offended holiness of God. The verb means "to appease," "to render favorable," "to conciliate," "to placate," or "to avert wrath." God's wrath against sin is taught in the Scriptures and this must be placated, appeased, satisfied, or propitiated before He can forgive and save sinners; and this happened at the cross where the wrath of God fell upon Christ for all believers.

11. Its acceptation by God 3:24. God sponsored this plan of justification and he has officially accepted it.
12. Its foundation on faith 3:25. This is the same as A and B above.
13. Its instrumentation by Christ's blood 3:25. Christ's death on the cross provided justification for us.
14. Its elimination of all human boasting 3:27. This plan of justification by faith gives all the glory to God and none to man. Faith is something we must exercise for salvation but it is not a meritorious thing we do. It is like the cry of the drowning man, which he must make for his salvation but which is not a grounds for boasting when he again is standing safely on board ship. In other words, he would be foolish to brag about how he saved himself because he cried so loudly. So also it would be just as stupid for the Christian to boast of how he saved himself because he believed. His faith is a receptive virtue, not a productive one.
15. Its equalization of both Jew and Gentile before God 3:29, 30. Both Jew and Gentile are on the same footing before God, as far as He is concerned.
16. Its effectualization of the law 3:31. This plan does not by-pass the law but rather establishes it or fulfills it. More will be said on how this is done later.

Appendix: Note the emphasis on grace and faith here in Romans 3:21-31.

II. The Contemplation of Christ's Offering, that is the intention or purpose of it

A. A demonstration of God's righteousness in passing over sins previously committed BY BELIEVERS.
This is a reference to God's disregarding the sins of Old Testament believers and letting them go unpunished. His purpose in setting Christ forth as a propitiation was to demonstrate His righteousness in passing over unpunished the sins of Old Testament believers. He withheld judgment with a view to Christ's payment on the cross. He passed over and forgave their sins ON CREDIT because no one had paid for those sins until later Christ did it.

B. A showing of His righteousness in this present time.
God did this by His judging of sins at the cross of Jesus Christ.

C. A maintenance of His own justice and His justifying of the one who has put his faith in Christ.
1. It is not that "God is righteous and yet declares the believer in Christ righteous."
There is no opposition between God's justice and His mercy, as this statement seems to imply. He does not justify us in spite of His righteousness.

2. But "God is righteous and therefore declares the believer in Jesus righteous."

God justifies us because of His righteousness. Our sins, as believers, have been paid for by an acceptable Substitute, Jesus Christ; and therefore God cannot punish two persons for the same crimes and remain true to His character as just. Someone must pay the penalty of death for sins; and for the believer, Jesus Christ paid that price.

III. **The Consequences of this Provision of Righteousness**
  A. The outlawing of boasting 3:27,28
     The "law" of faith here equals the "principle" of faith. This principle rules out any boasting on the part of the Christian. Faith is something we must exercise but it is not a meritorious work we perform. It is a RECEPTIVE virtue, not a PRODUCTIVE virtue. It is like the cry of the drowning man, "Save me, somebody, save me." His cry for help must go forth or he will not be saved. However, it is non-meritorious. The saved man cannot brag about how he saved himself because he cried so loudly. Even so, the Christian would not be saved apart from faith in the Lord Jesus; however, he cannot boast of how he saved himself because he believed. Again, faith is something we must exercise; but it is non-meritorious and certainly not grounds for boasting.
  B. The putting of Jew and Gentile on the same footing before God Rom. 3:29,30
     Both Jew and Gentile must come for salvation BY FAITH. This is clearly taught here. As Charles Hodge points out, the Greek expressions in these verses are different but there is no difference in meaning. Out of faith and by means of faith refer to the same instrument for our salvation.
  C. The establishment of the Law 3:31
     Another consequence of this provision of righteousness this way, via the cross of Christ, is that the law is established, not by-passed or abrogated. God's plan treats the law with the respect it deserves.
     1. First of all, there is an active establishment of the law by Christ who for thirty-three years lived here on earth and kept the law perfectly by what is called His ACTIVE OBEDIENCE. This is now put to the believer's account.
     2. Then there was the passive establishment by Christ who passively suffered the penalty of law-breaking by His death on the cross for all believers. God cannot remain righteous and just and play fast and loose with the law. Someone has to pay the penalty for sins, either the sinner himself or an acceptable Substitute, one acceptable to the Judge, viz.. God, and to the sinner himself.

50

Conclusion

"The Jew looked at the Old Testament, and he saw there Law, Obedience to Law or Works, Circumcision, Descent from Abraham. St. Paul said. Look again and look deeper, and you will see, not Law - but Promise, not works - but Faith, of which Circumcision is only the seal, not literal descent from Abraham but spiritual descent. All these things are realized in Christianity." (Used by permission: William Sanday and Arthur C. Headlam, The International Critical Commentary: Romans. 5th ed. (Edinburgh: T. & T. dark, 1950), p. 96.

Appendix: For a good summary of justification by faith, see Charles Hodge, Commentary on Romans, p. 81 and following.

    A. Justification is not simply pardon for sins committed.
A president may give a criminal a pardon and yet the criminal is not justified or declared righteous. A pardon is the release from the legal penalty of an offense, although the grounds for the punishment still exist.

    B. Justification is not simply pardon and the restoration to divine favor.
Here again the grounds for punishment still exist.

    C. Justification does not mean the MAKING of a person just or righteous inwardly.
When an accused person is declared righteous in the eyes of the law, his inner character is not changed.

    D. Justification is the declaring of a person just or righteous in the eyes of the court and the eyes of the Judge.

        1. It is a forensic term. A thing that is forensic is something belonging to, used in, or suitable to courts of law or to public discussion and debate. It is a declarative word in the Greek language.

        2. It is the opposite of condemnation.

        3. It involves God's imputation or reckoning of Christ's human righteousness or law-keeping to the believing sinner's account. Note that this is not God's righteousness but Christ's holy human righteousness put to the believing Christian's account. As Galatians 4:4 says, Jesus Christ was born... under the law to redeem those under the law.

        4. It is more than a mere pardon.

            a. Pardon involves the remission of punishment.

            b. Justification involves the declaration that no grounds for punishment exist. The grounds have been taken care of by our Substitute, Jesus Christ. We stand IN GOD'S SIGHT just as if we had never sinned. Keep in mind, however, that this is only true in God's sight. With all sinning, there are scars that remain as reaping; therefore, in many other ways we can never be today absolutely "just as if we had never sinned."

            c. Regeneration involves the changed heart, the new creation (II Corinthians 5:17).

Regeneration is the internal side to the external justification. Regeneration is done in us and justification is done for us. Regeneration is God's act within us while justification is God's act for us.

E. Appendix: How can God be true to His nature and declare a believing sinner righteous, who, in fact, is not experientially righteous?

Answer: The sinner's sins have already been paid for by Jesus Christ on the cross. God is just and cannot punish two persons for the same crime. Remember that Paul was writing to legally intelligent Romans who knew this principle. If God has accepted Jesus' death as the death of the believer, then it is obvious to those who know law that He cannot remain righteous and punish both Jesus and the sinner for the same sins.

Old Testament Illustrations of Justification by Faith ~ Romans 4:1-17a

> *¹What therefore shall we say that Abraham, our forefather according to the flesh, has found? ²For if [1st] Abraham out of works was justified, he is having grounds for boasting, but not before God [does he have grounds for boasting]. ³For what is the Scripture saying? "And Abraham believed God, and it was reckoned to him for righteousness." ⁴But to the one who is working, the reward is not reckoned according to grace but according to debt; ⁵but to the one who is not working but believing on the One who is justifying the ungodly [person], his faith is reckoned for righteousness; ⁶just as David also is saying regarding the blessedness of the man to whom God is reckoning righteousness apart from works:*
>
>> *⁷Blessed are [the ones] whose lawless acts have been forgiven and whose sins have been covered.*
>> *⁸Blessed is a man whose sin the Lord will never reckon [to him].*
>
> *⁹Was this blessedness [pronounced] therefore at [the time of] his circumcision or at [the time of] his uncircumcision? For we are saying, "Faith was reckoned to Abraham for righteousness." ¹⁰How therefore was it reckoned, while he was in circumcision or in uncircumcision? [It was] not in circumcision but in uncircumcision; ¹¹and [the] sign of circumcision he received [as] a seal of the righteousness of faith, that [which he had in a state] of uncircumcision, in order that he might continue being father of all the ones believing through [a state of] uncircumcision, in order that righteousness might be reckoned to them; ¹²and the father of circumcision to those not only from the circumcision [group] but also to those continuing to march in the footsteps of the faith of our father, Abraham, [which he had] in uncircumcision. ¹³For not by means of law was the promise to Abraham or to his seed [viz.,] that he was to be the heir of the world, but by means of a righteousness (stemming) from faith.*
>
> *¹⁴For if [1st] those out of law [are] heirs, faith has been emptied of meaning and the promise has been put out of business; ¹⁵for the law produces wrath; but where there is no law, neither is there transgression. ¹⁶Because of this it is by faith, in order that it may be according to grace, in order that the promise may continue being sure for all the seed, not only for the one [who is] of the law but also for the one [who is] of the faith of Abraham, who is father of all of us, ¹⁷even as it stands written, "A father of many nations I have appointed you (s)" before [the] God in whom he believed...*

Introduction: The key words in this passage have to do with reckoning, believing, and being justified or declared righteous.

I. The Case of Abraham   4:1-5,9-17a
    The following are the things told to us here about Abraham: He was...
    A. The father of the Jews according to the flesh
    B. A righteous man before God according to his faith
        Everyone admits that Abraham was a righteous man, i.e., he was justified. The only question was how that came about. So what does the Scripture, the final court of appeal for Paul, have to say on this. He then cites Genesis 15:6: "Abraham believed God and it, his belief, was reckoned to him for righteousness." The

verb "to reckon" means to count as equivalent to something else, which it is not. It means to have the force of or the weight of or the value of some thing else. For example, a check is not money but when it is properly filled out and signed, it is treated as money by the banks of our land. Faith or believing is not righteousness in the presence of God but it is reckoned as or treated as equivalent to righteousness on the books of heaven.

C. A man who had no grounds for boasting
Again, faith is something we must exercise but not a meritorious thing we do. Faith takes God at His Word and demonstrates its presence by an obeying of His commands. Faith has no saving merit but is the occasion upon which God justifies us. It is a RECEPTIVE virtue, not a PRODUCTIVE one. As Robert R. Williams writes, "When a man exercises his freedom to accept God's grace, it cannot be put to his credit; otherwise he is not saved by grace, and we are back with the legalists of every age. He needs no more will power than when he reaches out his hand to accept what is offered him from the other side of a counter in a store . .." (Robert R. Williams. A Guide to the Teachings of the Early Church Fathers, p. 168.)

D. A man whose faith was reckoned for righteousness 4:3-5
If one works for his righteous standing before God, then he gets it as a WAGE earned. But Paul's whole presentation here was meant to prove that no one can work for eternal life as it is necessary to work. If a righteous status before God is to be attained, it must be by grace on the basis of faith and faith alone. Some Jews were saying that you must earn God's favor. The Christian message says that you cannot do this. You must take God at His Word, which is faith.

E. A receiver of righteousness apart from circumcision 4:9-12
1. The time of his circumcision: This came 14 or 15 years after he was declared righteous.
Compare Genesis 15:6 and 17:24,25. Years before he was circumcised, Abraham was already declared righteous and therefore justified.
2. The significance of circumcision: His circumcision of himself and his whole household on one day was a sign and a seal of the righteousness he already had on the basis of faith alone. As the ark was a sign of Noah's faith, and the blood on the doorposts and the lintel was a sign of Israelite faith on Passover night, so was the circumcision of Abraham's household an evidence of his faith. God had said, "Circumcise your whole household," and Abraham did it, believing that God would protect his whole household during the time it would take for them to heal from that surgery. Later on a whole town was slaughtered by Simeon and Levi while it was healing from a similar operation.

54

See Gen. 34. Some were saying that one must become a Jew first by becoming circumcised before one can be justified. Paul says, "This is not true because Abraham wasn't." Abraham was circumcised and became a Jew after he had already been declared righteous some years before. Abraham was 99 and Ishmael 13 when they, with the rest, were circumcised.

    a.   This makes Abraham the spiritual father of the Gentiles who believe.

    b.   This makes him the father twice of the Jews who believe, naturally and spiritually.

    c.   This makes him according to Paul here, the father of all who believe.

F.   A receiver of the promise apart from law, i.e. apart from meritorious obedience to law 4:13-17

    1.   What promise? See the Abrahamic promise given and then reiterated in the following passages: Genesis 12:1-4; 17: 4,5; 18:18; 22:17,18.

        a.   Part 1: Abraham would have a son by Sarah.

        b.   Part 2: This son would have numerous descendants.

        c.   Part 3: In One of these descendants, viz., Jesus, the whole world would be blessed.

        d.   Part 4: Through this One, Abraham's seed would enjoy world-rule. Rom 4:13

            This verse indicates Abraham would be heir of the world.

        e.   Part 5: Abraham would become the father of many nations.

            And all he had to go on was the bare word of God. He did not even have a son by Sarah yet.

    2.   Why is it apart from law by faith?

        a.   Cause #1: The promise is apart from law and by faith because if the (perfect) obeyers of the law are heirs of the promise, faith is made void. Faith is emptied of meaning. The merit-method makes void the faith-method.

        b.   Cause #2: It is because thereby the promise is made of non-effect. This is because obedience to the law can only bring wrath and death, not eternal life and blessing. We are sinners.

            1.) No one can keep the law as it is necessary to keep it for justification. In other words, if the promise depends on keeping the law, the promise can never be fulfilled.

            2.) By the law's coming, it increases sin and guilt. There is sin and guilt before the operation of the law but not as much as there is after the coming of law. Ignorance of the law is no excuse: however, once the law is known, flagrant disobedience is even more guilt-worthy. Also, often when a prohibition is given, the natural man wants to break it. Therefore, Paul was right when he said that the entrance of law into a situation not only increases the guilt of a sin but often also increases the sinning.

    c.   Cause #3: It is because justification is according to God's grace, not man's obedience. Law knows no grace. One either keeps the law perfectly or he suffers the consequences of lawbreaking.

    d.   Cause #4: Justification is based on faith and then the promise is sure to all the seed. If justification is based on obeying the law, it can never be a sure thing. One never knows whether he has done enough. But since it is based on faith and not on obedience to law, it is sure to all the seed, both circumcised and uncircumcised believers.

II. **The Case of David** 4:6-8

  A. The reasons for including David's testimony

    1. Reason #1: The support of David's testimony adds the weight of another witness.

    2. Reason #2: It includes the testimony of another great Jewish hero from the Old Testament.

    3. Reason #3: It brings into view a person with an entirely different experience. Abraham was a relatively good man while David was a terrible sinner.

    4. Reason #4: It focuses on a man who lived after the Mosaic law was given. This would answer the assertion of any one who said that after the Mosaic Law was given, it was necessary then to keep it for justification.

  B. The results of his faith

    Note Paul's quoting of Psalm 32: 1,2a, the first part of one of David's penitential Psalms.

    1. Result #1: There would be no imputation of his sin to him by God, (although he REAPED the rest of his life for his adultery with Bathsheba.)

    2. Result #2: There would be forgiveness for his iniquities, and this was true even in the Old Testament. Their sins were forgiven ON CREDIT.

    3. Result #3: There was a covering of sins, which means forgiveness for them. Note the synonymous parallelisms here in this Hebrew poetry quoted.

    4. Result #4: There would be no reckoning of his sin to him and therefore he stood justified before God.

    Appendix: All of this, however, presupposes the confession of his sin to God. See I John 1:9.

Conclusion: General New Testament principles 4:4,5

  A. Principle #1: Rom. 4:4 To the one working, the reward is reckoned according to debt.

B. Principle #2: Rom. 4:5 To the one believing, his faith is reckoned or accounted as righteousness.
C. Appendix: The supposed conflict between Paul and James
The answer to the supposed conflict lies in two different references to works;
  1. Paul is strongly opposed to works of law whereby one attempts to merit his justification before God.
  2. James is supporting those works which are the lovely fruits of a real Christian experience; and Paul is solidly in favor of these as well. See Eph. 2:8-10 and all the practical sections of his epistles in which he describes "obedience that should stem from faith." See Romans 1:5 and 16:26 on the relation of obedience to faith.

The Characteristics of Abraham's Faith ~ Romans 4:17b-25

...who is the One giving life to the dead and calling the things which are not existing as though they are existing; ¹⁸who contrary to hope, on the basis of hope believed so that he became a father of many nations according to that which had been spoken, "Thus your (s) seed will be." ¹⁹And because he did not weaken in faith, he considered his own body as having become dead, because it was about a hundred years old, and the deadness of the womb of Sarah; ²⁰but at the promise of God, he did not waver with unbelief, but he became strengthened in faith, having given glory to God ²¹and having been fully convinced that what He has promised, He is also able to perform. ²²Therefore, also, it was reckoned to him for righteousness.

²³But it was not written on account of him alone, [viz.,] that it was reckoned to him ²⁴but also on account of us, to whom it is about to be reckoned, to those who continue believing on the One who raised Jesus, our Lord, from the dead, [Jesus] ²⁵who was delivered over on account of our transgressions and was raised on account of our justification.

Introduction: In Romans 4:17b-25 Paul describes the kind of faith which Abraham had and which God reckoned for righteousness.

I.   **Characteristic #1:** Abraham's faith was directed toward God Himself and God's promise that he would have a son through Sarah, through which son he would become the father of many nations. Note the importance of knowing and believing the specific promises of God that relate to us. Romans 4:17b

II. **Characteristic #2:** Abraham's faith was optimistic in the face of seeming hopelessness. Romans 4:18
     The promise of a son was given to Abraham and Sarah in their old age. That they should have a son was against all hope and reasonable expectation. Abraham was 100 years old and Sarah 90; furthermore, if they were married when Sarah was a teenager, she could have been barren for 75 years or more. See Genesis 17:17.

III. **Characteristic #3:** Abraham's faith was transcendent over reason. Romans 4:19,20
     His faith considered the obstacles to the fulfillment of the promise given him but refused to waver when facing them.
     A. The manuscript evidence
        1. The King James' version reads that he did NOT consider the deadness of his own body for begetting children and he did NOT consider the deadness of Sarah's womb.
        2. However, the best and oldest manuscripts say he did consider these obstacles without wavering. They omit the negative.
     B. The obstacles which Abraham considered while still believing were as follows:
        1. The deadness of his own body to beget children at the age of 100

58

      2. The deadness of Sarah's womb at the age of 90
      3. Appendix: And even when he offered Isaac, the seed of promise, on the altar on Mount Moriah, he did not waver in unbelief but believed that God could and would raise Isaac up from the dead to keep His word to him. See Hebrews 11:19 where God's Word specifically says this. Also see Genesis 22:5 where Abraham says to the two young men with him, "Stay here with the donkey, and I and the lad will go yonder and we will worship and we will return to you." Note the "we's" which are clear in the Hebrew and which clearly indicate Abraham's tremendous faith.

IV. **Characteristic #4**: Abraham's faith was confident in the supernatural. Romans 4:20
In the natural, Abraham and Sarah would have had no son. With the supernatural involved, they had Isaac. Paul says that Abraham did not waver or entertain any doubting thoughts regarding the son he was to have. He wavered a couple of times relative to Sarah when he lied regarding her relationship to him. See Genesis 12:10-20 and chapter 20. But in regard to a son from Sarah in his old age, he never doubted God. One problem relative to the confident faith of Abraham affirmed here is relative to Abraham's sexual relations with Hagar which produced Ishmael. (Genesis 15 & 16) Many scholars have seen a wavering of Abraham's faith at this point, although Paul says he never wavered in unbelief regarding the son which he was to have by Sarah. The following is the answer to the seeming discrepancy between the Genesis account and Romans 4:
A. The Genesis order of events is as follows:
      1. Genesis 12:1-3 God promises to make a great nation of Abraham and to bless him.
      2. Genesis 15:1-6 Abraham calls God's attention to the fact that he has no seed and refers to Eliezer, his steward, as a possible heir in keeping with the custom of that day. God promises Abraham that one born from his own loins will be his heir and that his seed will be as the stars of the heaven. Then comes Genesis 15:6 quoted by Paul in Romans 4: "Abraham believed God and that belief was reckoned to him for righteousness."
      3. Genesis 16:1ff. Then is recorded the planning of Ishmael's birth at Sarah's suggestion. It may be that they both felt that this would be God's way of providing seed from Abraham's loins, according to the earlier promise, since Sarah still had no son. Note that nothing up to this point has indicated that the son would come from Sarah, only that he would come from Abraham.
      4. Genesis 17:1ff. Here the promise is re-iterated to Abraham that he would be the father of many nations; and then apparently for the first time, Sarah is brought into the picture. (Genesis 17:15-19)
         a. Sarah's name was changed from Sarai.

        b.   God promised to give Abraham a son by her.

        c.   Then it says Abraham laughed, saying in his heart, "Shall a child be born unto him who is a hundred years old? And shall Sarah, who is ninety years old, bear?"

B.   Some personal observations regarding the above verses are as follows:

    1.   The promise of a son by Sarah is the promise which Paul says Abraham believed. The first suggestion regarding Eliezer as heir (Gen. 15:1-6) and the planning regarding Ishmael was apart from any divine indication that Sarah would be the mother. Eliezer was eliminated the moment God said the son would be from Abraham's loins. Ishmael was eliminated the moment God said that Sarah would be the mother. When Abraham heard this latter, Paul says, he believed, in spite of the biological problems naturally connected with it.

    2.   His laughter (IVA4c above) need not be laughter of unbelief but of joy. Whitelaw suggests it may have been an expression or exclamation of holy wonder or maybe an illustration of hardly being able to believe it for joy at the announcement. See Luke 24:41 where it says of the disciples regarding the resurrection: "And while they were still disbelieving from joy and wondering he said to them are you having here anything edible?" The laugh would appear to be caused by the fact that they could hardly believe their eyes and ears. Why could this not be true in Abraham's case also?

    3.   His request for Ishmael (IA4c above) need not be an indication that he would be satisfied with Ishmael with no Isaac needed; but rather that he was concerned lest Ishmael be left with no part in the blessings. Note that in v. 20 God promises to take care of Ishmael also, but THE COVENANT IS TO BE WITH ISAAC. Gen. 21:11 clearly indicates that Abraham did love his son, Ishmael, because he refused to send the boy and his mother away, as Sarah urged, until he had God's instructions to do so and God's promise that He would take care of them.

    4.   One needs to be careful in studying commentaries on Genesis and in using some of the translations and paraphrases of Genesis. Those who have worked on these works either have never tied in Genesis 17 with Romans 4 or, if they have, they have forgotten their findings. For example, note the Living Bible's paraphrase of Genesis 17:17: "Then Abraham threw himself down in worship before the Lord, but inside he was laughing in disbelief; 'Me, be a father?' he said in amusement. 'Me-100 years old? And Sarah, to have a baby at 90?'" Romans 4:20,21 indicates clearly that on the matter of a son from Sarah, Abraham never wavered in unbelief. Consequently, there must be another way to explain his laughter over the

promise and his plea for Ishmael in Genesis 17, other than as unbelief on his part. The hermeneutic principle of comparing Scripture with Scripture must always be followed for correct exegesis to result.

V. **Characteristic #5:** Abraham's faith glorified God. Romans 4:20 In no way could it take glory or credit to itself for the miracle that happened.

VI. **Characteristic #6:** Abraham's faith maintained full confidence in God that what He promises, He is fully able to carry out. God's promise for Abraham was just as good as the fulfillment of it. Romans   4:21

VII. **Characteristic #7:** Abraham's faith was successful in that it was reckoned as righteousness for the Hebrew patriarch. Romans 4:22 (Gen. 15:6) As said before, faith is not righteousness but it is treated as equivalent to righteousness. It is as if one lost the white queen belonging to a chess game. A button could replace the lost queen and the game could still be played, as long as both players understood the substitution. The button is not the queen but for purposes of the game, the button is reckoned as though it were, is moved like it, is captured like it, etc. Even so faith is not righteousness in God's sight but it is considered to be righteousness.

VIII. **Characteristic #8:** Abraham's faith demonstrated itself in actions of exact and immediate obedience. Romans 4:11,12 It is interesting to note that when Paul wanted an action of obedience to illustrate the faith which Abraham had, he did not cite the offering of Isaac on the altar described in Genesis 22. The reason may have been that that obedience was too great an act of obedience and it might have overshadowed the faith element, which Paul was stressing here. Rather Paul cites Abraham's circumcision of his whole household on one day. His doing this meant that he was trusting his God for protection during the healing of the males in his household from this surgery. This was proof that his faith was not just talk, as was also the offering of Isaac on the altar later.

Conclusion: Why was all this recorded in the Old Testament?
 A. Reason #1: It was an example that God does impute righteousness on the basis of faith, even in the Old Testament.
 B. Reason #2: It was to be an encouragement for us to trust God that the work has been done for us.
 C. Therefore, Paul concludes, let us believe in...
  1. God who delivered Jesus over to death for our trespasses; and
  2. Jesus who was raised again from the dead for our justification.

a. Christ's resurrection was conclusive proof that Christ was all He claimed to be.
b. His resurrection was proof of God's acceptance of Christ's work for our justification.

The Blessings of Justification ~ Romans 5:1-11

[1]Because, therefore, we have been justified by faith, we continue having peace with God by means of our Lord Jesus Christ, [2]by means of whom also we have had the introduction by faith into this grace in which we have come to stand; and we continue glorying because of the hope of the glory of God. [3]And not only [this], but we also continue glorying in tribulations, because we know that tribulation continues producing endurance, [4]and endurance [produces] approved character, and approved character [produces] hope; [5]and hope is not disappointing [us], because the love of God has been poured out in our hearts by means of [the] Holy Spirit who has been given to us. [6]Indeed, while we were yet weak, Christ died at the proper season on behalf of the ungodly. [7]For [the fact is that] only rarely on behalf of a righteous [person] will someone die; for on behalf of the good person someone might even dare to die; [8]but God is exhibiting His own love for us because, while we were yet sinners, Christ died on behalf of us. [9]Therefore, how much more rather, because we have been justified now by His blood, shall we be saved by means of Him from wrath. [10]For if [1st] while we were enemies, we were reconciled, shall we be saved by His life; [11]and not only [this], but (we are) also glorying in God by means of our Lord Jesus Christ, by means of whom now we have received the reconciliation.

Introduction: Therefore, because we have been justified or declared righteous by faith, we and all other Old and New Testament individuals justified by faith have the following...

I. A peace with God Romans 5:1
   A. This refers to a resultant union of man, who was once an enemy, with God the Father through the Son.
   B. This refers also to a change in God's relation to mankind.
   C. This means that God's wrath, which had been hanging over us, is now removed. See Romans 1:18.
   D. Appendix: This does not refer to "the peace of God" in the sense of inner peace of mind, although such a justified status does bring that also. See Phil. 4:7. In other words, the person justified by faith has both peace or reconciliation with God and the peace or tranquility which comes from a right relationship with Him.

II. **An official introduction into grace, which equals the justified relationship in which we have come to stand.** Romans 5:2a
   "Access" is too weak a translation.
   A. This is a place of justification.
   B. This is a place of privilege and responsibility.
   C. This is a place of divine favor.
   D. This is a place of divine help, much needed if we are to escape from divine wrath.

62

III. **A rejoicing in hope, probably the hope of the future glorified state in heaven** Romans 5:2b

The Greek word translated "rejoicing here" is the word that means elsewhere, "boasting," "glorying," or "exulting" with joy or triumph." It is used three (3) times in Romans 5:1-11.

Also it is important to remember that rejoicing is an action, not an emotion, and hence it is something one can do whether one feels like it or not.

IV. **A rejoicing in tribulations** Romans 5:3,4,5a

Note there is to be the same joy for both future glory and present tribulations and physical hardships. Paul glorified in these sufferings; we too often pity ourselves.

A. One result from this rejoicing: endurance, constancy, bravery, masculinity, activity, not passive patience (This is the picture of a veteran soldier in the midst of a hot battle.)

B. Another result: approvedness, which is the state of one who has stood the test

(As the International Critical Commentary describes this state, "It is the temper of a veteran rather than a raw recruit.")

C. Another result: hope for the future

D. A final result: unashamedness, the spiritual state which has proved itself under trial.

V. **The love of God which is poured out or distributed largely and abundantly within us** Romans 5:5b (Notice the logical reasoning.).

A. Mankind's unloveliness (Note how Paul's description of mankind gets worse and worse).

1. 5:6 Mankind is without strength, i.e., incapable of working out any righteous standing before God for themselves.

2. 5:5 Mankind is ungodly, i.e., bankrupt of all moral and spiritual inclinations toward God and holiness.

3. 5:8 Mankind is sinful, i.e., having missed God's mark of holiness totally.

4. 5:10 Mankind is an enemy of God. (This is a word that implies active hostility against God and His program.)

B. God's love

However, God's love overcame all of the above in the offering of His Son.

1. God's reconciliation of His enemies surely means He will save His friends. (See John Scott, Men Made New: An Exposition of Romans 5-8. Chicago: Inter-Varsity Press, 1966, p.20.

2. Christ's death for the ungodly is proof of God's love for His enemies because the most that human love will do is far less. (See James Denney, The Expositor's Greek Testament: Romans. Vol. II. Grand Rapids: Wm. B. Eerdman's Publishing Company, 1953, p. 625.

a. Paul indicates that someone may die for a coldly, legalistic, righteous individual. This is a person who is rigidly supportive of justice and does not deviate one bit from the right. He may gain one's admiration and respect but not his love.

b. Paul says that there is a greater possibility that someone might die for a warmer, good person. He is kinder and more benevolent.

c. But, says Paul, only Christ would die for an enemy. His love surpasses mankind's. As William R. Newell says it, God's love for us was "unasked for, undesired, and undeserved" and yet Christ died for us.

VI. **The presence of the Holy Spirit within the justified individual**
Romans 5: 5c-8 Remember that this blessing of justification by faith is for all the justified; and this includes the Old Testament believers as well as the New Testament ones. Paul has just used Abraham and David as examples of two Old Testament believers justified by faith.

VII. **A salvation from wrath** Romans 5:9
Paul's argument is that now that we have been justified by faith (the greater blessing) how much more shall we be saved from the wrath of God to come (the lesser blessing).

A. Deliverance from the wrath of God comes as a blessing of justification by faith. See Rom. 1:18.

B. This deliverance is the lesser benefit according to Paul here. His argument here is as follows: If the greater benefit (justification) is bestowed, the lesser benefit, salvation from wrath, will certainly follow.

VIII. **A reconciliation with God** Romans 5:10

A. This is a change in personal relations between God and mankind.

1. It is not wholly mankind's animosity against God which has to be taken care of.

2. It is also God's wrath toward the sins of sinners. He loves the sinner but hates the sins. It is God's wrath that needs to be propitiated or placated or appeased.

B. This secures for us the favor of God by the death of Christ, His Son.

C. This involves a change in God's relation to us, as well as a change in our relationship to Him.

IX. **An assurance of salvation now and in the future** Romans 5:10
Because we have been justified by faith, we have help for living now, not just a change in our present status before God. There is given a new aid and stimulus to enable the sinner to quit his sinning. See John 10:10 and Christ's statement that he came that we might have real living in the present, not just in the future.

64

X. **A rejoicing in God, which means a constant delight in God.**
    Romans 5:11

XI. **A reconciliation with God.** Romans 5:11
    A. Paul begins his list of blessings with this, calling it "peace with God."
    B. He reiterates it again within the list.
    C. Then he brings in the idea again toward the end of the list.

    Appendix: Reconciliation is a "bringing back together again" of the two parties that are estranged; and this has happened in the person of Christ in His death on the cross. Note that this is what God has done for us in Christ, not what we have done.

XII. **Appendix:** There are two additional blessings cited in the next section,   Romans 5:12-21.
    A. A removal of Adam's sin from our accounts on the books of heaven   (5:16-19).
    B. A reckoning of Christ's human righteousness to the accounts of all believers (5:16-19).

CHAPTER SIX

The Imputation of Adam's Sin to all in Adam and Christ's Righteousness to all in Christ Who are Receiving it
Romans 5:12-21

12Because of this, just as by means of one man sin entered into the world, and by means of sin, death, and thus death permeated all men, because all sinned-- 13for until [the] law, sin was in [the] world, but sin is not reckoned while law is not existing; 14but death reigned from Adam until Moses even over those who had not sinned after the likeness of the transgression of Adam, who is a type of the One coming. 15But not as the transgression, so also [is] the free gift; for if [1st] by the transgression of the one, the many died, how much more rather did the grace of God and the gift by grace, that of the one Man, Jesus Christ, for the many become available in abundance. 16And not as by means of one who sinned [is] the gift; for, on the one hand, judgment [was] from one [transgression] unto condemnation; but, on the other hand, the free gift [was] from many transgressions unto justification. 17For if [1st] by the transgression of the one, death reigned by means of the one, how much more rather will the ones receiving the abundance of grace and the gift of righteousness reign in life by means of One, Jesus Christ. 18Consequently therefore, as by means of one transgression [the judgment came] unto all mankind for condemnation, in the same manner also by means of one righteous act [the gift came] unto all mankind for a justification [characterized by] life. 19For just as by means of the disobedience of the one man, the many were put down [on the books] as sinners, in the same manner also by means of the obedience of the One, the many will be put down [as] righteous. 20But law entered in alongside in order that the transgression might become greater; but where sin became greater, grace became present in greater abundance; 21in order that, just as sin reigned by death, in the same manner also grace might reign by means of righteousness unto eternal life by means of Jesus Christ, our Lord.

Introduction: There is a contrast here: As it was with Adam, so it is not with Christ. If Adam was and is powerful for evil, Christ is more powerful for good.
   A.   In this passage there are another couple of blessings of justification by faith, namely, the removal of Adam's sin from the believer's account and the imputing there of Christ's human righteousness, his perfect law-keeping.
   B.   In this passage there is also an explanation of the way in which we get our righteous standing before God. In other words, the same way we are condemned in the first place is the way in which we also get our righteous standing before God.

I.   **The Commencement of the Comparison: the first member, Adam**
   A.   Adam was the responsible party for sin's entrance into the human race.
      1.   There have been several attempts to explain how he became this.

2. All that needs to be said here is that he was responsible for sin entering in the same way in which Christ was responsible for righteousness entering.
B. Adam was the responsible party (indirectly) for death's entrance.
   1. Death, according to the Scriptures, is a penal evil or punishment.
   2. Death is not a consequence of the original constitution of man. In other words, death is a damaging of human nature, not a demand of it.
   3. Death was not an essential part of human nature before the fall of mankind.
C. Adam was the responsible party for bringing death upon all men, because all sinned   5:12
   (THE BIG QUESTION is HOW?)
   1. View #1: All mankind sinned actually and personally.
      (Note that on this view nothing comes down from Adam.)
      a. This view is inconsistent with the Aorist tense of the verb "sinned" which is a tense of point or punctiliar activity. The durative Greek tenses would have been used had Paul intended this.
      b. It is inconsistent with the context of the text which makes Adam's sin, and not our many sins, the cause of death here. The emphasis here is on one man's SIN, not many men's SINS.
      c. It is inconsistent with vs. 13,14 which support v. 12. However, these verses do not support v. 12 if it is referring to the personal sins of all mankind.
      d. It is inconsistent with the penal evil of death which is more extensive than personal sin.
         1.) Paul's illustration here is that of the people between Adam and Moses, before the Mosaic law was given. They suffered the penal evil of death, but it could not have been because of breaking the law of Moses which had not been given out yet. Consequently, Adam's sin must have been the reason for their dying. Of course, someone might point out that they broke the law of God written on their hearts (Rom. 2:13-15) and for that reason they died.
         2.) However, one must remember, in addition, that infants and small children have not committed any actual sins and yet they die. And Paul would have explained this by saying that Adam's sin has been put in their accounts. So even though they have not sinned personally, they are involved with the sin problem and therefore suffer the punishment of death.

      ***e. It is destructive of the analogy between Adam and Christ being made here. If in justification, the righteousness which I possess is not mine personally; then, in the first place, the sin with which I start life here is not mine personally either. In both cases, the acts of other persons are imputed to my account, i.e., reckoned to me.

2.   View #2: All mankind have sinned mediately in that they have had Adam's sinful nature passed down the line to them. Adam defiled his own nature by sin and passed on that corrupt nature, the core of which is SELFISHNESS, to everyone who would be descended from him. This is called the mediate imputation theory and God condemns everyone in Adam on the basis of their inherent depravity.

      a. This view is inconsistent with the meaning of the Greek word which translates simply "All sinned," not "All became depraved."

      b. It is inconsistent with vv. 13, 14, where Paul is proving that all mankind sinned when Adam sinned, as far as God was concerned. And this is supported by the universality of the penal evil of death.

      c. It is inconsistent with vv. 15-19, where Adam's sin is the grounds of mankind's condemnation, not the sinful nature which we have gotten from him.

      d. It is inconsistent with the analogy between Adam and Christ being made here. If the righteousness of Christ is outside of us but only reckoned to us, so also must be the sinfulness spoken of here.

      e. Conclusion: It is true that the nature we receive from Adam is corrupt and depraved. This has been transmitted to us through our parents in a corrupt state; yet HERE it is not made the grounds of mankind's condemnation. ADAM'S SIN IS.

3.   View #3: All mankind sinned mystically in the loins of Adam, their ancestor. On this view, Adam's sin was considered to be the actual and personal sin of each person in Adam. This is called "the seminal headship view." Hebrews 7:4 and following is cited as biblical support for this position. There it is argued that the Levites paid tithes to Melchizedek by being in the loins of Abraham when he did it. See Genesis 14:18-20.

      a. This is inconsistent with our conscious experience. The Levites did not actually, personally or consciously pay tithes to Melchizedek.

      b. This is inconsistent with the analogy between Adam and Christ.
There is nothing biblically to support the view that we were in the loins of Christ while he was keeping the law perfectly and then paying the price for our sins on the cross by His death.

4. View #4: All mankind sinned representatively in the sight of God. This is called the "federal headship" view and is apparently the correct view according to points listed below. In other words, Adam's one sin was put to the accounts of all who would be in Adam. At the point of Adam's sinning, all in Adam were put down as sinners on the books of heaven.
   a. This view is consistent with the simple meaning of the words, "All sinned." It was at the point of Adam's sin that all to be in him were looked upon as sinners.
   b. It is consistent with vv. 13,14.
      1.) The infliction of punishment or penal evils implies the violation of law. When one sees another suffering the penalty of being behind bars, one concludes that he has broken the law. When one sees someone die, he concludes that he has sinned somehow.
      2.) The violation of the law of Moses does not account for the universality of death because men died before it was given.
      3.) Death presupposes transgression, but the law of Moses does not take into account any who died before it was given.
      4.) Therefore, men must be subject to the penal evils of death on account of something other than their own personal sin, viz.. the one sin of Adam.
      5.) Even the law on our hearts or conscience is not inclusive of all who die because babies die. Why do they? Paul would answer, "Because of the sin of Adam put in their accounts." It has to be this way because they have not reached an age where they have ever violated any law.
      6.) Conclusion: The difference between Adam's sin and the sin of others is that Adam sinned PERSONALLY AND ACTUALLY and others descended from him sinned REPRESENTATIVELY. The human race is a group of interrelated beings and hence an act of the head can be and was considered an act of all whom that head represents.
5. Summary
   a. We are not condemned in Romans 5:12ff. for our actual personal sins. See Rom. 1:18-3:20, where we are.
   b. We are not condemned here for our inherent corruption. See I John 1:8.
   c. We are not condemned here for our own sin which we are supposed to have committed in the loins of Adam. In fact, no where in the Bible are we condemned for this.

    d.   We are condemned here for Adam's sin which is put to the account of every member of the race descended from Adam.

II. **The Commentary on this Comparison** 5:15-17
Actually the cases of Adam and Christ are not alike in some ways. See the following.
    A.   Argument #1: If God requires that many suffer for the sin of one, much more we would expect that a just God would make provision that many shall be benefited by the merit of one. "The many" here = all mankind and is an antithesis to "the one." Note also that the "justification characterized by life (5:18) is conditioned for all mankind upon their continued receiving (Greek present tense) of "the abundance of grace and the gift of righteousness (5:17). As all in Adam by natural birth, apart from personal choice, die so also all in Christ will live by personally accepting by faith the second birth (Jn. 3:3,5).
    B.   Argument #2 (5:16) The sentence of condemnation which passed on all mankind for the sake of Adam, was for one offense, whereas we are justified by Christ from many offenses. "As it was by one man, antecedently to any concurrence on our own, that we were brought into a state of condemnation, so it is by one man, without any merit of our own, that we are delivered from this state. If the one event has happened, much more may we expect the other to occur. If we are thus involved in the condemnation of a sin in which we had no personal concern, much more shall we, who voluntarily receive the gift of righteousness, be not only saved from the consequences of the fall, but be made partakers of eternal life." (Charles Hodge, Commentary on the Epistle to the Romans. Grand Rapids: Wm. B. Eerdman's Publishing Company, 1953. pp. 168,169.)

III. **The Continuation of the Comparison** (from 5:12) 5:18,19
(The comparison, interrupted before, is now stated in full. "As we are condemned, so we are justified.")
    A.   The "all" or "the many" are SINNERS BY ONE MAN'S SIN and hence they die. They are put down on the books of heaven as sinners. The verb does not mean they are MADE sinners, just as Jesus Christ was not MADE a sinner for us. He was made SIN for us (II Cor. 5:21), meaning He was reckoned and treated as a sinner that we might be reckoned and treated as righteous individuals.
    B.   The "all" or "the many" will be treated as RIGHTEOUS ONES BY ONE MAN'S OBEDIENCE. Note this is not an absolute "all" for the following reasons:
        1.   Universal terms are always limited by the nature of the subject or their context. As examples of limited "all's," see Jn. 3:26. John "is baptizing and all are coming to Him." Luke 2:1, "...A census was to be taken of all the inhabited earth." Rom. 14:20 "All things are indeed pure."

70

2. Other Scriptures support the limiting of the "all" here by stating conditions.
See Rom. 3:2-5:11 where faith and believing are given as clear conditions for justification .
See also John 3:16 and Romans 10:9 and 13, plus many other verses.
3. Romans 5:17 itself contains a condition for salvation. Salvation is for all of those who continue receiving it by faith initially and continue in that receptive mode. Note the Greek present tense of the participle for the verb "receive."
4. Appendix: I Cor. 15:22
It is obvious that this verse means the following: "For as all in Adam die, so also all in Christ will be made alive. We become in Adam by no choice of our own but we enter into Christ by choice. Even the "all in Adam" is not absolute as Enoch and Elijah in the Old Testament did not die by the grace of God, and according to Paul, there will be a group of Christians at the end of the age at the coming of Christ who will be alive at His second coming and not die. See I Thess. 4:15 and 17.
C. Summary: A defense of the federal headship or representative view:
1. It fits the Aorist tense used for "sinned" in Rom. 5:12 (a point act).
2. It is easy to understand.
3. It carries out the analogy between Adam and condemnation and Christ and justification
4. It allows the analogy between Adam and Christ to be carried through consistently.
5. It involves the simple, natural meanings of the Greek words.
6. It creates no problem in dealing with the unsaved, if it is dealt with in proper sequence.
   a. One should begin with witnessing where Paul did in Romans, with a person's actual sins, and proceed to the sin of Adam. Start with Rom. 1:18-3:20 and then continue on to Romans 5:12-21.
   b. Then indicate that for the Christian, Romans 5:12-21 and the representative view is so much interesting and helpful information for the Christian, since Christ has taken care of the Christian's actual sins and also the sin of Adam reckoned to him from his birth.
7. Appendix: Charles Hodge, in his commentary, is excellent in his defense of this point of view. See Hodge, ibid., pp. 175,176.

IV. The Conclusion of the Discussion   5:20,21
A. The design of the law, as stated here, was to increase sin, as it was added to a plan already in operation
1. The design was not to blot out the program based on faith.

2. It was to give greater light, and hence greater responsibility to the lawbreaker.
3. It was to increase sinning. Often the forbidding of something increases the likelihood of its being attempted.
4. It was to bring men to Christ.
B. The results of the Gospel would hopefully be that grace would reign in the lives of people, i.e., it would be abundantly displayed

Summary Conclusion
A. Original sin in mankind can be identified as
1. sin that is derived from the original root of the race, Adam;
2. sin that is present in the life of every individual from his conception or origin;
3. sin that is the inward root of all actual sins;
   Sinners do not become sinners in the sight of God and on the books of heaven when they commit their first sin; they sin because they are sinners. (See Edward John Camell, The Case for Orthodox Theology. Philadelphia: The Westminster Press, 1959. p. 67.)
4. sin that involves the following:
   a. original guilt: the sin of Adam imputed to everyone in Adam
   b. original pollution: the absence of original righteousness (lost at the fall) and the presence of positive evil (selfishness)
   c. total depravity (which means:)
      1.) not that every man is as depraved as he can be
      2.) but that inherent corruption extends to every part of man's nature, although he or she is still free to cry out to God for help, in other words, to believe for salvation.
         The choice to believe the gospel, when it is presented to a person, is a choice that every sinner can make, at least initially. This is an act for which he is responsible but which is non-meritorious. It is like the cry of a drowning person. It is necessary for his salvation but cannot be the grounds of his boasting about how he saved himself because he cried so loudly. It is at this point that God respects the free will which He has given to mankind. He could violate it but in the matter of salvation, biblically He does not and apparently will not.
      3.) and that there is no spiritual good in the sinner at all
         See Rom. 3:9-20; Eph. 2:1; Jer. 7:9; I Jn. 1:8 and many other passages of Scripture.
   d. total inability (which means:)
      1.) that he can still perform naturally good things
      2.) that he can still perform civil good also

        3.) that he can still do externally religious things
        4.) that he cannot do any act which fundamentally meets with God's approval (Rom. 8:8; Heb. 11:6)
        5.) that he cannot change his fundamental preference for self to a love for God, or even approach such a change
        6.) that he has lost, in a sense, his liberty of choice (He cannot help himself out of his dilemma of sinfulness, but he can cry for help, which is another way of saying that he can believe.)

B. God's condemnation of mankind is for the following things, according to the Scriptures:
1. the sin of Adam (The sin of Adam, in God's sight, is the sin of all persons in Adam.)
2. his depraved, sinful nature
3. his personal sins
4. and his rejection of Christ
   All one needs to do to be lost is to do nothing. We do not go to hell because of the sin of Adam or even our own sins but because we have refused the remedy for our sins provided by Jesus Christ.

C. A vindication of God for thus treating mankind is as follows:
1. He is fair because of the solidarity of the race.
   The same solidarity by which we receive the effects of Adam's sin enables us to receive the fruit of Christ's victory on the cross; so we had better not knock that unity.
2. He is fair because He has provided justification by the same means, viz. imputation. If a person goes to hell, it will be in spite of all God has done to keep him from going there.

Review questions covering Romans 1-5

1. Who and what is introduced by Paul in the salutation?
2. What information is given in the information section of Chapter 1?
3. What various things are told us about the Gospel in 1:16,17?
4. For what specific sins does Paul condemn the Gentiles?
5. By what three ways do the Gentiles have light about God according to Romans 1 and 2?
6. How can God be just and punish with hell a heathen man who dies, having never heard of Jesus Christ?
7. What are the major characteristics of God's judgment as presented in 2:1-16?
8. What would you say to someone who said that Paul was teaching a justification by works in Romans 2?
9. For whom are the above principles of God's judgment relevant?
10. For what different things does Paul condemn the Jews?
11. What are the characteristics of the righteousness now revealed by which it is possible for a person to obtain a righteous standing before God?

12. According to 3:21-31, what is Christ with reference to the believer?
13. How can God be just and holy in character and also the justifier of an ungodly person when he puts faith in Christ?
14. Why does Paul refer to Abraham and David in Romans 4?
15. What are the various characteristics of Abraham's faith as it is described in Romans 4?
16. What two events in Abraham's life does Paul use to illustrate his tremendous faith?
17. What are the blessings enjoyed by every justified believer as given in Romans 5?
18. How is the tremendous love of God contrasted with man's love for man in this section?
19. Why is the imputation section included following Romans 5:1-11?
20. What are the various views as to the meaning of the phrase, "all sinned" in Romans 5:12? (Which is the preferred view presented in the outline study.)

CHAPTER SEVEN

The Sanctification of All Christians
Romans 6-8

The New Life Following Justification: Deliverance From a Life of Sin
~ Romans 6:1-14

¹What, therefore, shall we say? Shall we continue remaining in sin in order that grace may become greater? ²May it not be so! Since we indeed died to sin, how shall we any longer continue living in it? ³Or are you ignorant that as many of us as were baptized into Christ Jesus into His death were baptized? ⁴We were buried together, therefore, with Him by means of baptism unto [His] death in order that, just as Christ was raised from the dead by means of the glory of the Father, so also we ourselves in newness of life might walk. ⁵For if we have become planted together in the likeness of His death, yet also [in the likeness] of (His) resurrection we shall be; ⁶Because we are knowing this, that our old man was crucified together with (Him) in order that the body of sin might be put out of business, in order that we might no longer continue being a bond servant to sin; ⁷for the one who has died has been freed from sin. ⁸But if we died together with Christ, we are believing that we also shall live together with Him, ⁹because we know that Christ, because He has been raised from the dead, no longer is going to die, death no longer is lording it over Him. ¹⁰For [the death] which He died, to sin He died once for all; but [the life] which He is living, he continues living to God. ¹¹So also you yourselves, continue reckoning yourselves being dead indeed to sin but living to God in Christ Jesus.

¹²Therefore stop letting sin reign in your [pl] mortal body in order that you should continue obeying its desires, ¹³and stop presenting your [pl] members [as] weapons of unrighteousness to sin, but present yourselves to God as if living from [the] dead and your [pl] members [as] weapons of righteousness to God, ¹⁴for sin will not lord it over you [pl]; for you [pl] are not under law but under grace.

Introduction
A. The connection between 1:18-5:21 and 6: 1ff. is that 6:1 and following describes the new life which should follow justification by faith. If it is true that "where sin abounds, grace abounds much more," then why should we not continue sinning that grace may increase all the more? Paul's answer follows in Romans 6:1-14.
B. The emphasis here is on knowing we died to some things and continue living to other things being united together with Christ.
1. Emphasis #1: knowledge and knowing 6:3,6,9,16
2. Emphasis #2: death and dying
3. Emphasis #3: life and living
4. Emphasis #4: togetherness with Christ

I. Deliverance Through Our Expiration (Death) with Christ 6:2
Paul says that when we accepted Christ as Savior, ideally we died together with Christ.

75

A. The meaning of the verb: We died to sin at the point when we accepted Christ.

B. The tense of the verb: Aorist, which indicates a specific act at a specific time
Note that this is not an imperative to die, but a declaration that we have died. It is not an imperative, but an indicative, not a demand but a declaration. See pages 78-80 for a list of the verses which speak of the Christian as one who HAS DIED together with Christ.

II. **Deliverance Through Our Identification With Christ** 6:2
  A. Our identification with Him by our baptism6:3-5 AN ANALOGY
    1. Our baptism is a symbol of our death, burial and resurrection to a new kind of living. It does not produce our death to sin but pictures it. It does not produce our justification, only symbolizes it. Note that Paul has completed his discussion of justification by faith alone in 3:21-5:11 and consequently he has no fears that someone will read baptismal regeneration or baptism as a condition for justification into the symbol which he now uses in dealing with sanctification and death to sinning of all sorts. When we become Christians, Christ's death becomes our death and this is typified by our baptism by immersion. We die, are buried and come forth to new living ideally.
    2. Our baptism is a seal of the certainty of our death, even as our burial physically is a seal of our death physically.
    3. Our baptism typifies our union in Christ's death; it does not produce it. Not all baptized are necessarily justified.
    4. Our baptism is performed on the basis of the assumption that we actually believe what we profess about Christ and salvation.
    5. Appendix #1: In other words, what some teach is not supportable by these verses, viz., "The mystical union of the Christian with Christ dates from his baptism." There are too many clear verses of Scripture that base our union with Christ in salvation on faith and faith alone. See Romans 3:21-5:11 in defense of this.
    6. Appendix #2: Some scholars take the baptism here referred to as not water baptism but as the baptism by the Holy Spirit into the body of Christ, the Church. See I Corinthians 12:13. The rationale for this could be an attempt to avoid baptismal regeneration. As we have tried to show above, this is not necessary if one remembers that Paul has concluded his discussion of justification by faith alone in Romans 5 and that he is only using baptism here as a type or symbol, which does not produce justification but only pictures what happens in it.
  B. Our identification in Christ's crucifixion Romans 6: 6,7
    1. This means the crucifixion of "the old man."

76

a. This means the death of the old self, ourselves as we were before we became Christians.
The death of the old man is the death of the man of old. Gone ideally are the natural desires, the lusts, the hopes, the ambitions, and the judgments of the unsaved person and this old nature. See I Corinthians 5:17. We are new creations in Christ.

b. This means ideally the death of the ethical flesh, the carnal nature.
"The old man" and the flesh with its desires are crucified ideally for us on the cross. However, Paul will go on to say that we must now continue to reckon this truth practically true in experience. See Romans 6:11. This death of the ethical flesh is not an automatic thing except as it becomes so through habitual practice; and good habits are just as hard to break as bad ones.

2. This means the putting out of business of "the body of sin"

a. "The body of sin" has been variously identified. It has been taken to mean "the sinful body; however, the body is not sinful because it is physical. Nor does this expression mean "the mass of sin" or "the substance of sin" as some have variously interpreted it. Some have wrongfully taken the body here to refer to the sinful ethical flesh or the corrupt nature. One has taken the expression to indicate a personifying of sin by giving it a body. The best interpretation refers the expression to the physical body which can so easily become the instrument of sin. It seems that this is that to which Paul is referring here.

Note the New Testament's emphasis on the Christian's dying and death to sin with Christ.
Romans
6:2 Since we indeed died to sin, how shall we any longer continue living in it?
6:3 Or are you ignorant that as many of us as were baptized into Christ Jesus were baptized into his death?
6:4 We were buried together, therefore, with him by means of baptism into death . . .
6:5 For if have become planted together with (him) in the likeness of his death, certainly we also shall be (in the likeness) of (his) resurrection;
6:6 While we are knowing this, that our old man was crucified with (him), in order that the body of sin might be put out of business . . .
6:7 For the one having died has been justified from sin;

6:8 But if we died together with Christ, we are believing that we shall also continue living together with him . . .

6:11 So also you yourselves continue reckoning yourselves to be dead indeed to sin but living to God in Christ Jesus.

6:13 Stop presenting the members (of your body) as weapons of unrighteousness to sin; but present (once and for all) yourselves to God, as if living from the dead. . .

7:4 Therefore, my brethren, you yourselves also were made dead to the law by means of the body of Christ, in order that you might become another's, the One who was raised from the dead . . .

7:6 But now we have become discharged from the law, because we died to that by which we were being bound.

II Corinthians

5:14,15 For the love of Christ is constraining us, because we have determined this, that one died on behalf of all, therefore all died and he died on behalf of all, in order that the ones living should no longer continue living for themselves, but for the One who on behalf of them died and rose again.

Galatians

2:19,20 For I myself through the law died to law, in order that I might live for God. I have been crucified together with Christ; and it is no longer I who am living, but Christ is living in me ...

6:14 But far be it from me to continue glorying, except in the cross of our Lord Jesus Christ, by means of which the world has been crucified to me, and I (have been crucified) to the world.

Colossians

2:12 ...having been buried together with him in baptism, by which also you were raised together with him through faith in the working of God, the One who raised him from the dead.

2:20 If you died together with Christ from the rudiments of the world, why, as though living in the world, do you continue subjecting yourselves to ordinances....

3:1 If then you were raised together with Christ, continue seeking the things which are above, where Christ is sitting at the right hand of God.

3:3 For you died and your life has been hidden with Christ in God.

3:5 Therefore put to death your members, those upon the earth.

I Peter 2:24 ...who his own self bore our sins in his body upon the tree, in order that we, because we have died to sins, might live for righteousness . . .

4:1,2 Since then Christ suffered in the flesh, arm yourselves also with the same mind; for the one having suffered in the flesh has ceased from sin, in order that you no longer should live the rest of your time in the flesh for the lusts of men but for the will of God.

    b. "The putting out of business" of the body of sin refers to the physical body as the instrument of sin as having been put out of work or out of operation; and that which has been put out of business can come back into business. This does not mean that sin or the body of sin is destroyed or eradicated, as some have thought and taught.

    c. The principle behind the teaching here is that both our own death physically and our death with Christ will free us from sinning. Physical death, it goes without saying, will end one's sinning. Even so, our death with Christ ideally should do so also. It is important here that we remember the ideal and the practical, in other words the declarations of Scripture and the demands which accompany them.

C. Our identification in Christ's resurrection 6:8-10

    1. This implies a new kind of living after dying, just as it was true of Christ after His resurrection.

    2. This means that, according to the Scriptures, we are associated with Christ in His resurrection.

    3. This also includes a continuous living unto God. There is a contrast here between the death and dying which is an aorist, punctiliar act and the living which is a present, continuous procedure.

    4. This means that if he is continuing to live unto God, he is living a life which is separate from sin and holy in character. Sin has no claim on the Christian.

    5. Appendix #1: Note again all of the verses which stress the fact that the Christian has died to sinning and is alive to righteousness and holiness.

    6. Appendix #2: THUS FAR WE HAVE BEEN DEALING WITH THE IDEAL DECLARED IN THE SCRIPTURES. NOW WE TURN TO THE PRACTICAL SIDE OF THE CHRISTIAN LIFE DEMANDED OF US BY THE SCRIPTURES.

III. **Deliverance Through Our Consideration (Reckoning) of Ourselves as Dead to Sin but Alive to God** 6:11 This is the practical which is expected of us if we are to live consistent Christian lives.

A. The meaning of "reckon" here

1. The word itself means "to count a thing finished," "to regard something as complete," or "to reckon to be true what, in fact, is actually true." It means to act as if one is dead to sin and alive unto God and righteousness. This is one of the demands which balances the ideal seen in the declarations of the earlier verses of the chapter.
2. The tense of the imperative is present which means this is something which should be done continuously and repeatedly, i.e.. as often as one is tempted to sin.
3. The object of this reckoning is oneself, not the temptation or the sin. This is not a case of mind over matter because there is help from the Holy Spirit in the overcoming process. He will do His part if and when we do ours.
4. The illustrations of this solution of overcoming temptations are numerous in the Bible. Observe three of them, one negative and two positive ones:
   a. The negative one is David who, when tempted in regard to Bathsheba, failed to reckon himself dead to the temptation and committed adultery with her. See II Samuel 11:1-5.
   b. One positive one is Joseph who, when tempted by Potiphar's wife, reckoned himself dead to the temptation, fled the room, leaving his cloak behind but retaining his character. See Genesis 39:7-19.
   c. Another positive one is our Lord Himself when tempted in the wilderness by Satan. In all three temptations the Word of God came to His mind and He was able to reckon Himself dead to the sins being presented by quoting relevant Scriptures and then obeying them completely and immediately. See Matthew's account of the wilderness temptation of Jesus recorded in Matthew 4:1-11. There is something about repeated and immediate obedience given God's Word that baffles Satan.

B. The emphasis on death
   1. The teaching of this passage infers that as far as sin is concerned, we are corpses. The death of Christ is the death of the Christian who is in Christ. We died when we accepted Christ and now we must count on that fact as true.
   2. This means also that temptation and sin get no favorable response or reaction from us. It is as if we stuck a doll (or a corpse) with a needle. There would be no reaction.
   3. This does not mean that sin is eradicated or destroyed, or else why then do we find it so hard to reckon ourselves dead to temptation? We may not feel dead to sin but we must believe God's Word that we are and act on that truth. The reckoning does not make the fact true but is commanded in view of the fact. The habitual practice of reckoning here commanded by Paul can make us just as

dead to certain temptations, as some of us are today dead to cigarette smoke, or illicit drugs, or pornography. These things get no favorable response from us.

4. This does not mean that all temptations to sin will be over for the Christian. In fact, they may just be beginning in earnest. One must never confuse temptation to sin with sinning itself.

5. This does mean that we must follow the life-pattern of reckoning ourselves to be dead to sin and alive to God and righteousness, believing it to be true in actuality and then acting in keeping with that belief. According to the biblical declaration, God's grace will help us but we also have an obligation, according to the demand of Romans 6:11. The reckoning may take the form of literally running from the temptation, praying, quoting Scripture, seeking a friend for encouragement, etc. See I Cor. 10:13.

    a. Step #1: Never excuse sin.

    b. Step #2: Never expect to sin.

    c. Step #3: Never excite sin. (As someone has said, "What makes resisting temptation difficult for many people is that they do not want to discourage it completely.

    d. Appendix: Remember that God's will is never forced upon us.

C. The sphere of this death and new life is in Christ, in being members of the Body of Christ, His church. (Romans 6:11)

D. The psychology of this advice is that we tend to be very largely what we think.

1. The attitude we carry into the battle against sin largely determines the outcome of the battle, whether it will be a victory or a defeat.

2. This means that if we will practice Paul's command of repeated reckoning given here, we will become more resistant to evil and more pursuant of righteousness and holiness.

3. This means that we must "act as if" we are dead to sin and alive to righteousness, no matter how we may feel at a given time.

4. This means that we will look at a holy life as a moment-by-moment development, not as one large, impossible "whole." We must acquire the habit of walking with the Lord one step at a time.

    a. "Habits are built through use. They are broken through disuse. The disuse comes through resisting Satan over a period of time. Let a habit be abandoned for several weeks, even though it means a steady fight, and you will find that most of the fire has gone out of it." C. S. Lovett, Dealing with the Devil. Baldwin Park, CA Personal Christianity, 1967. p. 128.

    b.   The starting of a "habit bank" will free your mind from having to make certain decisions and will free it to work on other matters, those things for which you have no habits developed. Here are four steps to acquiring good habits:

       1.) Start your new habit off with the biggest shove you can. You may accidentally pick up some bad habits, but hardly any good ones come that way. Decide what habits you want to begin and go for them.

       2.) Never, never, never, never, never cheat. To allow yourself an exception "just once" is like a person . . . who suddenly drops the ball of string which he was just trying to wind. All of his previous work is immediately shot down in a second. Every time you are tempted to sin, reckon yourself dead to sin and alive to righteousness.

       3.) Welcome your first chance to practice your habit. People who say, "I'll start tomorrow," never do. Making a fresh resolution each day is like running up to jump a ditch but always stopping to go back for another (supposedly better) run.

       4.) Keep your momentum going by a little more-than necessary exercise each day. Go even beyond your minimums. Do it for no other reason than just the discipline of making yourself do it. Then, some day, when the heat of temptation is really high, you will be very glad for your extra reserve of discipline which you have in store and which can enable you to resist and achieve victory.

       5.) Appendix: See Campus Life Magazine. December, 1969 and the article entitled "Make Your Habits Work For You," written by Dean Merrill for a more extended development of the above points.

IV. Deliverance Through Our Presentation of Ourselves to God 6:12-14

However, before trying to take the practical step of reckoning, it is important, first of all, that we very practically present ourselves totally to God for his use. See Romans 6:12,13.

    A. This involves an immediate refusal to allow sin to go on reigning in our mortal bodies.

      1. This will involve a continued striving against temptation and sinning.

      2. It will involve a continued refusal to let sin lord it over us.

      3. It will involve a continued rejection of every temptation to sin that comes along. In other words, we must cease yielding to it.

      4. It will involve a recognition of our mortal bodies for what they are, still in a state of weakness.

B.   This involves an immediate refusal to present our members as weapons to sin for sin to use against God. We are to stop doing this, according to the Greek tense used.

C.   This will involve the presenting of our members as weapons belonging to righteousness for God to use to fight Satan and evil.

    1.   The tense is aorist which means that this is to be done immediately and decisively. This experience is one of crisis sanctification involving the putting of our members at God's disposal for His use.

    2.   The etymology of the word "present" includes the ideas of "standing beside one for their use," "being at hand for service," or "putting yourself at someone's disposal," in this instance. We become "checkers" on God's checker board for Him to use to win the battle of life against Satan.

    3.   The members involved are our bodily members, such as our hands, our feet, our eyes, our ears, our mind, and our other members, which become weapons for God and holiness.

    4.   The description of this total selling out of ourselves to God has been variously described:

        a.   It can be described as "saying the big yes" to God, which includes all the little yeses (the reckonings from 6:11) which will follow it. Many things in life which begin as a crisis (the presenting) must continue as a process (the reckonings).

        b.   It can be described as the "dedication of oneself to God by one decisive act, one resolute effort."

        c.   It is the submission of will that must precede and includes any successful reckoning of oneself dead to sin and alive to God following it.

        d.   It is the crisis act of becoming Spirit-filled, an experience in which one does not get more of the Holy Spirit but He gets ALL of the individual. A Spirit-filled person is one who is totally committed to God's will in advance of getting light from God.

        "A yieldedness to the will of God is not demonstrated by some one particular issue; it is rather a matter of having taken the will of God as the rule of one's life. To be in the will of God is simply to be willing to do His will without reference to any particular thing He may choose. It is electing His will to be final, even before we know what He may wish us to do. It is, therefore, not a question of being willing to do some one thing: it is a question of being willing to do anything, when, where, how, it may seem best in His heart of love ... It is quite natural to be saying: If He wishes me to do something, let Him tell me and I will then determine what I do. To a person in such an attitude of heart. He reveals nothing. There must be a covenant relationship of trust in which His will is assented to once for all and without reservation." Lewis Sperry Chafer. He That Is Spiritual, rev. ed. Philadelphia: Sunday School Times Company, 1922. p. 113.

    e.   It is the crisis experience of sanctification.

    f.   It has been described as an experience in which a person dies to self.

    g.   Appendix: There has been much debate over the names for this experience among theologians. What we need, however, is to end the bickering over the names for the experience and experience the experience. This was written to Christians for Christians and makes sanctification both a punctiliar and a progressive experience. It is a crisis and a process as the total presentation of ourselves and our continuous reckoning (6:11) indicates.

D.   Appendix: The reason for this reckoning and presenting: sin shall not have dominion over you, for you are not under law but under grace. In other words, you are not as you used to be, constantly bothered by attacks of sin aggravated by law of any kind. You are out from under law and under obligation to grace.

    1.   This means we are not under (the dominion of) law (of any kind)

        a.   The reason: Law has no power over a dead person.

        b.   The motive for living under law is FEAR lest we break the law of God and therefore suffer the consequences of law-breaking.

    2.   Paul says that we are under grace.

        a.   The meaning is clear that grace has its obligations also. This is the opposite of antinomianism and anarchy. FREEDOM FROM SIN DOES NOT MEAN FREEDOM TO SIN. When we become Christians, we are not free from all bondage but just change lords. We do not have a choice of whether we will be bondservants or not, just a choice of which master we will serve, sin or righteousness. We cannot be servants of sin and dead to sin at the same time.

        b.   The motive for living under grace is LOVE. Love takes all of the slavishness and gall out of the bondage of serving Christ and righteousness. As an illustration, take the marriage bond(age). Why are so many seeking marital bondage today, particularly in Christian circles? Ideally, the wedding ring cuts off your circulation. However, love has made this bondage attractive, just as it also makes our bond service to Christ and righteousness exciting and desirable.

Summary: By way of conclusion, Romans 6 teaches the following:

    A.   (6:1-14) We have deliverance from a life of sin by our death to it with Christ; and our baptism is the symbol of it.

        1.   Hold on to this by faith.

84

2. Believe the truth of it.
3. And act on the basis of that faith.
B. (6:15ff.) We have deliverance from individual acts of sin by a deliberate choice of a new Lord; and our being bondservants to righteousness for the furtherance of holiness is the evidence of it.

The New Life Following Justification: Deliverance From Individual Acts of Sin and From Bondage to Law ~ Romans 6:15-7:6

15What therefore? Shall we commit an act of sin because we are not under law but under grace? May it not be so! 16You [pl] know, do you [pl] not, that to whom you [pl] continue presenting yourselves [as] bond servants unto obedience, [his] bond servants you are whom you continue obeying, whether of sin unto death or of obedience unto righteousness? 17But thanks [be] to God that you used to be bond servants of sin, but you [pl] obeyed from [the] heart the pattern of teaching unto which you [pl] were delivered; 18and because you [pl] were made free from sin, you [pl] became bond servants to righteousness. 19I am speaking humanly because of the weakness of your [pl] flesh. For just as you [pl] presented your [pl] members subject to uncleanness and lawlessness for lawlessness, even so now present your [pl] members subject to righteousness for holiness. 20For when you [pl] used to be bond servants of sin, you [pl] were free with reference to righteousness. 21Therefore, what fruit did you used to have then [in the things] of which you are now being ashamed? For the end of those things is death. 22But now, because you [pl] have become free from sin and have become bond servants to God, you [pl] are continuing to have your [pl] fruit unto holiness, and the end, eternal life. 23For the wages of sin is death, but the free gift of God is life eternal in Christ Jesus, our Lord.

Romans 7
1Or are you continuing to be ignorant, brothers, (for I am speaking to ones who are knowing law) that the law lords it over man for as long a time as he is living? 2For the married woman has been bound by law to her husband while he is living; but if her husband dies, she has been discharged from the law relative to her husband. 3So then, while her husband is living, an adulteress she will be called, if she becomes another man's (wife); but if her husband dies, she is free from the law so that she is not an adulteress, although she becomes another man's [wife]. 4So then, my brothers, you yourselves also were made dead to the law by means of the body of Christ, in order that you might become another's [wife], the One who was raised from the dead, in order that we might produce fruit for God. 5For when we were in the flesh, the passions of sins, those which were by means of the law, kept on working in our members in order to produce fruit for death, 6But now we have become discharged from the law, because we died [to that] by which we were being bound, so that we continue being bond servants in newness of spirit and not in oldness of letter.

I. **The believer is a bond-slave of righteousness and no longer of sin.**
A. The introductory question: Although we should not continue on sinning, can we commit individual acts of sin now and then because we are no longer under law but under grace? The use of the aorist tense in 6:15 indicates that now Paul is referring to occasional acts of sin as opposed to living in sin.

85

B. The answer is #1: No, because you are then the bond-servants belonging to sin as your lord. This bond-service is characterized by the following: 6:16-20
  1. voluntariness 6:16 (It is freely chosen.)
  2. the furthering of uncleanness and iniquity 6:19
  3. freedom from righteousness as one's lord 6:20
     (In this paragraph, righteousness and sin are personified as lords of people's lives.)
  4. the payment of WAGES, which is death 6:21,23
C. The answer #2: No, because you are in actuality bond-servants belonging to righteousness as your lord. This bond-service is characterized by the following: 6:16,18
  1. voluntariness 6:16,19
  2. the furthering of righteousness and holiness
  3. the fruit of holiness and eternal life, fruit which is, however, a GIFT, not a wage
D. A summary of the answer: Christian freedom consists not in freedom to sin but in freedom from sin.
E. The solution to the problem is the presentation of your members as bond-servants to righteousness for the furtherance of holiness.
  1. The tense is aorist in 6:19. The way to victory here is the same as the way to victory over a life of sin. See 6:13.
  2. The meaning is that we should serve the new master, righteousness, with at least as much energy as we did the old one, sin. Note that there is no choice of whether one wants to be bondservant or not. The choice is just which lord will you serve.
  3. An appropriate illustration here is that of a ball player who has been traded from one team to another. How long would he be in organized ball if he wore the uniform of the new team but played ball for the old team when they came to town to play his new organization? Yet this is exactly what is going on in Christian circles. There are too many Christians wearing the Christian uniform and playing ball for the Devil and his crowd.

II. **The believer as dead to the law as a legalistic means of holiness or sanctification.** 7:1-7
The law, as an external code, cannot justify or sanctify a person; but it still remains as a mirror of love in action. IT CANNOT COERCE but it CAN GUIDE. See John 14:15. It is a guide to help us avoid sin (See Psalm 119:11.) and to give us a holy and a happy life.
A. An introductory question: Do you know that the law continues having dominion over a man as long as he lives? Consequently, if you are dead to law, it has no more hold on you.
B. The analogy of the marriage bond presented here is based on the legal maxim that death cancels all contracts for the deceased. The parts of the analogy which need identification are as follows:
  1. the married woman
  2. her first husband who dies physically

        3.   another man to whom she can be married after the death of her first husband

        4.   physical death, which breaks the marriage bond

        5.   the fruit of the first marriage

        6.   the fruit of the second marriage

C. The development of the comparison

        1.   The married woman is a person before she becomes a Christian and afterward.

           William R. Newell limits her to a Jewish believer, but this limitation is not necessary. The analogy fits both Jews and Gentiles.

        2.   The first husband is law of any kind in the legalistic sense of the word.

           Gifford identifies the first husband as "the old man" or the old nature; however, there does not seem to be any contextual reason for this. Law is the predominant emphasis in 7:1-6.

        3.   The other man to whom she can become married is Christ. To be married to Him means that she is under obligation and submission to Him.

        4.   The death spoken of here represents that which frees one of the partners so that that person can remarry without committing adultery.

        5.   The fruit of the first marriage is spiritual death.

        6.   The fruit of the second marriage is a life for God involving a change of living.

D. The teaching of the analogy

        1.   Christians are free from the law as a legalistic means of holiness because they have died together with Christ. The law cannot justify or sanctify.

        2.   They are free from the law by their identification with Christ in His death.

        3.   The fruit of their marriage to Christ is a holy, reformed life. It is only proper that we should expect to see the fruit of the new marriage in the life of the Christian.

        4.   The new marriage involves the substitution of new ties for the old ones. This does not mean the cessation of all ties, only a change of bond(age); and love takes all the galling or irritating aspects out of the "marriage bondage."

E. The inexactness of the analogy Paul gives needs to be explained.

        1.   In the analogy, the first husband dies, thus freeing his wife to be married to another man without committing adultery.

        2.   In the application, the believer dies together with Christ.

        3.   Appendix: If one tries to apply the elements of the analogy equally, he will have problems.

           a.   If the woman dies in the analogy, then she is no longer alive to be married again.

           b.   If the law dies in the application, then one runs the danger of encouraging antinomianism.

   c. Paul's emphasis here is on THE FACT of the Christian's freedom, not THE MEANS of it.

 F. The solution to the problem in this paragraph is that the Christian should continue reckoning himself dead to law as a legalistic means of holiness. Before we were Christians, we served in the minute particulars of legal observance. Now we serve in the newness of spirit (or the Spirit). However we do CONTINUE SERVING. Now we obey not because we fear a penalty but because we love a Person. In fact, our love compels more than the law commands. We are working OUT our own salvation with fear and trembling; but we are not working FOR it, because no one works for what he already has. See Phil. 2:12,13. (NOTE: With all Paul has said about law here, one must

not forget the didactic or teaching function of the law for the Christian. The commandments, both positive and negative, teach us how to love God and our fellowman. Paul will deal with this later in Romans 13:8-10.)

 G. Appendix: Several truths about marriage are presupposed by the teaching here in Romans 7:1-6:

  1. HERE AT LEAST, marriage is for life "until death do you part."

   It is to be a close, sacred, and permanent bond.

  2. The death of one of the marriage partners breaks the marriage bond, loosing the remaining partner and freeing him or her to marry again without sin.

  3. Not even adultery is grounds for divorce HERE. Neither is it made such in Mark 10:11,12, Luke 16:18 or I Corinthians 7:10,11.

Paul and the Law ~ Romans 7:1-25

¹Or are you continuing to be ignorant, brothers, (for I am speaking to ones who are knowing law) that the law lords it over man for as long a time as he is living? ²For the married woman has been bound by law to her husband while he is living; but if her husband dies, she has been discharged from the law relative to her husband. ³So then, while her husband is living, an adulteress she will be called, if she becomes another man's (wife); but if her husband dies, she is free from the law so that she is not an adulteress, although she becomes another man's [wife]. ⁴So then, my brothers, you yourselves also were made dead to the law by means of the body of Christ, in order that you might become another's [wife], the One who was raised from the dead, in order that we might produce fruit for God. ⁵For when we were in the flesh, the passions of sins, those which were by means of the law, kept on working in our members in order to produce fruit for death, ⁶But now we have become discharged from the law, because we died [to that] by which we were being bound, so that we continue being bond servants in newness of spirit and not in oldness of letter.

⁷What, therefore, shall we say? Is the law sin? May it not be so! But sin I did not know except by means of law. For I had not known about coveting except the law kept saying, "You [s] shall not covet"; ⁸but having taken [the] opportunity, sin by means of the commandment produced in me all [manner of] coveting; for apart from law, sin is dead. ⁹But I myself was living apart from law then; but, after the commandment came, sin came to life, and I myself died; ¹⁰and the commandment which was [to be] unto life, this was found by me [to be] unto death; ¹¹for sin having taken [the] opportunity by means of the commandment deceived me and by means of it killed [me]. ¹²So then, the law is indeed holy, and the commandment is holy and righteous and good.

¹³Did, therefore, that which is good become death for me? May it not be so! But sin [has become death for me], in order that it may appear sin, continuing to work death in me by means of that which is good, in order that sin by means of the commandment may become exceedingly sinful. ¹⁴For we know that the law is spiritual; but I myself am carnal, (I) who have been sold under sin. ¹⁵For what I continue doing, I am not [really] knowing; for not what I am desiring, this am I practicing; but what I am hating, this I am practicing. ¹⁶But if [1st] what I am not desiring, this I am practicing, I am consenting to the law that it is good. ¹⁷But now no longer am myself doing it but [it is] sin which is dwelling in me. ¹⁸For I know that [there is] not dwelling in me, that is in my flesh, [any] good thing; for to be desiring continues to be present with me, but to continue doing the good is not: ¹⁹for not good which I am desiring am I practicing, but evil which I am not desiring, this I am practicing. ²⁰But if [1st] what I myself am not desiring, this I myself am practicing, no longer am I myself doing it but sin which is dwelling in me. ²¹I am finding then the principle in me, the one who is desiring to be practicing good, that in me evil is continually present; ²²for I continue taking delight in the law of God with respect to the inner man, ²³but I continue seeing another law among my members which is continuing to war with the law of my mind and which is continually making me a prisoner to the law of sin which is among my members. ²⁴I am a miserable man; who will deliver me from the body of this death? ²⁵But thanks be to God, [deliverance is] through Jesus Christ, our Lord. So then, on the one hand, I myself with my mind am continuing to serve [the] law of God, but, on the other hand, with my flesh [the] law of sin.

I. **The Relationship of the Christian to Law** (As a Legalistic Means to Holiness) 7:1-6 (The Christian's obedience to the laws of God may start as an obligation but it will often and should end with loving desire. Then he will obey not because he has to but because he wants to. He will find out that it is always the best and most satisfying way to live.)

A. Question #1: Are you ignorant, brothers, that law hath dominion over a man for so long time as he lives? You are dead to law as a means of holiness, so reckon it so. We do not keep the law to merit our salvation or to earn anything, unless it may be rewards. We keep it because we love Him and want to demonstrate that love by our obedience. See John 14:15,21,23,24. The true function of God's law, wherever it exists, is not justification or sanctification but REVELATION. The Hebrew background of the word "Torah" is the Hebrew verb, to instruct. In other words, the law is our instructor to tell us what pleases God and what does not, to tell us what a maturing Christian does and does not do.

"By way of introduction it may help us to find our way through this difficult chapter of Romans if we think of the three possible attitudes to the law-attitudes represented first by the legalist, secondly by the libertine or antinomian, and thirdly by the law-abiding believer.

1. The legalist is a man in bondage to the law. He imagines that his relationship to God depends on his obedience to it. And as he seeks to be justified by the works of the law, he finds the law a harsh and inflexible taskmaster. In Paul's vocabulary he is 'under the law'.

2. The antinomian (sometimes synonymous with 'libertine') goes to the other extreme. He rejects the law altogether, and even blames it for most of man's moral and spiritual problems.

3. The law-abiding believer preserves the balance. He recognizes the weakness of the law (Romans 8:3. 'God has done what the law, weakened by the flesh, could not do'). The weakness of the law is that it can neither justify nor sanctify us, because in ourselves we are not capable of obeying it. Yet the law-abiding believer delights in the law as an expression of the will of God, and seeks by the power of the indwelling Spirit to obey it.

To sum up, the legalist fears the law and is in bondage to it; the antinomian hates the law and repudiates it; the law-abiding believer loves the law and obeys it. Directly or indirectly, the apostle portrays each of these three characters in Romans 7." John R. W. Stott, Men Made New. Grand Rapids: Baker Book House, 1984. pp. 59, 60.

II. **The Use and Character of Law**
   A. Question #2: Is law sinful (since you have to be delivered from it by your death to it and since sin makes use of law)? Isn't there something wrong with law since you have to die to it (7:1-6) as you do to sin and sinning (chapter 6)? Note that everything which has gone on before seems to stress a close connection between sin and law. "No!" is Paul's answer. Law is not sinful.
      1. Cause #1: The uses of law are good.
         a.   7:7-9 The law reveals what sin is and what it is not. It enlightens the sinner's conscience but is not itself sinful. It is designed to REVEAL sin, not to RELIEVE it. It is like the X-ray machine which reveals the cancer in the lungs but is not therefore cancerous. In fact, the better picture the X-ray machine presents of the tumor, the better the machine is doing its job. Paul goes on to state the following facts:
            1.) Sin is dead, i.e. unobserved, as far as the sinner is concerned prior to the operation of law. Without the operation of law, there are no guilt feelings within, although sin is still there and working secretly. It is as a tumor which may be growing secretly until the X-ray machine shows its presence.
            2.) Sin is known only after one knows the standard and recognizes how far short of it he falls.
            3.) Sin exists, but apart from law, it has no means of producing guilt. However, the entrance of law gives sin the opportunity it wants to take over in the life, the "beachhead" for which it is looking to capture the life. The Greek word used here is one which is used for a base of operation in a military sense.
            4.) Appendix: When was Paul actually living apart from law? Was this actually an experience of Paul about which he is writing? Could this be a gnomic use of the pronoun "I"?
               a.) Some think Paul was referring to the ante-Mosaic period, the period before the law of Moses was given. Then obviously he could not have been referring here to his own personal experience.
               b.) Some think he was referring to the childhood state before the consciousness of the meaning of the law has taken hold of the individual.
               c.) Probably he was referring to the pre-salvation experience before the law has come to an individual's understanding in its full sense, as it does after his salvation. For example, before Paul was a Christian, he thought himself blameless with respect to the law. See Phil. 3:6.

After his conversion, he wrote at the end of his ministry for Christ, "I am a chief of sinners." See I Tim. 1:15.

   d.) Appendix: It was in Paul's post-salvation experience that he became aware of the full implications of the law through his study of and meditation on the Word of God. He came to se it through the eyes of Christ, who condemned both murder AND HATRED, adultery AND LUST, in other words, the sin and the sinful attitude that can lead to it.

b.   7:10 The law leads to life ideally, although actually it leads to death.
   1.) The law should lead to life. In Adam's case, it would have if he had obeyed it. In Christ's case, it did.
   2.) The law actually has evil consequences, viz.. death, because no one can keep it.
   3.) The law is unable to save the sinner and give him real life.
   4.) The law was designed to make people happy and holy. See John 10:10. The laws of God are the rules for the game of life given to us by God, the playground to protect the children from harm and to help them have the most fun out of the playground equipment.
   5.) The law is unable to give the help necessary to accomplish what it commands.
   6.) The law leads indirectly to actual death ultimately and a living death immediately.

Thayer's Greek-English Lexicon of the New Testament defines thanatos or death here as a state of being deprived of real life. It can be a reference to the living death described in the end of Romans 7. It is the loss of that which alone is worthy of the name "life". It is the misery of soul arising from sin, causing the person in the throes of it to cry out, "I am a miserable man; who will deliver me from the body of this death?" See Romans 7:24.

c.   7:11-13 The law makes sin exceedingly sinful. Although ignorance of any law is no excuse, the deliberate violation of a known law is far worse than the breaking of a law unknowingly. A penalty for the breaking of a law ignorantly will be less than that for a flagrant violation of a law known by the lawbreaker.

2.   Cause #2: The character of law is not sinful. Note that everything which Paul has to say about law here is good.
   a.   Char. #1   The law is revealing what God's will is.
   b.   Char. #2   It is life-bringing ideally.
   c.   Char. #3   It is holy.

d. Char. #4   It is righteous.
e. Char. #5   It is good.
f. Char. #6   It is spiritual, in that it is Spirit-caused and Spirit-given.
g. Char. #7   However, it is used by sin.
Never forget the following thought. An X-ray machine could be used to murder someone but that does not make the machine a murderer.

B. Question #3: Did that which is good become death unto me? No, because sin, and not law. is the cause of death. 7:13-25

III. The effect of the law in a Christian's experience is that it creates a conflict with sin dwelling in his flesh.

A. The problems for Paul or whoever the person in this conflict is are as follows:
1. Item #1: Law is indirectly responsible for the trouble.
   a. Law prescribes a holy walk.
   It was never intended to GIVE life but only to GUIDE life.
   b. Law is helpless to give the power to live the life it prescribes. It cannot help us do what it demands.
   c. Law cannot secure a holy walk for the Christian.
2. Item #2: Indwelling sin is directly responsible for the conflict.
   See the many references to this in the end of chapter 7:17,18,20,21,23,25.
   a. The conflict is not the fault of law at all. All Paul says about law is good and proper.
   b. The conflict is the fault of the flesh, sin dwelling in the bodily members. The law is good but the instrument with which it has to work is bad. In other words, the believer in this life is still involved with indwelling sin in his bodily members.
3 Item #3: "I" trouble is the key to this person's spiritual difficulties. Note that there are approximately fifty "I's," "me's" and "my's" in chapter 7 and the Holy Spirit is conspicuous by his absence; and there are 14 references to the Holy Spirit in the first 17 verses of Romans 8.
4 Item #4: A "will" problem is at the core of the conflict. The "wretched man" does not have his will set to obey God. He does not want to do so badly enough.

B The person in this conflict is a Christian.
Some even go so far as to say that this is Paul in his regenerate state. If this is true then we do not know when in his Christian experience he went through this carnal period. See Romans 7:14.
1. Reason #1 is that many Christians go through this experience after their conversions. It is as if they are walking civil wars with the Spirit fighting the sin dwelling in their members.

2. Reason #2 is the incapability of assigning certain statements made here to an unregenerate person.
   a. This person hates evil, although he is somehow practicing it.
   b. He consents to the goodness of the law.
   c He delights in the law after the inner man.
   d. He is crying out for deliverance from the power of indwelling sin in his members, not from its guilt and penalty.
   e. He is serving God and God's law with his mind but with the flesh the principle of sin.
3. Reason #3 is the description of this individual as CARNAL in 7:14.
   This is the Greek word sarkinos. which is clearly used of Christian people, although, not good ones, in I Corinthians 3:1.
4. Reason #4 is the context of this passage. We have long since left the section of Romans dealing with justification (3:21-5:11) and are now dealing with the doctrine of sanctification (chaps. 6-8).

C. The points discovered by the Christian from this conflict are as follows:
   1. There is sin dwelling in his bodily members, although he delights in the law of God.
   2 His own will is powerless against that indwelling sin unaided. He does the things he does not really want to do (sins of commission).
   3. He does not do the things which he seemingly wants to do (sins of omission).
   4. His sinful self is not his real self, although he still feels to blame for his lack of right living. His wretchedness comes from knowing that he is responsible.
   5. He is conscious of the spiritual weakness in himself. 7:18 He knows what to do but cannot perform. Maybe it is better to say that he will not.
   6. He calls his spiritual defeat a "captivity." 7:23
   7. He knows that the deliverance from the body of this death is THROUGH JESUS CHRIST. It comes immediately through our identification of ourselves with Christ through reckoning and will come ultimately at the rapture of the church through the resurrection body then received. One writer has described the wretched life here pictured as the life of the Christian between experiencing John 3:16 and Romans 12:1.
   8. Appendix 7:25b
      Why does Paul close this chapter with the declaration in 7:25b rather than with the victory cry of 7:25a. The declaration which closes the chapter is as follows: "So then,

on the one hand, with my mind I myself am continuing to serve the law of God, but, on the other hand, with my flesh the principle of sin."

Answer: Paul does not answer the question raised but the answer may lie in the fact that to know the means to victory does not mean automatic victory. You may be aware of the fact that the medicine in the bottle has the potential of making you well; however, if you refuse to take the medicine, it should not surprise you if you do not regain your health. Diagnosis is not enough. The means to victory must be appropriated. You have to take the "medicine."

D. The power for Paul's victory and OURS over indwelling sin in our members is...

1. Not through obedience to law but through death to law as a legalistic means to a holy life. (It is not through meritorious and legalistic striving to obey the letter of the law.)

2. Through simple faith in Christ's work on the cross and in our lives. (It is through applying the practical demands of Romans 6:11-14, viz, "presenting" and "reckoning."

3. Through simple faith in the indwelling presence and power of the Holy Spirit. (One will not dwell on what the law demands but oh what the Spirit would do in his place. As one has said, we are just "suits of working clothes" which the Holy Spirit wears AND MY CLOTHES DO NOT DIRECT MY ACTIVITIES, TELLING ME WHAT I CAN AND CANNOT DO WITH THEM.)

4. Through reckoning oneself dead to sin and law (Present yourself to God with one resolute effort and continue reckoning regularly. Our wills are involved but only as they are completely yielded to the Holy Spirit's will. Our desire is "not our will but His will be done.")

Conclusion

A. Chap. 6 Continue reckoning dead "the old man," "the old adamic nature," the "sin in our members."

B. Chap. 7 Continue reckoning yourself dead to law as a means of sanctification or holy living. (Again, the law is not for justification or sanctification, but only for revelation regarding what pleases God and what does not.)

C. Chap. 8 Continue allowing the Spirit to live his life out through you. As a Christian, you are in the Spirit. Now make sure that with His indwelling help, you continue living according to the Spirit. This is the Spirit-led life of Romans 8.

D. Appendix:

One of the unique features of Christianity is "the unique feature of the moral teaching of our Lord. That uniqueness does not lie in the type of conduct which is produced in men; other great ethical systems set similar ideals before their pupils. The real distinctiveness of the Christian ethic lies in the means whereby the good life is attained. It is not, as it is in all other systems, the result of long training, stern repression of human desires and even instincts, but a change in the outlook and direction of life. In other words, it does not say 'Be good and you may get into contact with God', but 'get into contact with God and He will help you to be good'." T. H. Robinson, "The Old Testament and the Modem World," The Old Testament and Modem Study. H. H. Rowley(ed.) London: Oxford University Press, 1967. p. 360.

On to Victory ~ Romans 8:1-13

¹There is, therefore, now no condemnation to those who are in Christ Jesus. ²For the law of the Spirit of life in Christ Jesus has freed you [s] from the law of sin and death. ³As for that which was impossible for the law because it was being weakened by means of the flesh, God, who sent His own Son in the likeness of flesh of sin and for a sin offering, condemned sin the flesh, ⁴in order that the righteous requirement of the law might be fulfilled in us who are not continuing to walk according to the flesh but according to the Spirit. ⁵For they who are according to the flesh continue setting their minds on the things of the flesh, but those who are according to the Spirit [continue setting their minds] on the things of the Spirit. ⁶For the manner of thinking belonging to the flesh is death, but the manner of thinking belonging to the Spirit is life and peace. ⁷Therefore, the manner of thinking belonging to the flesh is hostile toward God; for to the law of God it is not subjecting itself for neither is it able [to be subjecting itself.] ⁸But those who are in the flesh are not being able to please God. ⁹But you, yourselves, are not in [the] flesh but in [the] Spirit, if [1st] indeed [the] Spirit of God is dwelling you. But if [1st] anyone is not possessing [the] Spirit of Christ, this one is not His. ¹⁰But if [1st] Christ is in you [pl], on the one hand, your body is dead because of sin, but, on the other hand, your spirit is life because of righteousness. ¹¹And if [1st] the Spirit of the One who raised Jesus from [the] dead is dwelling in you [pl], the One who raised Christ Jesus from [the] dead will also quicken your [pl] mortal bodies by means of His Spirit who continues dwelling in you [pl].

¹²So then, brothers, we are debtors, not to the flesh in order to continue living according to [the] flesh; ¹³for if [1st] according to [the] flesh you continue living, you [pl] are about to be dying; but if [1st] by [the] Spirit, the practices of the body you [pl] continue putting to death, you [pl] will live.

Introduction
A. A review of chapters 6 and 7: THE NEW LIFE FOLLOWING JUSTIFICATION:
  1. deliverance from a life of sin 6:1-14 (THE BAPTISM ANALOGY)
     a. His expiration with Christ
     b. His identification with Christ
     c. His consideration of himself to be dead to sin but alive to God every time he is tempted
     d. His presentation of himself and his members to God as weapons to fight sin at a specific time
  2. Deliverance from individual acts of sin 6:15-23 (THE BONDSERVANT ANALOGY) His presentation of his members as weapons to righteousness and to God)

3. Deliverance from bondage to law as a means of holiness ch. 7
(THE BOND OF MARRIAGE)
   a. The relation of the Christian to law: his death to it.Romans 7:1-6
   b. The character and use of law: all said is good. Romans 7:7-13
   c. The effect of law in the carnal Christian: an internal war 7:14-25
4. Deliverance from a carnal life lived according to the flesh and an introduction to a life lived in and according to the Spirit
B. A relating of Romans 8 to Romans 7-8 is an enlarged discussion of the victory cry in Romans 7:25a. There is victory through Jesus Christ.
C. Appendix: Note the similarity of the teaching of Howard Guinness in the following quotation to that of Paul in Romans 6 and 7 and his teaching on "presenting" and "reckoning."

When I receive Christ as my Savior, the attitude of my heart and will must be that of simple trust and unconditional surrender. Nothing less than this swings wide the door for Him to enter, for He is a King. Failure to realize this sometimes leads to false conversions and subsequent falling away. At the moment of conversion, therefore, Christ is not only received but enthroned, and I am "filled with the Holy Spirit." There is no reason why I should not progress in the life of this fullness right from that moment, but the fact is that most of us fail to do so through disobedience or unbelief, with the result that Christ is dethroned and "self takes His place. He does not leave us at such moments, however, but waits sorrowfully for us to see our mistake and return to Him in penitence and surrender. With many of us there comes a conscious time-or period of time-sometimes after we have been defeated Christians for several years, when we re-enthrone the Savior and are freed from self and sin by the in flooding power of the Holy Spirit. There is one vital difference between these parallel truths of receiving and enthroning Christ however. The first is done once for all and I become "born of God;" the second is not done once for all, but is a moment by moment experience which, started by a definite act, and at first continued by many similar acts, finally becomes habitual through the settled attitude of my will. Many acts lead on to a constant attitude. A crisis starts a process. This does not secure for us "sinless perfection"-the inability to sin; but it does secure freedom-the ability not to sin. Howard Guinness, Sacrifice. Chicago: Inter-Varsity Christian Fellowship, 1947. pp. 55,56.

I. The Road to Victory in the Struggle of 7:14-25 THE KEY: FAITH
   A. 8:1 There must be a realization that we are in Christ Jesus.
   B. 8:2 There must also be a realization that we are free from the principle of sin and death.
   C. 8:4 There must be a sincere attempt on our part to walk according to the leading of the Holy Spirit through the Word of God.
   D. 8:9 There must be a realization of what we are in the Spirit and a living like it.

II. The Realm of This Victory: Being in the Spirit
   A. The three possible conditions of an individual today:

1. Condition #1: Being in the flesh and walking according to the flesh, which is the condition of the unsaved or "sensuous" person. He is the psuchikos person of I Corinthians 2:14 and Jude 19, who does not have the Holy Spirit living within him. See Romans 8:9.
2. Condition #2: Being in the Spirit but walking according to the flesh, which is the condition of the carnal Christian. Some Christians are living this way ignorantly and others intentionally.
   a. There are two dangers one must avoid when admitting that this kind of a Christian can exist.
      1.) Danger #1 is that of reducing justification to nothingness while sanctification is magnified. This is done in some "holiness" circles. Some of them cannot even admit that the carnal Christian state exists since some hold to the Wesleyan doctrine that the moment one commits a sin, defined as a voluntary transgression of a known law, he loses his salvation. Rather than increasing the difference between the experience of salvation and sanctification, one ought to diminish it.
      2.) Danger #2 is that of encouraging the Christian to keep on living on this plane spiritually. Some who admit this condition of carnal Christian living exists even describe it as the normal Christian experience. Note Romans 8:12, 13 where Paul gives a solemn warning to brothers and sisters in Christ who might like to continue living according to the flesh and to accept Jesus Christ only as a fire- escape from hell.
   b. There are three clear illustrations of carnal Christians in the Bible.
      1.) The Corinthians, to whom Paul wrote I Corinthians, were practicing sinful things, as tolerating divisions within their ranks, taking Christians to law before heathen judges, practicing fornication with prostitutes, abusing the Lord's supper, hurting weaker Christians, and the like. Yet Paul writes to them in I Corinthians 6:19,20, "You know, don't you, that your bodies are the sanctuaries of the Holy Spirit who is in you and that you do not belong to yourselves...Therefore, glorify God with your bodies." In other words, he addresses them as Christians, but not good ones.
      2.) The Hebrew Christians to whom the book of Hebrews was written, had retrogressed in their Christian lives. The writer writes to them, rebuking them with his statement that "they had become having need of milk again, not solid food. See Hebrews 5:12. He wants them to

leave the basics of Christianity and press on to maturity in their Christian lives. See Hebrews 6:1,2.

      3.) The carnal Christian of Romans 7:14 and following is another case in point. He is a "walking civil war" and a very "wretched" person. See Romans 7:24.

  3. Condition #3: Being in the Spirit and walking according to the Spirit, which is the condition of the spiritual person or the Spirit-filled person. (Note that this person can be recognized. When they wanted deacons in Acts 6, one of the criteria was that they be Spirit-filled. See also Galatians 6:1. It goes without saying. The one looks for people exhibiting the fruit of the Spirit. See Galatians 5:22,23.

    a. Life on this spiritual plane is always the goal of the Holy Spirit in a life. This is the life of Romans 8.

    b. It is the life of rapid spiritual growth and maturity, not of spiritual arrival and stagnation.

    c. It is the life which experiences the full blessings of Romans 8. (Some of these are true of the carnal Christian as well, but to a lesser degree without full appreciation.

    d. It is the normal Christian life of the book of Acts and should be for Christians of every age.

    e. Appendix: This kind of Christian becomes just "a suit of working clothes" for the Holy Spirit to wear. He has as little will of his own as the pants or the jacket he wears. How foolish it would be for the "clothes" to tell the Holy Spirit what He can do.

B. There are different ways of describing this victorious position of the believer

  1. This can be described as "dwelling in Christ Jesus." It is like members of a body being in the body or branches of a vine being in a vine. 8:1

  2. This life involves having the Spirit of God, who is the Spirit of Christ, living within a person. 8:9,11

  3. This life involves having Christ living or, in other words, being at home in a person. 8:10

  4. This life involves having the entire Trinity living within by means of the person of the Holy Spirit of God. We must realize this, we must believe it, and then we must act like it.

  5. Appendix #1: William R. Newell in his commentary, Romans Verse by Verse pp. 300, 301 is mistaken here. He writes, "Those who are Christians either have or will have the Spirit." Paul teaches here that every Christian does have the Spirit within. There is nothing futuristic about it.

  6. Appendix #2: Romans 8 discusses primarily condition #3 described above, that of the Spirit- filled Christian. It can be said that the carnal Christian has the blessings positionally

but is not enjoying them experientially. The Spirit-filled Christian is enjoying the privileges both positionally and experientially. See the following chart.

The following has been developed from Romans 8:1-1

The Unsaved Person	The Carnal Person In Christ Jesus v. 1	The Spiritual Person In Christ Jesus v. 1
Condemnation positionally and experientially	No condemnation positionally but condemnation experientially	No condemnation positionally or experientially v. 1
Continuing to walk according to the flesh v. 4	Continuing to walk according tothe flesh (miserable)	Enjoying life as he continues to walk acc. to the Spirit v. 4
No freedom from the law law of of sin and death v. 2	Freedom from the sin and death v. 2	Freedom from the law of sin and death v. 2
Continuing to set his on things of the flesh v. 5	Continuing to set his mind on things of the flesh v. 5	Continuing to set his mind on things of the Spirit v. 5
Inability to please God v.8	Ability to please God but isn't	Ability to please God, and is
Existence in the flesh v. 8,9	Existence in the Spirit v. 9	Existence in the Spirit 8:9
No presence of the Spirit indwelling v. 9	Possession of the Spirit indwelling but not controlling v. 9	Possession of the Spirit indwelling and controlling v. 9
No possession by Christ v. 10	Possession by Christ v. 10	Possession by Christ v.10
No expectation of a new body	His spirit alive but body dead because of sin v. 10	His spirit alive body dead because of sin v. 10
Living acc. to the flesh and destined to die vv.12,13 a	Expectation of a new v. 11	Expectation of a new body v. 11
	Indwelling by the Spirit but living acc. to the flesh and on the brink of dying (again) v. 12,13a	Indwelling by the Spirit and living according to the Spirit v. 13b
		Continuing to put to death the doings of the body and is destined to live v.13b
		Is continuing to be led bythe Spirit v. 14

III. The Rewards of Such a Victory

A. There is freedom from condemnation of every kind, including the kind seen in the end of Romans 7. In fact, a carnal Christian is a walking civil war. He is like a square circle or a four-angled triangle. Paul discusses being "in Christ" here as if the carnal Christian condition did not exist as a possibility.

B. There is freedom from the principle of sin and death including the death described in the end of Romans 7, death defined as the absence of real living.

C. There is the fulfillment of the righteous ordinance or demand of the law in us, i.e. in our cases. The law no longer binds us as a way to acceptance by God but we are obliged to keep it as a way of holiness. It is no longer binding for our acceptance before God, since we are no longer under law but under grace; but it is binding upon us as a Christian standard of conduct; and we seek to keep it as we walk according to the Spirit and His leading via the Word of God. See John R.W. Stott, Men Made New. pp. 82,83.

D. There is a change of mind. This person delights to think on the things of the Spirit now. This means a change of ambitions, of interests, and of preoccupations.

E. There is now real peace and real living. There is no experiential peace or enjoyable living at the end of Romans 7 for the carnal Christian.

IV. The Requirement for Such Victory: The coming of Christ the first time

A. The purpose of His coming the first time: to do what the law could not do, not because the law has something wrong with it but because we have something wrong with us.

B. The manner of His coming the first time: "in the likeness of flesh of sin"
Note Paul's careful phrasing here. Jesus was like us in everything essential to being a true human being.

   1. Paul did not say He came "in likeness of flesh." Then He would not have been a true man. He would only have been "like" us.

   2. He did not say "in flesh" because the word "flesh" since the fall has sinful connotations which he did not want to convey.

   3. He was very careful not to say "in sinful flesh." This would have been Gnostic in flavor, suggesting that matter is somehow evil.

   *4. By saying that He came "in the likeness of flesh of sin," he described Christ as a true man, yet without sin. In other words, Christ's human nature was exactly like Adam's was before he fell into sin. Again, sin is a DAMAGING of human nature, not a DEMAND of it.

C. The occasion for Christ's first coming was that He might be an offering for sin.
D. The effect of His first coming was that God condemned sin in the flesh. How this was done has been variously described:
   1. Christ condemned sin by his very presence in the flesh, showing it is possible to live a sinless life in the flesh, thus leaving us inexcusable. The text says God condemned the sin in the flesh, not Christ.
   2. Christ destroyed the reigning power of sin in the flesh; however, this is much stronger than the text would imply. Furthermore, it is Christ again doing it and not God the Father.
   *3. God condemned sin in the flesh by sending Christ to die for it, i.e.. to suffer its penalty. He condemned it in the sense that He punished it, meting out upon Christ the penalty of death prescribed by law. God condemned our sin in the person of Christ, our Substitute, so that there would not need to be any condemnation for us.
E. The ultimate object of Christ's first coming was that the righteous demand or requirement of the law might be satisfied or fulfilled in our case. The righteous demand of the law is that the sinner must die. God provided Christ to be an acceptable Substitute for us that He might declare us righteous.
F. The condition in order that Christ's first coming might achieve this for us is that we continue walking not according to the flesh but according to the Spirit. The Gospel is not antinomian in character, but rather encourages lawful and holy living.

V. **The Relation of Flesh to the Spirit**
   A. There is a difference of interest.
      1. Those who are in the flesh have their minds, affections and wills set on the things of the flesh.
      2. Those who are in the Spirit have their minds, affections and wills set on the things of the Spirit (and the spiritual realm).
   B. There is a difference of result.
      1. The result for the unsaved person is death.
      2. The results for the saved individual are life, peace, and the ultimate resurrection with a quickened body. Romans 8:11
   C. There is a difference in relation to God and His law:
      1. The unsaved person is insubordinate to God's law and is unacceptable to God. See Romans 8:8. Those in the flesh cannot do anything meritorious which will ultimately please God. They are totally unable to do so.
      2. The saved person is capable of obeying God's law and of pleasing him and has the righteous demand of the law fulfilled for him by Christ, His Substitute.
   D. Appendix:
      1. The flesh spoken of here is not the material body, which can be acceptable to God.

2. The flesh spoken of here is the power of sinfulness working in the members of our body and this can never be acceptable to God. The core of this indwelling sin is SELFISHNESS, something with which we are born.

Conclusion

A. Romans 8:9 Note that the Holy Spirit indwells every believer. The difference between the carnal Christian and the Spirit-filled Christian has to do with the matter of control.
To be Spirit-filled is to be Spirit-controlled; and not all Christians are allowing him to direct their lives.

B. Romans 8:12,13 Note the "red light" given in these verses to carnal Christians. The carnal Christian is not spiritually dead but it would appear that Paul is warning such that this could happen. They are on the brink of dying all over again. Paul is warning such believers of a very live possibility.

Check also I Corinthians 3:1-3 and other places in the book where Paul was attempting to get the Corinthians off of the carnal plane of living on to the Spirit-filled. The writer to the Hebrews was also concerned because the Hebrew Christians seemed to him to have retrogressed spiritually from the Spirit-filled plane of Christian living to the carnal. See Hebrews 5:11-14 and 10:32-39. By so doing, he warns them they are coming close to an unpardonable state. (Heb. 6:4-6:10:26-31.)

The Life According to the Spirit ~ Romans 8

14For as many as are continuing to be led by [the] Spirit of God, these are sons of God. 15For you [pl] did not receive again [the] spirit of bondage unto fear, but you [pl] received [the] Spirit of adoption, by whom we continue crying out, "Abba, Father." 16(And) the Spirit Himself continues bearing witness together with our spirit that we are children of God. 17And since [we are] children, [we are] also heirs, on the one hand, heirs of God, and, on the other hand, fellow heirs together with Christ, if [1st] indeed we continue suffering together with Him that we may also be glorified together with Him.

18For I am reckoning that the sufferings of the present season are not worthy [to be compared] with the coming glory to be revealed unto us. 19For the eager expectation of the creation is waiting eagerly for the revelation of the sons of God. 20For the creation was subjected to frustration, not willingly but because of the One who subjected [it], on the basis of hope 21because the creation itself also will be freed from the bondage of the corruption unto the freedom of the glory of the children of God. 22For we know that all the creation continues groaning together and travailing together until the present, 23and not only [this], but we ourselves also, who continue having the first-fruits of the Spirit, even we, ourselves, in ourselves are groaning, while we are waiting for the adoption, the redemption of our body. 24For hope we were saved; but hope which is being seen is not hope; for, who continues hoping for what he is seeing; 25But if for what we are not seeing we continue hoping for, [then] by means of endurance we continue waiting [for it].

26And likewise also the Spirit continues helping [us] together in our weakness; for we do not know for what we should pray as is proper, but the Spirit Himself continues interceding on our behalf with indescribable groanings; 27and the One who continually searches the hearts knows what the Spirit's manner of thinking is, because according to [the will of] God He continues making intercession on behalf of the saints. 28And we know that, for those who are continuing to love God, all things He continues working together for good, for those who are according to [His] purpose being called. 29Because those whom He foreknew, He also foreordained [to be] conformed together to the image of His Son, in order that He might be firstborn among many brothers; 30and those whom He foreordained, these also He called; and those whom He called, these also He justified; and those whom He justified, these He also glorified.

31What then shall we say to these things? Since God is on our side, who [is] against us? 32He, who indeed His own Son did not spare but on behalf of us all delivered Him up, how will He not together with Him all things freely offer us? 33Who will bring a charge against [the] elect of God? He who is justifying is God. 34Who is the One condemning? [It is] Christ Jesus, who died, but more, who was raised, who is also at [the] right hand of God, who is also interceding on behalf of us. 35Who will separate us from Christ's love? [Will] tribulation or distress or persecution or famine or lack of clothing or peril or sword? 36Even as it stands written,

> *On account of you [s], we continue being put to death all the day;*
> *We were reckoned as sheep for butchering.*

37But in all these things we continue being more than [merely] conquering by means of the One who loved us. 38For I stand persuaded that neither death nor life nor angels nor rulers nor things present nor things future nor powers 39nor height nor depth nor any other created thing will be able to separate us from God's love, which is in Christ Jesus, our Lord.

Introduction: The following names have been given to the life in the Spirit and lived according to the Spirit:

    A.   The transformed life
    B.   The separated life
    C.   The abiding life
    D.   The sanctified life
    E.   The Spirit-filled life
    F.   The deeper life
    G.   The victorious life
    H.   The Spirit-led life

I.   **The Conduct of the Christian living this life** Romans 8:12,13

    A. We, as Christians, are not debtors to live our lives according to the flesh, i.e., the old nature.

    B. We are to continue putting to death the doings of the body by the help of the Holy Spirit. This is another way of saying we are to continue reckoning ourselves dead to sin and alive to God in Christ Jesus. See Rom. 6:11. Dr. Stott writes, "Mortification (putting to death by the power of the Spirit the deeds of the body) means a ruthless rejection of all practices we know now to be wrong; a daily repentance, turning from all known sins of habit, practice, association or thought; a plucking out of the eye, a cutting off of the hand or foot, if temptation comes to us through what we see or do or where we go. The only attitude to adopt towards the flesh is to kill it." John Stott, Men Made New, p.91.

II. **The Concerns of the Spirit** (the entire chapter)

   In other words, the work of the Holy Spirit on behalf of the Spirit-led Christian is as follows:

    A. He frees us from condemnation of all kinds, both positional and experiential. 8:1

    B. He makes possible our freedom from the principle of sin and death. 8:2 (We are now following the "faith" plan, not the "obey" plan.)

    C. He makes possible the accomplishment of the righteous demand of the law in our cases. 8:4

    D. He indwells every believer. 8:9

    E. He will quicken our mortal bodies, probably at the time of their resurrection. 8:11

    F. He leads the sons of God, although this does not mean that He will force his guidance upon any Christian. Our free wills are still involved. God will not lead anyone who does not want to be led. 8:14-17.

    G. He, as the Spirit of adoption, makes us the children of God. 8:15

(It is because of His work that we can use the most familiar name for God, Abba. This is the Aramaic word for "father" and so familiar a name that the rabbis did not use it for God. Our English correspondents would be "daddy" or "papa," although the Greek "father" is also used by Paul here.

H. He bears witness with our spirits that we are sons of God. 8:16
1. Note the many references to our sonship. See 8:14,15,16, 17,19, 21 and 23.
2. Note the words used here:
   a. The Greek word for "son" emphasizes the rank and privilege of our legal status.
   b. The Greek word for "child" emphasizes our kinship to God by nature, in other words, our natural status.
3. The comparison is that of the relation of a child to his parent. There is no fear, in a normal father-child relationship, when the child is called into the presence of his father. The normal relation is one of love, not fearfulness.

I. He helps us in our praying. 8:26
The idea in the Greek word "help" is one of his getting into the other side of a yoke with us and helping us pray, as one ox helps the other in pulling a wagon. See Luke 10:40 where the same verb is used by Martha when she desires Mary's assistance. Note that He helps us in our praying but He does not do it for us.

J. He is unquestionably also involved in God's working all things together for the good of those who are continuing to love God and who are being called according to His purpose.
1. The Christian must remember, however, that loving God equals obeying God. See John 14:15, 21, 23, 24.
2. The "being called" means not merely receiving the call but responding to it affirmatively. The calling does not automatically produce the desired effect but demands a positive response to it from us.

K. Appendix
All of these workings of the Holy Spirit are true to some degree of all Christians, both the carnal and the Spirit-filled. However, they are known in their fullness only by those who are not only in the Spirit (saved) but who are walking according to the Spirit's leading by the Bible (Spirit-filled). These latter are righteous both positionally and experientially.

Ill. The Cry of Creation
Paul's mention of suffering preparatory to glorification (8:17) leads on into his discussion of the sufferings of the present time as compared to the coming glory.
A. A cry in nature itself (8:18-22) is indicative of the longing of nature for the revelation of the sons of God when Christ returns and nature will be changed and "freed from the bondage of corruption."

1. There is a mysterious sympathy between nature and man.
2. Nature here includes animate and inanimate creation, excluding man
3. The reference here is to the Edenic experience when nature was subjected to frustration by God with the hope that it would be freed later on.
4. The involuntary subjection of all nature to vanity took place following the sin of Adam and Eve recorded in Genesis 3.
5. The subjection of all nature thus was to be only temporary.
6. All nature is waiting for the transformation of the sons of God at the return of Christ and then all nature will be freed from the curse.
7. Appendix: Note the references to suffering and groanings in these verses: 8:22,23,26. Suffering marks the road to glory, like the birth pangs before the birth of a baby.

B. The cry in us ourselves (8:23-25) is also indicative of the longing for the coming of Christ and the change in us.
1. This cry grows out of our being new creations in Christ with our citizenship in heaven.
2. It comes from the presence of the Holy Spirit in us as a "first fruits" of the coming inheritance.
3. It is a cry or groaning for that inheritance from within us. The fact that the new life of heaven has been begun in us already intensifies the longing for the new glorified life to begin.

IV. **The Calling of the Christian**   CONFORMATION TO THE IMAGE OF GOD'S SON, JESUS CHRIST. 8:29,30 (The final conformation will come when Jesus Christ returns; but even now we should be striving with His help to become more like Him.)

A. There is a beginning of this conformation in the foreknowledge of God. (See also I Peter 1:1,2 where Christians are said to be elect according to the foreknowledge of God.)
1. The reference is to the divine foreknowledge of all things, both actual and possible.
2. The meaning is that God knows beforehand what choices people will make with their free wills; and on that basis the rest of the actions mentioned in these verses take place. We must remember that foreknowledge is not CAUSATIVE but only COGNITIVE. We do not do an act because God foreknows we will do it, but He foreknows the act because we shall freely choose to do it. Prophecies given on the basis of God's knowledge ahead of time do not determine what one must do but only declare what one will do. Examples of this can be seen in Jesus' telling Peter ahead of time that he would betray him. As Robert Shank indicates, Jesus' own life was an illustration of the cognitive nature of God's divine foreknowledge operating through the Old Testament prophets who spoke of Jesus'

work ahead of time. He writes, "As the Son of man, Jesus' life did not automatically unfold in the fulfillment of God's will without the necessity of His own deliberate decision and earnest striving. There was nothing artificial or merely hypothetical about His temptations and testings.... It is true that His redemptive career had been foretold and, having been written "the Scriptures must be fulfilled." But the prophecies were given, not to determine what He must do, but to declare what He would do. Jesus' fulfillment of the Scriptures was entirely voluntary. The fact that He could have turned aside from the path of His redemptive mission was declared by our Savior in His words to Peter in Gethsemane. "Put up thy sword thinkest thou that I cannot now pray to my Father and he will immediately send me more than twelve legions of angel? But how then shall the Scriptures be fulfilled, that thus it must be? ... He asserted that the fulfillment of the Scriptures with respect to His redemptive career as Messiah was to be determined by His personal decision alone. All therefore that Jesus endured and achieved in His redemptive career was purely voluntary on His part, rather than the inevitable unfolding of some inexorable divine decree. From Nazareth to Calvary, Jesus was under no constraint or coercion other than His own desire to fulfill the will of His Father ... See Robert Shank. Life in the Son. (Springfield, Missouri Westcott Publishers, 1960), pp. 246,247.

3. The manner of speaking is anthropomorphic. Actually there is no foreknowledge in God for He knows things in one eternal NOW. This way of talking is the same kind of a figure of speech as when the Bible says of God, who cannot change, that He repents. See Gen. 6:6.

B. The next step in our conformation to His Son is God's foreordination.
   1. The reference here is to God's fore ordering of how the life of single individuals will end up. Note that foreordination is a biblical doctrine which is conditioned upon God's foreknowledge.
   2. The meaning is that God, on the basis of His foreknowledge of man's free choices, has ordained beforehand where that person will spend eternity.
   3. The synonym for foreordination is predestination. To summarize. God foreordains or predestines some men to heaven and some to hell because He, by his foreknowledge, knows in advance what their free choices with regard to Christ will be. Therefore, men go to hell, not primarily because God foreordains that they go there, but because they freely choose to go there. To put it another way, men go to hell not because God sends them there but in spite of all a holy and loving God can do to keep them from hell. God is not willing that any should perish (II Peter 3:9).

If this is His will and desire and He is all-powerful, why do men perish? Can't God save all men? If not, why not? THE ANSWER LIES IN OUR FREE WILLS, WHICH GOD COULD VIOLATE BUT HE WON'T. And this principle holds true for both Christians and non-Christians. IF A PERSON GOES TO HELL, IT WILL BE OVER CHRIST'S DEAD BODY. Furthermore, this view does not detract from the sovereignty of God, for it was His sovereign plan to create man with a little area over which he could be sovereign. God could violate this, but does not.

C. S. Lewis writes, "The sin, both of men and of angels, was rendered possible by the fact that God gave them free will: thus surrendering a portion of His omnipotence . . . because He saw that from a world of free creatures, even though they fell. He could work out... a deeper happiness and a fuller splendor than any world of automats (robots) would admit. See C. S. Lewis. Miracles. (New York: The MacMillan Company, 1948), p. 147.

C. A further step is in God's calling those whom He has foreknown and foreordained. Cf. I Cor. 7:15,18. This is not an effectual calling that effects anything automatically apart from our wills. It involves God's invitation to accept Christ and our acceptance of that invitation by faith, as described in Romans 3:21-5:21.

D. An additional step is in God's justifying of individuals. He declares them righteous on the basis of their faith in His Son.

E. The concluding step results in God's glorifying His own. This is apparently what is called a gnomic aorist, by which something not yet realized is stated as having already taken place. The truth is so certain of occurring that it can be stated as though it has already happened. This has to do with the reception of the heavenly state to be experienced by the Christian at the return of Christ.

F. THE END is conformation to the image or complete likeness to Jesus Christ, God's Son. What Christ is, we are to be. We will be reflections of the original. See I John 3:2,3.

G. Appendix: However, this is not an automatic progression toward a necessary or forced end. It is "what has happened and will happen to the foreknown believer," whose faith in Christ has been foreseen by God.

1. The process begins with God's divine foreknowledge of the FREE choices of mankind; and then God ordains that all who will believe will be justified. On the matter of the Lord's foreknowledge, see John 6:64.

2. Then there must be an acceptance of the call or invitation to salvation.

3. This acceptance of the call takes the form of faith for justification.

4. However, faith is not an act but a life of acceptance. Perseverance in faith must then follow for glorification. See I Corinthians 9:24-10:12.

V. **The Confidence of the Christian** 8:31-39
   A. A question regarding our divine support; Since God is for us, who is against us? 8:31 Here there is an argument from the greater to the lesser. If (or since) God did the great thing for us, i.e.. delivering up His own Son for us, He will, will He not, also give us freely all the blessings he has just named? Of course is the answer Paul expects.
   B. A question regarding our freedom from condemnation: Who shall lay anything to the charge of God's select? 8:33 Condemnation may come from Satan, other people, and even our own consciences; but God, the highest Judge and Ground of Appeal, has been satisfied and He is the only one who matters.
   C. A question regarding the one who condemns us: Who is he that condemns? 8:34
      Answer: It is Jesus Christ:
      1. He who died for us
      2. He who was raised for us
      3. He who is sitting at the right hand of God for us
      4. He who is interceding for us, and that is a far cry from CONDEMNING us.
   D. A question regarding that which can separate us from Christ's love and God's love: Who will separate us from Christ's love and God's love which is in Christ Jesus? 8:35,39.
      Answer: No one and nothing can separate us from their love for us because we are more than merely conquering the following things:
      1. Tribulation
      2. Anguish
      3. Persecution
      4. Famine
      5. Nakedness
      6. Peril
      7. Sword
      8. Death (which cuts us off from the world)
      9. Life (with all of its dangers)
      10. Angels
      11. Principalities (spiritual powers)
      12. Present dangers
      13. Future dangers
      14. Powers
      15. Height
      16. Depth
      17. Any other kind of created thing, i.e., anything else he may have overlooked

18. Appendix: Note, as some have, that all of the above things are EXTERNAL to the Christian. Note the quotes following from H. P. Liddon and F. Godet.
    a. HP. Liddon
        This passage (31-39) does not afford countenance to that theory of the Final Perseverance of the Saints which makes their salvation independent of responsibility and free will. That forfeiture of Grace which God the Father and our Lord never will, and which no external power of circumstance ever can effect, may be brought about by the free will of the Christian himself. H. P. Liddon. Explanatory Analysis of St. Paul's Epistle to the Romans. (Grand Rapids: Zondervan Publishing House, 1961). p.146.
    b. F. Godet
        It is a fact of the moral life which is in question, and in this life, liberty has always its part to play. . . from the first moment of faith. What Paul means is that nothing will tear us from the arms of Christ against our will, and so long as we shall not refuse to abide in them ourselves. F. Godet. Commentary on St. Paul's Epistle to the Romans. Vol. II. (Edinburgh: T. & T. dark, 1881). pp. 123, 124.

Conclusion

Paul begins Romans 8 with the life in the Spirit and according to the Spirit and winds up with Father and the Son. THE BLESSINGS AT THE END DEPEND ON THE LIFE AT THE BEGINNING.

The prayer of Dr. Walter L. Wilson (M.D.), recorded in his pamphlet, "Whose Body Is Yours?" is a fitting conclusion to this section of Romans, which discusses the Spirit-led life and sanctification. The pathway to spiritual victory is the praying of this prayer willingly and sincerely. The whole drive of Romans 6-8 is to bring us to the place where we can offer this prayer ourselves AND MEAN IT!

My Lord, I have mistreated You all my Christian life. I have treated You like a servant. When I wanted You I called for You; when I was about to engage in some work I beckoned You to come and help me perform my task. I have kept You in the place of a servant. I have sought to use You only as a willing servant to help me in my self-appointed and chosen work. I shall do so no more. Just now I give You my limbs, my eyes and lips, my brain; all that I am within and without, I hand over to You for You to live in it the life that You please. You may send this body to Africa, or lay it on a bed with cancer. You may blind the eyes, or send me with Your message to Tibet. You may take this body to the Eskimos, or send it to a hospital with pneumonia. It is your body from this moment on. Help Yourself to it. Thank you, my Lord, I believe You have accepted it, for in Romans twelve and one You said "acceptable unto God." Thank you again, my Lord, for taking me. We now belong to each other.

CHAPTER EIGHT

The Relation of Israel to the Righteousness from God by Faith: Her Renunciation of it but Her Ultimate Salvation
Romans 9-11

Israel's Relation to the Righteousness From God by Faith ~ Romans 9:1-33

¹I am speaking truth in Christ, I am not lying, because my conscience is bearing witness to me by the Holy Spirit, ²that [there] is for me great grief and unceasing sorrow in my heart. ³For I could wish that I myself would be accursed from Christ on behalf of my brothers, my kinsmen according to [the] flesh, ⁴who are Israelites, whose are the adoption and the glory and the covenants and the giving of the law and the service and the promises, ⁵whose are the fathers, and from whom [is] the Christ according to the flesh, God, the One being over all things blessed forever. Amen

⁶But by no means has the word of God failed. For [as for] all those from Israel, these are not Israel, ⁷neither because they are seed of Abraham, [are they] all children, but "in Isaac will your [s] seed be called." ⁸That is, [as for] the children of the flesh, these are not children of God, but the children of the promise are being reckoned for seed. ⁹For the word of promise is this, "At this season I shall come and [there] will be a son for Sarah." ¹⁰And not only [this], but also Rebecca, while by one [man] she was conceiving, Isaac, our father-- ¹¹([for the children], although they were not yet born nor had done anything good or foolish, in order that the purpose of God might continue remaining according to [the principle] of election, not by works, but by the One calling) -- ¹²it was said to her, "The elder will serve the younger"; ¹³even as it stands written, "Jacob I loved, but Esau I hated."

¹⁴What then shall we say? [There] is no unrighteousness with God, is there? May it not be so! ¹⁵For to Moses, He is saying, "I will have mercy on whomever I am having mercy, and I will have compassion on whomever I am having compassion." ¹⁶So then [it is] not of the one willing nor of the one running but of the One showing mercy, [viz.], God. ¹⁷For the Scripture is saying to Pharaoh, "For this very [purpose] I raised you [s] up, in order that I might show forth in you [s] My power, and in order that My name might be spread abroad in all the land." ¹⁸So then He is having mercy on whom He is willing, and whom He is willing He is hardening.

¹⁹You [s] will say to me then, "Why is He still finding fault? For who has resisted His will?" ²⁰O man, on the contrary, who are you [s], the one answering back to God? The thing formed will not say to the one who has formed it, "Why did you [s] make me this way," will it? ²¹The potter is having authority over the clay, does he not, to make out the same lump, this one a vessel for honor and that one [a vessel] for dishonor? ²²But, [what will you say then] if God, although He was desiring to show forth wrath and to make known His power, endured with much longsuffering vessels [deserving] of wrath which prepared themselves for destruction, ²³and [that] in order that He

113

*might make known the riches of His glory upon vessels [deserving] of mercy,
which He prepared beforehand for glory, ²⁴even us whom He called not only
from Jews but also from Gentiles? ²⁵As also in Hosea He is saying,*

> *I will call that which is not my people "my people,"
> And her who is not beloved "beloved."
> ²⁶And it will be in the place where it was said to them,
> "You yourselves are not my people,"
> There they will be called sons of [the] living God.*

²⁷And Isaiah is crying on behalf of Israel:

> *If the number of the sons of Israel should be as the sand of the sea,
> the remnant (only) will be saved.
> ²⁸For [His] word [the] Lord will perform upon the earth, accomplishing
> it and executing it quickly.*

²⁹And, just as Isaiah has foretold,

> *Except [the] Lord of Hosts had left behind a seed for us,
> As Sodom we would have become and we would have become like
> Gomorrah.*

*³⁰What then shall we say? [It is this], that [the] Gentiles, who were not
pursuing righteousness, overtook righteousness, but a righteousness which
is by faith; ³¹and Israel, who was pursuing a law [which was to produce]
righteousness did not reach [that] law. ³²Because of what? Because [they
pursued] not by faith but, as it were, by works; for they stumbled over the
stone of stumbling, ³³even as it stands written:*

> *Behold, I am going to lay in Zion a stone of stumbling and a rock
> of offense; But everyone continuing to believe on Him will not be
> disappointed.*

Introduction
    A. Question #1 answered in Romans 9-11: What is the relationship
of the physical Israelites to the whole plan of justification by
faith?

    B. Question #2: How is this "justification by faith" consistent with
the privileged position of the Israelites?

    C. Question #3: Since Israel was chosen but has now apparently
been rejected because she refused this justification by faith, is
not God unfaithful to His promises to Israel?

I. **The Sorrow of Paul for Israel is first of all expressed.** 9:1-3 His
sorrow is characterized by the following:

    A. Char. #1: intensity
Note that Paul puts himself under oath by calling to his witness
three witnesses: Jesus Christ, his own conscience, and the Holy
Spirit.

    B. Char. #2: solemnity
Note that his oath gives solemnity and support to an otherwise
hard to believe statement.

114

C. Char. #3: sincerity
   Note that the way Paul makes this statement makes it
   practically impossible for anyone to doubt his sincerity.
D. Char. #4: continuance
   Paul speaks of his unceasing sorrow for Israel's lostness and
   refusal to accept justification by faith.
E. Char. #5: severity
   Note the lengths to which Paul says he is willing to go if more
   of his kinsmen, the Jews, might accept the Lord.
   1. The reference is to the Jews who were some of his worst
      tormentors on his missionary journeys. See the book of
      Acts.
   2. The word is the word "Anathema" meaning "cursed" or
      "devoted to destruction." In other words, he says he would
      be willing to go to hell if more of his fellow-Jews could
      thereby come to know the Lord. Is it any wonder that he
      put himself under oath to stress his sincerity!
   3. The language is the language of feeling and emotions
      which overwhelmed him. See the following tract entitled
      "Are Missionaries Unbalanced?" which stresses rightfully
      the uniqueness of the missionary passion for lost souls.
      Would to God more had this burden today!

ARE MISSIONARIES UNBALANCED? by T. Norton Sterrett
Are missionaries unbalanced? Of course they are. I'm one. I ought to
know. A missionary probably began as an ordinary person. He dressed
like other people, he liked to play tennis and listen to music. But
even before leaving for the field he became "different." Admired by
some, pitied by others, he was known as one who was leaving parents,
prospects and home for - a vision. So he seemed to be a visionary.

Now that he's come home again he's even more different. To him some
things - big things - just don't seem important. Even the World Series or
the Davis Cup matches don't interest him especially. And apparently he
doesn't see things as other people see them. The chance of a lifetime - to
meet Isaac Stern personally seems to leave him cold. It makes you want
to ask where he's been.

Well, where has he been? Where the conflict with evil is open and
intense, a fight not a fashion - where clothes don't matter, because
there's little time to take care of them - where people are dying for help
he might give, most of them not even knowing he has the help - where
the sun means 120 in the shade, and he can't spend his time in the
shade. But not only space; time too seems to have passed him by. When
you talk about the Beatles he looks puzzled. When you mention Batman
he asks who he is. You wonder how long he's been away.

All right, how long has he been away? Long enough for thirty million
people to go into eternity without Christ, with no chance to hear
the gospel - and some of them went right before his eyes: when that

flimsy riverboat overturned; when that cholera epidemic struck; when that Hindu-Muslim riot broke out. How long has he been gone? Long enough to have had two sieges of amoebic dysentery, to nurse his wife through repeated attacks of malaria, to get the news of his mother's death before he knew she was sick. How long? Long enough to see a few outcaste men and women turn to Christ, to see them drink in the Bible teaching he gave them, to struggle and suffer with them through the persecution that developed from non-Christian relatives, to see them grow into a sturdy band of believers conducting their own worship, to see this group develop an indigenous church that is reaching out to the community. Yes, he's been away a long time.

So he's different. But unnecessarily so now, it seems. At least, since he's in this country, he could pay more attention to his clothes, to what's going on around the country, to recreation, to social life. Of course he could, But he can't forget–at least most of the time–that the price of a new suit would buy 3,200 Gospels; that while an American spends one day in business, 5,000 Indians or Chinese go into eternity without Christ.

So when a missionary comes to your church or your Christian group, remember he will probably be different. If he stumbles for a word now and then, he may have been speaking a foreign tongue almost exclusively for several years, and possibly is fluent in it. If he isn't in the orator class, he may not have had a chance to speak English from a pulpit for awhile.   He may be eloquent on the street of an Indian bazaar. If he doesn't seem to warm up as quickly as you want, if he seems less approachable than a youth evangelist or college professor, remember he's been under a radically different social system since before you started high school, and maybe is unfamiliar with casual conversation.

Sure the missionary is unbalanced. But by whose scales? Yours or God's?
Reprinted by permission from HIS, student magazine of Inter-Varsity Christian Fellowship, copyrighted 1948.

II. **The Status of the Israelites is next presented by Paul** 9:4,5
     He lists their privileges which made them different and explains somewhat why he had such a desire for their salvation.
     A. One special privilege was their divine national adoption. God's choice was to do something wonderful in and through the Israelite nation.
     B. Another was the shekinah glory which accompanied Israel through the wilderness in the seeable form of a cloud. This was a special sign of God's visible presence among his people.
     C. Another was the covenant which God made with His people. It was one original covenant renewed and made more detailed as it was repeated.
          1. The Abrahamic covenant
          2. The Mosaic covenant

116

3. The Davidic covenant
4. The "new" covenant of Jeremiah 31 and Ezekiel 36 and 37
D. Another was the giving of the law or Torah to Israel via Moses.
E. Another privilege was the possession of the service of God connected with the Tabernacle and later the Temple worship.
F. Another was the giving of the promises directly to Israel, such as the promises of salvation, the coming of the Messiah, and the restoration of the kingdom to Israel.
G. Another was Israel's possession of the fathers, namely Abraham, Isaac, Jacob, Joseph, and Judah.
H. Of course, the outstanding privilege was that the Christ, the Messiah, as far as His flesh was concerned, came from Israel. What an outstanding honor. However, He came to His own things and His own people rejected Him. See John 1:11.
I. Appendix: Paul's purposes in listing the above privileges were apparently for the following:
1. Purpose #1 to explain the basis for his great sorrow, because the greater the privileges one has, the greater are the responsibilities.
2. Purpose #2: to emphasize the bigness of the problem facing him, since Israel's Messiah had come and she had rejected Him. Consequently now she seemingly was cut off from the blessings which she had brought into the world through her Messiah. Paul will now attempt to answer this.

III. **The Surety of God's Word relative to Israel** 9:6-13
A. Question: Does not God's rejection of Israel mean that God's promises to Abraham, Isaac, and Jacob have failed?
B. The answer: NO!
1. Cause #1: because not all belonging to physical Israel are the true Israel
2. Cause #2: because not all the physical children of Abraham are the true seed of Abraham
a. The line of promise came through Isaac and Jacob since theirs was the seed of promise.
b. Physical descent from Abraham is not enough because, if it is, one must also include the descendants from Ishmael and Esau as elect.
c. The election here was to higher privileges in the case of Jacob, in contrast with Esau. God had chosen to work through the Israelites, not the Ishmaelites or the Edomites.
d. Note, however, this election was not arbitrary but was based on divine foreknowledge.
GOD FOREKNEW the characters of Ishmael and Esau BEFORE THEY WERE BORN, although THIS IS NOT STATED IN THIS PASSAGE, a passage which is stressing divine sovereignty, not human free will.

3.	Cause #3: God never promised to save all Israelites but only those who followed in the footsteps of the faith of Abraham, although, this is NOT STATED IN THIS PASSAGE EITHER. The emphasis on free will be made in 9:26-ch. 10 of Romans. See Romans 4:10-17 and Galatians 3:7. Many Jews believed that they had a covenant with God that nothing could dissolve. Paul says, "No!" God's covenant was with believers, those following in the faith of Father Abraham.

4.	Appendix
a.	Abraham had two sons, Ishmael and Isaac, and God chose to work through Isaac.
b.	Isaac had two sons, Esau and Jacob, and God chose to work through Jacob, whose other name was Israel.
c.	Jacob or Israel had two types of children, unbelieving Israelites (who were trusting in their name, their physical circumcision and their possession of the law for their justification) and believing Israelites or the remnant (who were believing in the promises of God for their justification). God chose to work through the latter. 9:8

IV.	**The Sovereignty of God with Reference to Israel** 9:14-24
A.	Another question: Does not this mean that there is unrighteousness with God because He chooses one and not another? 9:14
(Remember that this choice by God does not override the free will of mankind, or else this passage contradicts all the passages which say that people are responsible for their sins and also their own destinies. God has simply bypassed the principle of lineage and has chosen to honor the principle of faith.)
B.	The answer: NO!
1.	Cause #1: God is sovereign in dispensing mercy and judgment.
No one has a hold on God entitling them to salvation because He is sovereign in all His choices.
a.	This is seen in the message given to Moses: "I will have mercy on whom I am having mercy, and I will have compassion on whom I am having compassion."
b.	This is seen in His message to God-defying, godless, Pharaoh, who kept on hardening his own heart until God finally confirmed him in his defiant way: "For this very purpose I raised you up, in order that I might show forth in you my power and in order that my name might be spread abroad in all the land."
c.	Conclusion: 9:18 "So then He has mercy on whom He wills, and whom He wills He hardens."
2.	Cause #2: However, God does not do this arbitrarily

118

This is not discussed here, however, as Paul is still isolating the doctrine of divine sovereignty in 9:1-25. Later, in Romans 10, he will emphasize the free will of mankind and mankind's responsibility for his own reception of salvation by faith. With the doctrine of predestination or election, one must always consider the teaching of Romans 8:29,30 and I Peter 1:1,2 where foreknowledge, not causative but cognitive, is the condition for the doctrine.

3. Appendix: Paul is here in Romans 9:1-25 "isolating one side of the divine nature; and in making deductions from his language [,] these passages must be balanced by others which imply the Divine love and human freedom." William Sanday and Arthur C. Headlam, The International Critical Commentary: Romans. 5th ed. Edinburgh: T. & T. dark, 1950. p. 257.

C. Another question: Why does God find fault with us then since no one is resisting God's will nor is able to do so?
In other words, if there is no resistance being offered by the person who disobeys God and he is only doing what God has willed that he should do, how can God blame people who are simply victims of His divine decree?

D. The answers given here in this chapter which is emphasizing divine sovereignty:

1. A rebuke: 9:20 "Oh man...who are you, the one answering back to God? The thing formed will not say to the one who has formed it, 'Why did you make me this way, will it?'" The obvious answer Paul expects is "Of course not."

2. A response: 9:21 "The potter has authority over the clay, does he not, to make out of the SAME lump this one a vessel for honor and that one a vessel for dishonor?" The answer expected is "Of course."

3. A revelation: 9:22,23. But "God endured vessels of wrath which fitted themselves (a Greek perfect participle in the middle voice) for destruction, "vessels like Pharaoh, in order that He might make known the riches of His glory upon vessels (deserving) of mercy which He prepared beforehand for glory." Please note that even in a strong sovereignty section, Paul cannot bring himself to write that God prepares people for destruction. Even if this participle be taken to be a Greek passive participle, which it may be, it still does not ascribe the action of preparation to a loving God.

V. **The Salvation of the Gentiles** 9:25-33
Paul now turns to his emphasis on free will when he says that the salvation of many Gentiles implies the rejection of many Israelites.

A. The salvation of the Gentiles, says Paul, is not a new doctrine but can be found in the Old Testament.

1. Hosea 2:23 and 1:10 claim that the Gentiles, who were not God's people, will some day be called His people.

119

2. Isaiah 10:22. 23 and Isaiah 1:9 claim that only a remnant of Israel will be saved, a fact which implies that many of Israel according to the flesh will be rejected.
B. The fact of the salvation of the Gentiles is then declared by Paul.
1. The Gentiles who were not pursuing righteousness according to the (Mosaic) Law will receive it by faith when it is offered to them.
2. The Israelites who were seeking after the law which should give them righteousness did not reach that righteousness before God.
C. The reason for this is that faith is the key to righteousness before God; and the Israelites, in the majority of cases, were trying to get a righteous standing by works, an impossible task. 9:32, 33 In fact, they thought they had it by virtue of being natural children of Abraham and by performing good works; and they stumbled over the teaching of their own prophet, Isaiah, who taught that everyone continuing to believe on the Lord will not be disappointed (Isaiah 28:16).

Israel's Rejection of the Righteousness From God by Faith ~ *Romans 10:1-21*

[1]Brothers, really the good will of my heart and [my] supplication to God on behalf of them is for [their] salvation. [2]For I continue bearing witness with reference to them that they continue to have a zeal for God, but not according to knowledge; [3]for, because they were ignorant of the righteousness from God and because they were seeking their own [righteousness] to establish, to the righteousness from God they were not subjected. [4]For Christ is the termination of law for righteousness to everyone who is believing. [5]For Moses writes that the man who has done the righteousness which is out of law will live by it; [6]but the righteousness which is out of faith is speaking in this manner: Do not say in your [s] heart, "Who will go up into the heaven?" that is in order to bring Christ down; [7]or "Who will descend into the abyss?" that is, in order to bring Christ up from the dead. [8]But what is it saying? "The spoken word is near you [s], in your [s] mouth and in your [s] heart, that is, the spoken word concerning faith which we are preaching, [9][viz.] that if [3rd] you [s] confess with your [s] mouth Jesus [to be] Lord and you [s] believe with your [s] heart that God raised Him from the dead, you [s] will be saved; [10]for with [the] heart one continues believing for righteousness and with [the] mouth confession is being made for salvation." [11]For the Scripture is saying "Everyone who is believing on Him will not be disappointed." [12]For there is no distinction between Jew and Greek. For the same Lord is [Lord] of all, He who is being rich toward all the ones who continue calling upon Him; [13]for everyone who calls upon the name of the Lord will be saved.

[14]How then will they call [on Him] in whom they have not believed? And how shall they believe [on Him] of whom they have not heard? And how shall they hear without [someone] preaching? [15]And how shall they preach if [3rd] they are not sent forth? Even as it stands written, "How beautiful are the feet of those who are preaching the gospel of good things." [16]But not all hearkened to the gospel. For Isaiah is saying, "Lord who believed our report?" [17]So then faith is from hearing, and hearing is by means of the spoken word concerning Christ. [18]But I am saying they all have heard, have they not? Indeed,

120

Into all the earth their sound went out,
And unto the ends of the inhabited earth their spoken words.

[19]*But I am saying, Israel knew, did she not? First of all, Moses is saying,*

I myself will make you jealous with [that which is] not a nation,
And with a senseless nation I will make you angry.

[20]*And Isaiah is being bold and is saying,*

I was found by those who were not seeking me,
I became manifest to those who were not inquiring after me.

[21]*But to Israel, he is saying "During the whole day, I stretched out my hands to a people who continue being disobedient and obstinate."*

Introduction:
The gist of this chapter is that the Word of God has not failed; the people of Israel have.

I. The Reasons Why They Rejected This Righteousness 10:1-5
    They were characterized by the following:
    A. A misguided zeal for God
        Zeal must not be mistaken for knowledge.
    B. An ignorance of the righteousness from God based on faith
    C. A selfishness that sought to establish their own righteousness
        before God; a self-righteousness. Note the emphasis on free will
        here, in contrast to the heavy stress on divine sovereignty in
        Romans 9. The two must be balanced.
    D. A pride in themselves which refused to subject themselves to
        the righteousness from God.
    E. An obstinacy which refused to subject themselves to the
        righteousness from God
    F. A shortsightedness that failed to see Christ as the end or the
        goal of the law for righteousness for all who are believing. The
        law was designed to lead mankind to despair so that they would
        turn to Christ for eternal life.
    G. A blindness that overlooked the message of faith, which was
        near them 10:9,10 (Note the emphasis on mouth and heart in
        this passage.)
        1. Condition #1 of the message: If you will confess with your
            mouth Jesus to be Lord,
        2. Condition #2 of the message: If you will believe in your
            heart that God raised Jesus from the dead,
        Conclusion: THEN you will be saved.

II. The Righteousness They Rejected 10:6-15
    (Note the emphasis on believing and faith in this whole section,
    two words which emphasize freedom of choice.)

A. A righteousness close to them This closeness is emphasized by the use of the proverbial words from Deuteronomy 30:11-14, words that meant by Paul's time something very close.
    1. No one needs to go up and bring the Messiah down from heaven. (He has already come down from there.)
    2. No one needs to go into the abyss to bring the Messiah, Christ, up from the dead. (He has already come out of the abyss, another word for Sheol or Hades, the place of the dead.)
    3. Christ, the Object of faith and the source of faith-righteousness, is present with them, as close as the message which Paul was preaching.
    4. However, the Jews failed to believe on the Messiah and hence were not saved. They had freedom of choice but exercised it the wrong way.
B. A righteousness preached
C. A righteousness based on confession and faith 10:8-10
   The entrance into eternal life and salvation has two sides:
    1. The external: a public confession of Jesus to be Lord, the Yahweh of their Old Testament. They must confess Jesus to be more than Messiah. He was and is God and this must be declared outwardly. They must publicly express the truth that Jesus, the Man from Nazareth, was and is Jehovah.
    2. The internal: a change of heart, which belief in Jesus' resurrection indicates. In other words, by believing in the resurrection, they are admitting that Jesus was all He claimed to be, and they were wrong. They crucified their Messiah.
D. A righteousness effective in salvation
E. A righteousness applicable to all who will believe 10:11-13
   See Joel 2:32. Note the prevalence of universal terms in these verses and their context.
F. A righteousness requiring proclamation
   The word usually translated "preaching" here is better translated "proclamation" or "heralding" forth news. This is not necessarily formal preaching from a pulpit done by a minister. This heralding of news can be done by anyone.
    1. Condition #1 in the salvation of anyone: the sending of someone to do the announcing
    2. Condition #2: the proclaiming or the heralding forth of the message
    3. Condition #3: the hearing of the message
       All must hear to have even the possibility of being saved. The method is through proclamation.
    4. Condition #4: the believing of the message heard by the hearer
    5. Condition #5: the calling for help by the hearer
    6. The result: salvation

Note the implication that without messengers to proclaim the message, people generally cannot be saved. God has ordained the method of proclamation whereby people are saved.

7. Appendix
   To believe and to call for salvation demands hearing. Paul goes on to show that Israel's problem was not that they had not heard, but they had not believed the message they heard, they had not called, and hence were not saved. Israel was not willing to meet conditions 4 and 5 above. Paul quotes their own Old Testament as proof of their obstinacy in refusing the righteousness from God by faith in Jesus Christ.

III. Their Actual Rejection of This Righteousness: Partial, although all had heard in some way or another 10:16-21
   A. O.T. support from Isaiah 53:1: Isaiah
      Only a few believed the message when they heard it. Most of Israel refused the good news of the Gospel when they heard it; and no one can be saved apart from hearing, believing, and calling. 10:17
   B. O.T. support from Psalm 19:4: the Psalmist
      Everyone has heard in some way or another. V. 18 emphasizes how universally the works of nature glorify God. All might not have heard but all had the opportunity of hearing from the light about God from nature. See Romans 1:18-20.
   C. O.T. support from Deuteronomy 32:21: Moses
      Hopefully Israel would be provoked to jealousy by the Gentiles, "that which was not a nation," as the Gentiles accepted righteousness by faith, when it was offered to them. The Gentiles were not even considered a nation when compared with the privileged position of the Jewish nation. 10:19
   D. O.T. support from Isaiah 65:1: Isaiah
      The Lord declares through the prophet Isaiah, "I was found of them who did not seek me (the Gentiles); I became manifest to those who did not ask of me (the Gentiles). 10:20
   E. O.T. support from Isaiah 65:2: Isaiah
      But Israel disobeyed and contradicted the message of justification by faith, even though she had heard the message. 10:21

Conclusion: Note the stress on two items in Romans 9 and 10:
   A. Divine sovereignty is stressed in Romans 9:1-25.
   B. Human responsibility on the part of Israel is stressed in Romans 9:26- 10:21.
   C. There is no contradiction here: God's divine foreknowledge of saving faith is the key to as much of an understanding of these two items as it is possible for us to grasp with our finite minds.

Note also that saving faith is not just an act of the moment but a life that must continue. Then, with this emphasis on divine foreknowledge of free choice,

1. one avoids blaming God for sending people to hell. (They make their own choice. One must remember that foreknowledge is not causative, only cognitive. Because something is foreknown does not force that thing to occur.)
2. and one avoids the extreme of people surprising God with anything they do with their free wills.

Israel's Reception of Her Promised Messiah ~ Romans 11:1-36

¹I am saying, therefore, "God did not reject His people, did He?" May it not be so! For I myself also am an Israelite, out from the seed of Abraham, from the tribe of Benjamin. ²God did not reject His people whom he foreknew. Or, you [pl] know, do you not, in [the passage referring to] Elijah, what the Scripture is saying, how he continues pleading to God against Israel? ³"Lord, your [s] prophets they killed, your [s] altars they destroyed, and I myself have been left alone and they continue seeking my life." ⁴But what does the divine answer say to him? "I have kept for Myself seven thousand men who did not bow [the] knee to Baal." ⁵In this manner, therefore, also at the present time a remnant according to the election of grace has come into being; ⁶but since it is by grace, it is no longer by works; for otherwise grace becomes no longer grace. ⁷What then? That for which Israel is seeking, this she did not obtain, but the election obtained [it]; but the remaining ones were hardened; ⁸just as it stands written,

> *God gave to them a spirit of [spiritual] insensibility,*
> *eyes in order that they might stop seeing and ears in order*
> *that they might stop hearing, until this very day.*

⁹And David is saying,

> *Let their table become a snare and a trap*
> *and a stumbling block and a recompense to them;*
> *¹⁰Let their eyes be darkened in order that they may stop seeing,*
> *and bow down their back continually.*

¹¹I am saying, therefore, "They did not stumble in order that they might fall [into ruin], did they?" May it not be so! But by their transgression, salvation [came] to the Gentiles in order that it might make them jealous. ¹²But if [1st] their transgression is riches for the world and their defeat is riches for the Gentiles, how much more [will be] their completed number. ¹³But I am speaking to you [pl], the Gentiles. Because I myself am, therefore, an apostle of the Gentiles, my ministry I am glorifying, ¹⁴if [1st] somehow I may make my flesh, [i.e., my fellow countrymen], jealous and may save some of them. ¹⁵For if [1st] the casting away of them is the reconciliation of the world, what will the acceptance [of them by God] be except life from the dead? ¹⁶And if [1st] the first fruits are holy, [so] also is the lump; and if [1st] the root is holy, [so] also are the branches.

17But if [1st] certain ones of the branches were broken off, and you [s] yourself, although you [s] belonged to a wild olive tree, were grafted in among them and became a fellow-partaker [with them] of the root of the fatness of the olive tree, 18stop boasting over the branches; but if [1st] you [s] are boasting, you [s] yourself are not bearing the root but the root [is bearing] you [s]. 19Therefore, you [s] will say, "Branches were broken off in order that I myself might be grafted in." 20Well, because of unbelief they were broken off, but you [s] yourself have come to stand because of faith. Stop being proud, but continue fearing; 21for if [1st] God the natural branches did not spare, neither will He spare you [s]. 22Behold, therefore, the goodness and the severity of God; on the one hand, toward those who have fallen, severity, but toward you [s], the goodness of God, if [3rd] you [s] continue on remaining in His goodness; otherwise, you yourself also will be cut out. 23And those also, if [3rd] they do not continue remaining in unbelief, will be grafted in; for God is able to graft them in again. 24For if [1st] you [s] yourself were cut out of that which was naturally a wild olive tree, and, contrary to nature, were grafted into a cultivated olive tree, how much more rather will these which are the natural [branches] be grafted back into their own olive tree?

25For I am not desiring you [pl] to continue being ignorant, brothers, with reference to this mystery, lest you [pl] continue being wise in yourselves, that a hardening in part has come to pass for Israel until the full number of the Gentiles enter; 26and in like manner all Israel will be saved, even as it stands written,

> *The Deliverer will come out of Zion;*
> *He will take away ungodliness from Jacob.*
> *27And this is for them the covenant from Me,*
> *Whenever I shall take away their sins.*

28On the one hand, according to the gospel, [they are] enemies on account of you [pl]; but, on the other hand, according to the election, [they are] beloved on account of the fathers. 29For irrevocable [i.e. lit. without regret] are the free gifts and the calling of God. 30For just as you yourselves formerly were disobedient to God, but now have been shown mercy because of the disobedience of these, 31so also have these now been disobedient in order that by the [same] mercy [shown to] you they themselves also now may be shown mercy. 32For God has imprisoned them all unto disobedience in order that upon all He might have mercy.

> *33O, the depth of the riches and wisdom and knowledge of God; how unsearchable are His decrees and how incomprehensible are His ways!*
> *34For who has known [the] mind of [the] Lord? Or who has become His counselor? 35Or who gave to Him first, and it will be paid back to Him?*

36Because out from Him, and by means of Him, and for Him are all things; to Him be the glory forever. Amen.

I. **The remnant of Israel (believing Jews) were never cast off by God.** Romans 11:1-6
    A. Question #1: God has not cast away His people, has He?
    B. Answer #1: No, because then how did Paul become accepted and saved, for he was an Israelite.

C.   Answer #2: No, because a remnant, as existed in the days of Elijah, has been saved by grace, not by works. (Note that the reference to the remnant emphasizes the fact that righteousness is an individual matter, not a national one.)

II.   **The rejecters in Israel (unbelieving Jews) were cut off.** 11:7-15
A.   Question #2: What then?
B.   Answer: All Israel did not receive the message of justification by faith but the elect did, with the rest being hardened.
C.   Reason: God blinded their eyes. Note the emphasis on divine sovereignty. In spite of the existence of a remnant, it is still true that Israel as a nation failed to attain the goal God had for her, namely, righteousness by faith.
1.   Isaiah 29:10: Isaiah
God gave them a spirit of stupor, eyes to see not and ears to hear not, down to this very day.
2.   Psalm 69:22,23: David
Let their table become a snare and a trap, and a stumbling block and a retribution to them. Let their eyes be darkened to see not and bend their backs forever.
D.   Question #3: They did not stumble that they might (irrevocably) fall and never get up again, did they?   No. !!
1.   This fall is not a final falling away of Israel. (Anyone who falls down may never get up or may recover himself.)
2.   This fall means the salvation of many Gentiles. (Note in Acts that Paul's preaching to the Gentiles was often occasioned by the Jewish rejection of his message.)
3.   This fall of Israel and the turning to the Gentiles hopefully would result in provoking Israel to jealousy so that she would come back and accept the message.
4. This fall will mean greater blessing for the world when Israel is restored.

III. **The Relationship of the Gentiles to the Jews, both believing and unbelieving** 11:16-25 (THE OLIVE-TREE ANALOGY)
A.   Introductory Matters
1.   The dough/bread analogy: If the "first fruit" or the first portion of dough from which several loaves of bread are made is holy (free from leaven), the lump is holy. In other words, the first of the dough given to the Lord means the consecration of the whole lump of dough to the Lord.
2.   The root/branches analogy: If the root of the olive tree is holy, so are the branches attached to the root.
B.   The parts of the tree which need analysis are as follows:
1.   The natural olive root = Abraham, who was to be a blessing to all nations He was the root from which both Christian Jews and Gentiles receive their nourishment. See Romans 4:16.

    2. The olive tree = the true seed of Abraham, Isaac, and Jacob who are believing, both Israelite and Gentile, specifically the Church

    3. The branches = the individual members of the Church, both natural branches and those grafted into the tree

    4. The original branches belonging to the tree = believing Israelites

    5. The original branches cut out = unbelieving Israelites (Note: Here is where the analogy breaks down because unbelieving Israelites were never in the tree in the first place.)

    6. The wild olive tree = the Gentile world

    7. The branches of the wild olive tree grafted in = Gentile believers (These are the Gentiles following in the footsteps of their father, Abraham's faith. See Rom. 4:10-12.)

    8. The fatness of the olive tree = the blessings of being connected with Abraham

C. The warning given to the Gentile believers here is as follows:

    1. You Gentiles were grafted in among the natural Jewish branches. 11:17

    2. You partake of the root of the fatness of the olive tree. 11:17

    3. You must not boast of your position because the root bears you, not vice versa. 11:18

    4. You stand in the natural olive tree by faith, not your own merit. 11:19,20

    5. You can be cut out also, if you fail in your faith. 11:20,21 (Faith is an individual matter, not a collective one. It is also something that must continue without stopping.)

D. The teaching regarding Israel here is as follows:

    1. Israel was broken off on account of unbelief. 11:20,21 (She, with all of her divine blessings, was not spared by God.)

    2. She was hardened only in part. 11:25 (A remnant always existed in any day.)

    3. She can and will be grafted back in, when she as a nation of individuals believes. 11:23

    4. She was cut out of the olive tree until the fullness of the Gentiles has come in, that is, until the full number of the Gentiles is saved.

    5. Then she will be grafted back in again, since she will not continue in unbelief. (This will be at the time when the Deliverer comes out of Zion. cf. Jeremiah 31 and Ezekiel 37. "Zion" here refers to heaven.)

IV. The Restoration of Israel in the Last Days 11:26-32

A. The manner: "so" "in like manner"

    1. Either restoration through envy and jealousy of the Gentiles who are being saved

    *2. Or, more probably, restoration by faith, i.e., in the way just described or spoken of, if they continue not in their unbelief   (11:23).

> Godet: Paul speaks of a collective movement which shall take hold of the nation of Israel in general and bring them to Him in faith. Individual resistance still remains possible.

   B.   The persons: "all Israel"
   1. not such Jews as believe, viz. the remnant All Israel is used here in contrast to the remnant.
   2. not spiritual Israel, which includes both Jews and Gentiles. There is a difference in the context between Jews and Gentiles.
   *3. Israel as a whole, as a nation. This refers to the mass of Israelites, although this does not necessarily include every individual Israelite alive at the time.

   C.   The time: "after the fullness of the Gentiles is come in" Compare Luke 21:24. This will be at the time when the Deliverer, Jesus, comes out of Zion or heaven. See Acts 1:6,7.

   D.   The kind: a spiritual salvation not a physical, national one The Israelis are already going back to Palestine but in unbelief for the most part.

   E.   The result: the taking away of Israel's sins, but this is an individual matter, not a national collective one

   F.   The conclusion: 11:30-32. All are sinners and God chooses to show his goodness to all.
   1. The Gentiles were disobedient once and yet God showed mercy to them.
   2. The Jews were disobedient also.
   3. The plan of God was to make disobedience an opportunity of His showing mercy.

Consequently, all can equally become recipients of divine mercy.

V.   The Riches of God identified in a benediction 11:33-36
   A.   God's wisdom
   B.   His knowledge
   C.   His unsearchable judgments
   D.   His ways
   E.   His inscrutable mind
   F.   His lack of need for a counselor
   G.   The conclusion: He is the source, channel, and the goal of all things.

Appendix: Here is what Paul has shown in Romans 9-11:
   A.   The rejection of Israel is not contrary to divine justice or divine promises to Israel.
   B.   The rejection of Israel is her own fault and on her own head; however, there has been in every day a remnant who were believing.
   C.   Historically the rejection of Israel was the cause of preaching the Gospel to the Gentiles. See the book of Acts.
   D.   The restoration of Israel will be a time of even greater blessing to the world. (NOTE GOD IS NOT THROUGH WITH ISRAEL.)

Appendix: There is a tendency in theology to go from one extreme to another, here, from the Calvinistic emphasis on divine sovereignty to the Pelagian emphasis on man's free will. Once more Romans 9-11 brings the scholar back to the "middle of the road" position.

The Calvinistic emphasis is on sovereignty:	The Pauline emphasis in Romans 9-11 is on free-will and sovereignty	The Pelagian emphasis on free will
The total depravity of Mankind	Total depravity (with mankind's will still free to choose but not able to save itself)	The inherent goodness of mankind with no depravity
Unconditional election	Conditional election (based on man's faith known in advance by God)	Conditional election
Limited atonement with the elect in view	Unlimited atonement with all mankind in view	Unlimited atonement with all mankind in view
Irresistible grace	Resistible grace both before salvation and after	Resistible grace both before salvation and after
Perseverance of the Saints	Perseverance through 1. The help of the Holy Spirit	Emphasis on human effort
Salvation by faith alone	2. The cooperation of the human Salvation by good will through continuing faith alone	Salvation by good works

"Two great truths pervade the whole Bible: namely that if we are saved, it is entirely of God's grace, and if we are lost, it will be entirely from ourselves." William Jay

"Although much has taken place in theology in the intervening centuries, there are many Christians today whose religious thinking has been molded by the Armenian tradition. They would do well to examine the careful work done by the founder of that tradition, and they will find there firm support for resisting an easy- going, culture-Protestantism which confuses man's work with God's. And those who call themselves Calvinists will discover that it is too simple to dismiss Arminius as a Pelagian who did not see clearly the issue of sola gratia. They may find themselves closer to him than they had supposed." Carl Bangs,"Arminius: An Anniversary Report," Christianity Today. V (October 10, 1960), p. 19.

Review projects covering Romans 6-11

1. Sum up in your own words the teaching of Paul regarding
    A. the relationship of the believer to a life of sin, using the analogy of baptism 6:1-11
    B. the relationship of the believer to individual acts of sin, using the analogy of the bond-servant 6:15-23
    C. the relationship of the believer to law, using the bond of marriage 7:1-6
2. In Romans 6:11,13 what is the significance in the Christian's experience of the Greek present tense of the verb "to reckon"? When will such reckoning be necessary? What is the significance of the Greek aorist tense of the verb to present" the second time it is used? How do these three verses teach that it is necessary for the Christian to have a sanctifying experience with God following his conversion? What is the relationship of "reckoning" to this experience of "presenting"?
3. How does Paul characterize the law in Romans 7? Why does he feel it is necessary to defend its character? How can he claim it is holy when it is involved with the sin problem? What is wrong with the law? Explain your answer.
4. What is the conflict described by Paul in Romans 7:7-25? What things did Paul discover in this conflict which waged within himself? How do you know that this must have been the conflict of a regenerate man? Wherein does the victory lie? How does this section relate to Romans 8:1-11, which follows?
5. What are the three possible states in which we find individuals today? Cite a biblical example of an individual or specific group of individuals whom you would classify in each. What is the end of a life lived on each of the three levels? How do you know this? What Scriptures do you have to support your statements?
6. Why is the emphasis on God's foreknowledge in 8:29 so important for the series of divine acts which follow it? What happens when you put God's foreordination first? List the verbs in 8:29, 30 and describe in one sentence to what specific divine activity each points.
7. How would you answer someone who quoted the end of Romans 8 in support of the view that once you accepted Christ, you could then sin without fear of punishment since nothing can separate you from God, not even sinning?
8. List the various works of the Spirit in Romans 8 as they are related especially to the Spirit-filled believer.
9. How does Paul answer the following questions in Romans 9?
    A. Does not God's rejection of Israel, since she has refused to come by faith for justification, mean that God's promises to Abraham, Isaac, and Jacob have failed? Give Paul's reason for the answer.
    B. Is there not unrighteousness with God because He has no regard for the principle of lineage and favors the principle of faith? Give Paul's reason for the answer.
    C. Why does God find fault with us since no one is resisting God's will nor is able to do so?

10. What reasons does Paul give in Romans 10 regarding why the Jews rejected the righteousness based on faith? What things were true of the righteousness which the Jews rejected? How is 9:30-10:21 a good balance for 9:1-29? Why must this balance be kept in the Christian's thinking, even though he may not fully understand it?

11. Discuss the olive-tree analogy in Romans 11 by listing the parts of the analogy and that to which each refers. List the hints in this chapter that Israel as a whole will some day be saved. How will this come to pass?

12. List the points (to be gleaned from your class notes on Romans 6-11) which you could give to a person who claimed that one experience with God in salvation was sufficient and that it did not matter how you lived from that time on. You were saved, and absolutely nothing could change this (List 9 or 10 points).

CHAPTER NINE

The Conversation (or the Conduct) of the Justified Person in Various Life Relationships
Romans 12:1-15:5

Introductory Pleas ~ Romans 12:1-2

> *¹I am beseeching you [pl], therefore, brothers, in view of the mercies of God, to present your [pl] bodies [as] a sacrifice, [which is] living, holy, well-pleasing to God, your [pl] reasonable service; ²and stop conforming yourselves to this age but continue permitting yourselves to be transformed by the renewing of [your] mind, in order that you [pl] may continue discovering what the will of God is, that [will] which is good and well-pleasing and perfect.*

Introduction
Romans 12:1,2 is the beginning of the practical section of Romans, the usual way in which Paul concludes his other Pauline epistles.
A. How far back does the "therefore" of Romans 12:1 point?
    It points back to the doctrinal discussion of justification and sanctification. Paul believed strongly that since one has been justified by faith and put into a new relationship with God, he ought to live like it in the various relationships of daily life. Romans 12:1-15;5 is the practical development of the theoretical teaching of Romans 6-8.
    The correlation between Romans 6:11-14 and Romans 12:1,2 is more than coincidental. The verb "present" is the same Greek verb in 6:13 and 12:1. In chapter 6 we are commanded, with an aorist imperative, to present our members to God as weapons for His use against Satan. In 12:1, we are exhorted, with an aorist infinitive, to present our bodies to God as living sacrifices. In 6:11, we are commanded with a present imperative to continue on reckoning ourselves to be dead indeed to sin and to be living to God. In 12:2 we are commanded to stop conforming ourselves (i.e. our living) to this present age but to continue permitting ourselves to be transformed by the renewing of our minds . . . The Spirit-controlled life begins as a crisis, both theoretically and practically, and must then continue on as a process. In other words, the theory of Romans 6:11-14 is repeated in Romans 12:1,2, before Paul applies it in various personal relationships, arbitrarily chosen, in Romans 12:3-15;5.
B. On what basis does Paul appeal to the Roman Christians?
    His appeal is on the basis of the mercies of God extended to both Jews and Gentiles. Note the emphasis on the mercies of God in Romans 11:31,32 and Romans 12:1. Although the Greek

words for "mercies" are different, they carry the same idea. In fact, they are used synonymously in Romans 9:15. See Vine's Dictionary of New Testament Words for a complete treatment.

C. Why does Paul exhort them to present their bodies when they already belong to Him? See I Corinthians 6:19, 20 where the declaration is made. Here the corresponding demand is made: "Now present once and for all your body to God." Give Him complete control. Too many Christians' bodies don't indicate that they belong to God. (Note: A great illustration of someone who made the total presentation of her body to God for His use was Mary, the mother of Jesus. See Luke 2:38.)

D. What kind of a sacrifice of the Christians' bodies is this to be according to Paul here?
   1. It is to be an absolute sacrifice.
      The aorist tense used indicates that it is to be a crisis experience without any reservations at all. He may be Savior of the life, but he is not Lord at all unless He is Lord of all.
   2. It is to be a definite sacrifice.
      For most Christians, it will take place at a specific time and place. The use of the aorist tense points to that.
   3. It is to be a complete sacrifice.
      It will involve the putting of all of the members of your body at God's disposal. The verb means to "stand alongside" and implies one is waiting for orders from his Master.
   4. It is to be an immediate sacrifice.
      The aorist imperative expresses urgency. The sooner the Lord gets our sacrifice the more He will be able to do with us. One does not buy a gift for a friend, get all the good out of it he can, and then give it as a present to his friend.
   5. It is a costly sacrifice.
      And the Lord knows this. Any true sacrifice we make will cost us something; and this one will cost the ultimate: "We give up ourselves totally to the Lord for His use completely.
   6. It is a living sacrifice.
      a. It is different from the Old Testament ones, which were dead and only useful for a brief time.
      b. It can be of real use to God.
      c. It can be of daily and continual use to God.
      d. It carries the implication of its being a lasting and perpetual sacrifice.
   7. It is a holy sacrifice. The Christian's body is a sanctuary in which the Holy Spirit dwells. I Corinthians 6:19, 20
   8. It is a well-pleasing sacrifice. It is something that God desires us to give Him freely for His use.
   9. It is a rational and spiritual sacrifice.
      a. It is rational, not irrational as the Old Testament sacrifices were.

   b. It is spiritual, not material, as the animals of the Old Testament era were.

  10. It is a voluntary sacrifice. It is commanded of us, not compelled or coerced from us. It is not wrenched from us against our wills.

  11. It is a personal sacrifice.
   This is something which each individual must do for himself or herself. No one can do this for someone else.

 E. What kind of an effort after holiness is theirs to be following their presentation (aorist).

  1. It is to be a continuous effort, as indicated by the present tense of the imperative. It is like the "reckonings" of Romans 6:11.

   a. Command #1: Stop conforming yourselves to this age. We are not to let this age "squeeze" us into its mold. If we obey this command, it will affect every area of our lives, our dress, our driving, our speech, our spending, our Sunday observance, our dating, our marriage, our job, our entertainment, our thought life, etc.

   b. Command #2: Continue on permitting yourselves to be transformed by the renewing of your mind. Continue on letting the Lord make your mind new again. This will involve an inward as well as an outward change. The word used here is the same Greek word that is used in Matthew 17:2 of Jesus' transfiguration on the mount.

  2. It is to be a voluntary effort.
   Again, this is commanded, not compelled or coerced. There is something we must do about this, if we really want to do it. The beginning of this obedience is a regular, thorough study of the Bible and then a continuous dedication of ourselves to do all that we find therein. See Psalm 119:11.

  3. It will be a purposeful effort.
   The purpose for obeying here is in order that we may continue (all our lives) discovering what the will of God is for us, that will which is good, acceptable, and perfect. Too many Christians cannot discern the will of God for their lives because they have not met the demands given here for knowing it.
   "This passage involves two facts: first, that God has a plan for our lives, which He is very willing and desirous we should discover; and, second, that only those who surrender themselves to Him, rejecting conformity to this age, can discover that will." William R. Newell, Romans Verse bv Verse. Chicago: used by permission of Moody Press, Moody Bible Institute of Chicago, 1938. p. 456.

"If we learn to obey God where His will is obvious, we'll develop the ability to sense His will where the specific Word is not so obvious. The more we live in joyful obedience to the best Lord, the more we'll discern His likes and dislikes." Robert Oerter, Undebatable Guidance HIS May, 1962.

F. Appendix: We ourselves are members of the body of Christ, the Head. Only as you present your body for His use as a member of His body can He do anything in the world. A healthy body is one in which all of the bodily members are in complete subjection to the directions of the head.

Conclusion

Romans 12:1,2 calls for a determined, crisis presentation of all of our bodily members as a living sacrifice to God for His use, this followed by a continuous refusal to conform ourselves to this age and by a continuous allowing of the Lord to transform our minds.

Then Romans 12:3-15:5 is a description of how such a totally presented Christian will live in various relationships, probably chosen arbitrarily by the apostle. Other relationships not dealt with here can be found in the practical sections of his other epistles. For example, Paul deals with the proper Christian marriage relationship in Ephesians 5:22-33. He deals with proper home relations in Ephesians 6:1-4. For how a Christian should deal with a brother who has fallen, see Galatians 6:1.

The relations which Paul will deal with in Romans 12:3-15:5 are as follows:

A. A Christian and his PARTNERS within the church body   12:3-8
B. A Christian and his PURSUIT of his work for Christ   12:9-13
C. A Christian and PEOPLE in general   12:14-16
D. A Christian and PERSECUTORS in particular   12:17-21
E. A Christian and the POWERS that be, the government   13:1-7
F. A Christian and the PRESCRIPTIONS of God, His laws   13:8-10
G. A Christian and the PRESENT PERIOD, this age   13:11-14
H. A Christian and his PARTNERS in the church, whether they be weaker or stronger   13:11-14

Appendix: From Romans 12:1 and 2 it is possible to know the following about God's will for each Christian:

A. The will of God is something that will be taken seriously by serious Christians.
B. It involves a total presentation of his body to God as a sacrifice for His exclusive use.
C. It always involves a refusal on his part to let this age squeeze him into its mold or pattern of living.
D. It will mean that he will live his life differently than the child of this present age.
E. It will involve not only the above crisis but a continual process of transformation within his life by the renewing of his mind.

F. It means that he will come to think differently about things than the child of this age thinks and to act differently than he acts.
G. It will affect all of his living and his endeavors.
H. It is discoverable continuously throughout life by the right kind of Christian.
I. It is something that the Christian continues discovering since it is not made known to him all at once or all of a sudden.
J. It is good, well-pleasing and perfect, since it is God's plan for the Christian.
K. It is something that God is very willing for every Christian to discover.
L. It will not be forced by God upon any Christian but should be freely accepted by every Christian as the best and only way to have a holy AND A HAPPY life.

I. **The Walk of the totally presented Christian relative to those in the Church: His PARTNERS in Christ 12:3-8**

> *3For I am saying, by means of the grace which has been given to me, to everyone who is among you [pl] not to be thinking more highly [of himself] than what he ought to be thinking; but to continue thinking soberly, as to each one God has assigned a measure of faith. 4For just as in one body, we customarily have many members but all the members are not having the same function, 5so we, the many, are one body in Christ and everyone members one of another. 6And because [we are] having free gifts [which are] different according to the grace which has been given to us--whether prophecy, [let us prophesy] according to the proportion of [our] faith; 7or ministry, [let us give ourselves] to [our] ministry; or the one teaching, to his teaching; 8or the one exhorting, to his exhortation; [as for] that one who is sharing with [someone], [let him do it] with sincerity; [as for] that one who is superintending, [let him do it] with diligence; [as for] that one who is showing mercy, [let him do it] with gladness.*

What is to characterize our walk relative to our partners in Christ?
A. Modesty and humility in service v. 3
    This is not, however, a running down of one's abilities. This means a humble assessment of one's gifts or abilities. It is as much a sin to remain in the background when God wants you in the foreground leading, as it is to be in the foreground leading when God wants you to be a follower.
B. Soberness in judgment regarding one's abilities
    One needs to accept oneself as God has made him and this includes one's sex as well as one's gifts.
C. Unity in mind and purpose for the benefit of the whole church body
    The Body of Christ, the Church, has many members with differing abilities. There must be a unity with diversity for the good of the whole. The various gifts Paul lists are as follows:
    1. The gift of prophecy or forth telling, involving the communication of truth from God

136

2. The gift of ministering or practical service, involving ministering to the material needs of other people.
3. The gift of teaching or explaining the truth for the minds of others
4. The gift of being able to exhort and console others who need encouragement
5. The gift of being able to give with singleness of heart and motive out of one's private means (There is a gift in knowing how to give as well as to receive.)
6. The gift of administration or superintending the work of others
7. The gift of being able to show mercy without making the receiver feel that it is charity
8. Appendix: There are undoubtedly many other gifts not listed here or in the other biblical lists, two lists in I Corinthians 12 and one list in Ephesians 4. No one of the four lists has all of the gifts in the others. There are such gifts as musical gifts and the gifts of cooking, working with computers, cars, etc. that all can be used in the service of the church and of the Lord, although not mentioned in the Bible.
D. Single-mindedness in giving without mixed motives v. 8
E. Diligence in administration v. 8
F. Cheerfulness in showing mercy v. 8
G. Appendix: What is the "faith" of verse 3 ?
    1. Not confidence or trust in God
    2. Not the truth of the Gospel, what is believed
    3. But a gift, since no gift is exercised apart from faith

II. The Walk of the totally presented Christian relative to his work for Christ: His PURSUIT of his work for Christ 12:9-13

⁹[Let] love be without hypocrisy. Continue abhorring that which is evil; continue cleaving to that which is good. ¹⁰With brotherly love, [be] loving tenderly; with reference to honor, continue regarding one another more highly [than oneself]; ¹¹in diligence, not being lazy; in spirit being zealous; continuing to serve the Lord; ¹²in hope continuing to rejoice; in tribulation continuing to endure, in prayer continuing to persevere; ¹³in the needs of the saints continuing to become a partner; [and] hospitality continuing to pursue.

What things are to characterize his walk relative to his pursuit of Christ's work?
A. Sincerity in love v. 9
   He is not a play actor or a hypocrite.
B. Abhorrence of evil v. 9
   What many people hate is not evil itself but the consequences of it.
C. Cleave to that which is good v. 9
   The idea here is being glued to the good in people.
D. Love for the brothers, i.e., fellow-Christians v. 10

The word used here is the word for the natural affection which ought to exist between close family members. The church is a family and the loving relationship of the family ought to exist among the members.

E. Humility with reference to one another v. 10

F. Diligence in the Lord's service v. 11
Such a person will throw everything he has into his work for Christ. He will not just seek to get by with as little effort as possible.

G. Fervency in spirit v. 11
He will be enthusiastic and desperately in earnest about his work for Christ. Some people are never enthused about anything.

H. Joyfulness in hope v. 12

I. Endurance in tribulation v. 12
This refers to a triumphant fortitude that will remain standing firm under any trial.

J. Perseverance in prayer v. 12

K. Sympathy with the saints v. 13
The Greek word used carries the meaning of communicating to the needs of the saints. Consequently it is not just an emotion but also an action. It involves doing something, not just feeling it.

L. Hospitality, especially toward the saints, v. 13
The Christians needed this in their traveling since the inns of the day were notoriously crowded, filthy, and even immoral places.

III. **The Walk of the totally presented Christian Relative to Others in General: PEOPLE in general** 12:14-16

14Continue speaking well of those who are persecuting; continue speaking well and stop cursing. 15Continue rejoicing with ones who are rejoicing; continue weeping with ones who are weeping. 16The same thing with reference to one another continue thinking, not continuing to think high things but continually allowing yourselves to be occupied with lowly things. Stop becoming wise among yourselves, [i.e., in your own estimation].

What things are to characterize our walk relative to people in general?

A. Forgiveness of persecutors v. 14
Many people are saved today because they saw how a Christian could forgive. Augustine said that the church owes Paul to the prayer of Stephen.

B. Sympathy and sharing in the experience of others
Note that it is relatively easy to empathize with people going through defeats, griefs, and hardships. It can be very hard to rejoice sincerely with them in their victories. We are too self-centered by nature and therefore we find it relatively easy to condole but rather difficult to congratulate.

C. Harmony and unity with other people

138

D. Humility which will give itself wholeheartedly to the humblest and demeaning of tasks

IV. The Walk of the totally presented Christian relative to his enemies: His PERSECUTORS in particular 12:17-21

17Stop paying back to anyone evil for evil; continue taking thought for things that are good in the sight of all mankind; 18if it is possible, as far as you [are concerned], with all mankind continue living at peace; 19stop avenging yourselves, beloved, but make room for the wrath [of God], for it stands written,

To me vengeance belongs, I myself will pay back, the Lord is saying.

20But if [3rd] your [s] enemy is hungering, continue feeding him; if [3rd] he is thirsting, continue giving him [something] to drink; for by doing this coals of fire [s] you will heap upon his head. 21Stop being overcome by evil [done to you], but continually overcome by goodness that evil.

Please note that Paul is teaching here about private, personal ethics, not governmental or official.

What things are to characterize our walk relative to our persecutors?

A. Forgiveness (and forgetfulness)
He will get rid of his enemies by making them his friends. He will do away with enemies by doing away with enmity. And the forgetting of the wrongs done does not mean he can or will wipe them from his memory, only that he will never bring them up against them again.

B. Concern for the opinions of other people
He will seek to be involved in Christian action which can be approved by all, Christians or not. He knows that he will never win them as a pal unless they like him as a person.

C. Peaceableness with everyone, as much as is possible
He has a love for peace and a strong desire to make peace. He may be involved in conflict but will try not to be the cause of it. This peaceable attitude does not mean, however, that he will compromise with evil and error. It is never peace at any price.

D. Love: Why is this love commanded, a love which can result in heaping coals of fire upon the heads of our enemies?
1. Suggestion #1: "The coals of fire" are some outstanding act of kindness. Loads in the olden days were often carried on the heads of people. The idea some have seen here is that the pan for carrying coals would be carried on the head; and instead of giving one or two coals, which might go out on the way home, the benefactor would "heap coals of fire" into the pan carried on the head of the needy individual. This view would correspond with Jesus' words of giving your tunic as well as your outer cloak when you are sued for the one or going the second mile when forced by someone to go only one. See Matthew 5:40,41.

2. Suggestion #2: "The coals of fire" are a physical pain of some kind, "the coals of red hot love." One woman was abused by her husband and told by her pastor to be patient with her spouse, set him a good example, and in that way "heap coals of fire on his head." She replied, "That won't do any good. I've already poured boiling water on him, and it doesn't even take the dandruff out of his hair."

3. Suggestion #3: "The coals of fire" are divine punishment of some kind, as if we are thinking, "I will get out of the way and let divine retribution take its course." The consolation is that one's enemies will be punished and that more severely by God than we, as human beings, could ever punish them. This may happen but this should never be one's motive for his good actions.

4. Suggestion #4: "The coals of fire" are the mental pain and torture which we intend and hope our good actions will bring upon our enemies. Again, this may be a by-product of our good deeds but certainly should not be the intent or driving force behind them. We should not want to hurt our enemies but help them.

5. Suggestion #5: The correct view is this one. The coals of fire heaped upon the head of the supposed enemies are the pain of shame that our good actions may cause; however, the pain is not the purpose of our good actions but may be the result of them; and there is a difference. Jesus never performed miracles in order that or for the purpose that people would marvel. He did them to help people so that, as a result, people were marveling. The result could not be helped. I am sure He would rather they had believed on Him instead of being struck with wonder and amazement. On views 3 and 4 above we are doing the punishing; on view 5, if any punishing with pain is to be carried out, God will have to do it, not we. We will show our enemies sincere love in action with the only motive being to win them as friends.

E. Forbearance to give place for God's wrath to operate
There is no desire on the Christian's part for evil to befall his enemies but he will not usurp God's prerogative of punishment, if there is to be any meted out.

F. Trust in God that any punishment to come will be from Him and will be fair and just

G. Action, since actions always speak louder than words
Biblical love is more a volitional matter than an emotional. We are commanded to love our enemies and feelings cannot be commanded. Actions alone can. Note how Paul here couples love with action. If one's enemy is hungry, continue feeding him. If he is thirsty, continue giving him a drink. Note that the command is not to like the enemy but to do something for him. And one can do something whether he likes to do it or not.

140

H. Victory
    Paul closes the chapter by commanding, "Stop being overcome
    by evil (done to you) but overcome that evil with goodness, i.e..
    good actions. When we allow feelings of revenge to overcome
    us, we let the evil done to us gain the victory over us.

The Reader's Digest published an article written by J. P. McEvoy entitled
"Love Your Enemies - It'll Drive 'Em Crazy." See The Reader's Digest.
December, 1957, pp. 52-54. The article closes with a beautiful illustration
of how love for enemies can "destroy" them by making them friends.
The author of the article, a Cuban immigrant came to the United States,
bringing with him his two little girls. Pat and Peggy. They had a tough
time with English and hence also with their colleagues in the first and
second grades in the public school to which they were assigned. One
stocky little girl, daughter of the village barber, little "Lolla," tormented
them worst of all. She was older and the ringleader "Terror of the Tiny
Tots." But let the author of the article tell the story.

> Pat and Peggy came home crying almost every day, so I decided
> to cheer them up. "Let's have a party," I said. Pat and Peggy's
> tears dried magically. Right away they got creative: "Ice cream!
> Cake, and big red balloons!" "And friends?" I said. The tears
> started again. "We haven't got any friends," Pat blubbered.

> Peggy wailed. "Nothing but enemies." Then I had one of my
> rare inspirations. "Let's have an enemy party. Let's invite all
> your enemies — especially the worst ones — and we'll fill'em
> up with ice cream and cake and give'em big red balloons to
> take home."

> Little Pat and Peggy exchanged knowing looks, and one of
> them said with an eloquent Spanish gesture, "Que pasa al
> viejo?" (What goes with the Old One?)

> Now the angels who have the special job of watching over
> children's parties must have been pleased to see that the
> "Enemy Party" was a mad, merry success, and the best time
> was had by the biggest enemy, little "Lolla," who rolled on the
> floor and shrieked with delight.

> Pat and Peggy never came crying home from school anymore.
> Their biggest enemy had turned into their staunchest
> champion. Nobody dared lift a finger to them...little "Lolla"
> would have broken it off, pronto. One day "Lolla's father
> dropped by to see me. "I come to thank you for asking my little
> girl to the party," he said. Then he added, mystified, "Why did
> you do it?" "Why not?" I told him. "She's a solid little citizen
> and she likes ice cream, cake and big red balloons, just like any
> other little girl. Yes?" "Oh, yes," he said, "but do you know
> something? Nobody ever asked her to a party before. Why?"

A good question. Are the "Lollas" left out because they are enemies, or do they become enemies because they are left out? There are several schools of thought working on this, but the Great Teacher settled it long ago. "Love your enemies, pray for them that persecute you, do good to those that hate you...."

V. The walk of the totally presented Christian relative to his government: The POWERS that be Romans 13:1-7

¹Let every soul to the authorities who are over him continue subjecting himself; for there is no authority except by God and those which by God stand appointed. ²So then he who continues resisting the authority, against the ordinance of God he has set himself; and those who have set themselves against [this] will receive for themselves [penal] judgment. ³For those who are ruling are not a cause for fear to the good work but to the evil. You [s] do not want to continue fearing the authority, do you [s]? [Then] goodness continue practicing, and you [s] will have praise from it [i.e., the authority]; ⁴for a minister of God it is for you [s] for good. But if [3rd] you continue doing that which is evil, keep on fearing; for it is not without just cause wearing the sword. For a minister of God it is, a punisher for [the execution of] wrath on the one who is practicing evil. 5Therefore, it is necessary to continue subjecting one's self, not only because of [a fear of] wrath but also because of conscience. ⁶For because of this also tribute continue paying; for ministers of God they are who are busily engaging [themselves] with this very thing. ⁷Pay back to all their dues: tribute to the one [entitled to receive] tribute, custom to whom custom, fear to whom fear, and honor to whom honor.

A.   Introductory Matters
   1.   Early in Nero's reign, when the epistle to the Romans was probably written, the Christians were well-treated by the Romans. The magistrates then were, for Paul, administrators who kept order and restrained evil and evildoers.
   2.   Later the situation changed and persecution of the church began, especially in A.D. 64, when the fire that burned down 10 of the 14 wards of the city of Rome was blamed on the Christians.
   3.   Later the teaching of Paul relative to the government did not change. Some have suggested that had Paul been writing the epistle later he would have changed his teaching; however, from one of his other epistles and one of Peter's, we know that the principle of obedience to government was never abrogated. The character of the government or of the government leaders made no difference. Obedience was the order of the day, as long as what was being required did not involve the breaking

142

of commandments from God. For the church, obedience to man must never take the place of obedience to God. We must never pay to Caesar what we owe Christ. Note the teaching relative to the government and its officials presented in the following epistles, written later in Paul's and Peter's lives, after government persecution of the church had begun.

    a.   Titus 3:1: Continue reminding them to continue subjecting themselves to rulers (and) to authorities, to continue being obedient, to continue being ready for every good work. (This was written later after Paul's first imprisonment in Rome recorded in Acts 28.)

    b.   I Peter 2:13-17: Be subject to every human ordinance because of the Lord, whether to the king, as supreme, or to governors as being sent by him ... For so it is the will of God, that by well-doing, you should continue putting to silence the ignorance of foolish men... Honor all. Continue loving the brotherhood. Continue reverencing God. Continue honoring the king. (This was written by Peter near the close of his life.)

B.   The Purpose of Civil government according to Paul here in Romans 13:1-7

    1.   The promoting of the well-being of its citizenry

    2.   The praising of the good work and the doing of good work

    3.   The punishing of the evildoer

    This is not in contradiction to Romans 12:19, which claims that vengeance belongs to God and He will repay evil. Actually, according to Romans 13:1-7, the government is the extended arm of the Lord meting out judgment on the doers of wickedness during this age. See also I Peter 2:14, where he writes that governors are sent by the king for the punishment of evildoers and the praise of those who do the right. In like manner, the avenger of blood in Old Testament times was the instrument used by God to punish with death the convicted murderer. See Num. 35:9-28; Deut. 19:1-13; and Josh. 20:1-9.

    a.   Verse 2 "judgment"

    In verse 2, the Greek word krima has been interpreted to mean three different things:

        1.) Damnation, meaning eternal hell, is too strong.

        2.) The judgment of God is against the context.

        3.) The probable meaning is the judgment of the magistrate or the civil official.

    b.   Verse 4 "sword"

    In verse 4, the Greek word machaira. translated "sword," is the following:

        1.) an emblem symbolizing capital punishment

        2.) not the sword worn as a sign of one's magisterial office, the xiphos

3.) an instrument whose sole purpose was punishment, not reformation
It was an instrument used to vindicate the law, not to reform the criminal or even to prevent more crime from taking place.

4.) Conclusion: See Eccl. 8:11 where the reason is given why capital punishment and punishments for other crimes are not deterrents to evildoing. The author of Ecclesiastes writes, "Because the sentence against an evil deed is not executed quickly, therefore the hearts of the sons of men among them are given fully to doing evil."

4. Appendix:
Many today, using the English translation for the sixth commandment, "You shall not kill," teach that capital punishment is a violation of that commandment and hence should be abolished today. What these need to be told is the following:

a. The Hebrew and Greek words used by the biblical writers referring to the sixth commandment are not the general words for "kill" but the more specific words for "murder in any degree;"

b. Furthermore, following Exodus 20 where the Ten Commandments are recorded, is Exodus 21 in which appear several crimes to which God specifically assigned the death penalty (21: 12,14,15,16,17, and 23); consequently He apparently did not consider such a penalty a violation of the sixth commandment.

c. In addition, the humaneness of the method of such death did not seem to concern God since two methods of capital punishment were burning (Lev. 20:9,14) and stoning (Lev. 20:2,21; 24:23; and Deut. 22:21, 24);

d. Also, the word "kill" cannot be understood to rule out absolutely all killing of every sort.' (If "you shall not kill" is to be taken absolutely, one cannot eat a piece of meat, cut flowers for a bouquet, eat a radish, or swat a mosquito or a fly.)

e. According to the Bible, what is forbidden by the sixth commandment is murder in any degree; and to such a crime, capital punishment was assigned long before the Mosaic law was given. See Gen. 9:3,4.

1.) The sixth commandment does not therefore ban the killing of animals for food or sacrifice.

2.) It does not prohibit the putting to death of criminals duly convicted and sentenced for capital crimes.

3.) It does not prohibit the defensive killing of aggressors in time of war.
(Remember that God Himself commanded Israel to go to war and to kill on those occasions.)

           4.) It does not ban the killing of housebreakers when they are caught breaking into one's home and threatening one's family. (In other words, self-defense is permissible under certain circumstances; and such may result in the taking of a life. See Exodus 22:2,3.)

           5.) Obviously, the sixth commandment does not refer to accidental manslaughter, which is unintentional and, we assume, unavoidable.

C. The Biblical Principles Relative to Civil Government

    1. Civil government and all civil power have divine sanction. Civil authority is ordained of God. Anarchy is not. Two times in Rom. 13:1-7 the civil authority is called the servant of God and once the minister of God.

    2. To resist such power is to resist and sin against God, generally speaking.
This is an obvious deduction from point #1 above.

    3. The Christian should render unto Caesar the things that are Caesar's, and unto God the things that are God's. See Matthew 22:21 and Jesus' words recorded there. God has obligations which need to be paid also; and we dare not pay to Caesar (the government) what we owe only to God.

    4. The Christian should obey God rather than man, when it is a question of one or the other. See Acts 4:18,19 and 5:29. Note the following biblical illustrations when people chose to obey God rather than men who were clearly in the wrong.

       a. In Exodus 1, the Hebrew midwives in Egypt refused to murder the boy babies as commanded by Pharaoh.

       b. In Exodus 2, Moses' parents refused to murder Moses in obedience to Pharaoh.

       c. In I Samuel 22, Saul's guards refused to murder a city of priests at the command of their king, Saul.

       d. In Daniel 3, the three Hebrew young men refused to bow down in idolatry to the image at the command of Nebuchadnezzar, their king.

       e. In Daniel 6, Daniel refused to obey the king's command not to pray to anyone but the king for a month.

       f. In Matthew 2, the Magi refused to go back to Herod, as he had commanded, to report to him the whereabouts of the Christ-child.

       g. In Acts 4:15-20 and 5:29, the apostles refused to obey the Jewish rulers who commanded them not to speak in the name of Jesus Christ any more.

       h. Appendix: HOWEVER, NOTE that in every case where disobedience took place, it was only and always when those disobeying were sure that the government was clearly in the wrong.

D. The Payment of the Christian to Civil Government

The Christian citizen's obligations to his government as seen here are:

1. Subjecting himself to his government officials
   Obedience to the laws of his government officials is a requirement. Note also that character of the government in power is not a consideration; the kinds of demands are. Paul does not exhort, "Obey good leaders or good government." A generally bad government may make good and legitimate demands and a generally good government can enact bad ones. The following are types of laws to which the Christian citizen must give attention: traffic laws, pedestrian laws, fire-arm laws, family support laws, tax laws, public demonstration laws, and public or military service laws.

2. Paying financial support
   Tribute is a tax paid directly to the state, like our income taxes. Custom is a tax which is paid indirectly to the state, such as our current sales tax.

3. Offering of honor and respect to our government officials
   Note Paul's rebuking of the high priest of his people in Acts 23:3-5 and his immediate apology when he realized what he had done. Compare Exodus 22:28.

4. Fear of disobeying
   Paul mentions here the fear of the external pains of governmental punishment and also the internal pains of a conscience worked on by the Holy Spirit through the Scriptures.

5. Appendix: Along with these obligations could be added other responsibilities of good citizens, such as intelligent voting for officers (where such is a practice), office-holding if one is able to do so and is desired by the citizenry, prayer for those in office, and a patriotic support of one's government when one can morally and conscientiously do this.

E. A Predicament Relative to the Christian and Civil Government
   1. A problem any Christian faces when he accepts Christ is that he leaves the ethic of this present age and he becomes a citizen of the age to come, with its new set of principles by which to live.
      a. Should he ever resist an evil-doer?
      b. Does the Bible teach that he should always demonstrate a pacifistic attitude toward evil-doers?
      c. Must he become a conscientious objector to all war because he is now a Christian and a participant in the life of the age to come?
   2. An answer from the Bible
      a. A use of force against evildoers is taught as legitimate in the Bible.

146

1.) Force is to be exercised against evildoers. Along with many other Scriptures, see Romans 13:1-7, where the magistrate is given the authority to wield the sword in resistance to evil, even to the extreme of meting out capital punishment where warranted.

2.) Furthermore, the use of force can be an indication of love for the evildoer rather than a violation of it. A father in a home may use force of two different kinds.

    a.) He may try the moral force of persuasion to shame his child into good behavior. For example, he may say, "A good little girl would not do a thing like that."

    b.) However, if that doesn't work, than he may have to use more forceful persuasion of a spanking or other disciplinary action. This is not because he does not love his child but because he does and wants to help him or her avoid other more severe problems in the future.

b. The problem of international conflict

  1.) Family trouble should be biblically handled by the father, the responsible party before God for the home (Eph. 5:22-33).

  2.) State or national trouble should be settled by the civil authorities in charge (Romans 13:1-7).

  3.) International trouble should ideally be handled by some kind of an international police force since, by inference, that force should be to the international community what the armed forces are to its nation or the police force is to its city.

c. The problem relative to Christ's words "We are not to resist an evil person," is very clear (Matthew 5:39a). Can a Christian at any time serve as head of a home, a state or national official, or a soldier in an armed force since all at some time or other will have "to result in resisting an evil person?"

  1.) The answer lies in the difference between personal conduct and official conduct. What a person may do officially he may not be allowed to do personally; and it is up to each individual to determine how he will act on any given occasion. See the Sermon on the Mount (Matt. 5-7) and Rom. 12:17-21 for examples of personal ethics. See Romans 13:1-7 for an example of official ethics being taught.

  2.) Example #1: A pastor and his church board may have to excommunicate a member.

Personally, they love him; but officially they have to seem to treat him rather roughly. "Love roofs over the faults of others (I Cor. 13:7) but officially people who personally love may have to hold a church member's faults up to view and judge them.

    3.) Example #2: A faculty member personally loves his students; unfortunately, officially he may have to fail one of them. Too often what has been done officially is taken personally by the one failed.

    4.) Example #3: A Christian police officer or soldier may have to shoot an evildoer officially, although, he loves the offender personally. There is a difference between the two kinds of ethics.

    5.) Example #4: God himself personally loves all mankind, even his enemies, but in the end time He will have to punish officially with hell all who have refused salvation through His Son.

    6.) Appendix: And the final decision under which ethics to operate must be left for the individual Christian to make on specific occasions.

  3. An exhortation relative to the above matters: Many pacifists would not agree with the difference between personal and official ethics. They place a strong emphasis on loving the world to Christ. Any resistance of an evildoer, for them, is a sign of a lack of love. We must love those who disagree with the above distinction between personal and official practice. Many strict pacifists are better Christians than many who are not.

F. A Restatement of the Biblical Principle
  1. Obey your government (Rom. 13:1-7), unless it involves you in compromise (other Scriptures).
  2. In cases of compromise, obey God, rather than man, whatever it may cost you.
  In individual situations, depend upon God to lead you regarding how to react, whether personally or officially.

As Daniel Webster once said, "Whatever makes persons good Christians makes them good citizens."

VI. **His Walk relative to the law of God: the PRESCRIPTIONS of God**
Rom. 13:8-10

[8]Do not continue owing anyone anything except to continue loving one another; for the one who is loving the other has fulfilled the law. [9]For [as for] this, you [s] shall not commit adultery, you [s] shall not commit murder, you [s] shall not steal, you [s] shall not covet, and if there is any other commandment, in this saying it is customarily summed up, in this, you [s] shall love your [s] neighbor as yourself. [10]Love does not work evil for its neighbor; therefore, love is the fulfillment of the law.

148

What things are to characterize our walk relative to God's prescriptions?
A.   Romans 13:8-10 Love for others:
   1.   This love for others is the only debt which the Christian
        can allow to remain since he can never fully pay it off.
        a.   An explanation is needed here in the light of several
             translations of Rom. 13:8, which imply that all owing
             of money is a violation of God's Word. For example,
             "Owe no one anything but to love." The Greek, with
             its use of the present tense, does not condemn the
             INITIATION of a debt but the CONTINUATION of it. A
             better handling of the original would read, "Stop owing
             anyone anything but to continue loving one another.
             "In other words, it is our obligation, should we enter
             into a debt with anyone, to be continually striving to
             pay it off, even though it may a very small sum each
             pay period.
        b.   A quotation which supports this translation and
             interpretation is as follows: "Let your only debt that
             is unpaid be that of love — a debt which you should
             always be attempting to discharge in full, but will never
             succeed in discharging." (Sanday and Headlam, The
             International Critical Commentary, p. 373.)
        c.   Another quotation supporting the explanation given
             above is as follows: "The force of the imperative is that
             we are to have no unpaid debts; that we are not to be
             in debt to any. In accord with the analogy of Scripture
             this cannot be taken to mean that we may never incur
             financial obligations, that we may not borrow from
             others in case of need" (cf. Exod. 22:25; Psalm 37:26;
             Matt. 5:42; Luke 6:35).
             But it does condemn the looseness with which we
             contract debts and particularly the indifference so often
             displayed in the discharging of them. "The wicked
             borroweth, and payeth not again" (Psalm 37:21).
             Few things bring greater reproach upon the Christian
             profession than the accumulation of debts and refusal
             to pay them." (John Murray, The New International
             Commentary: Romans. Vol. II, pp. 158,159.)
   2.   This love for others is the fulfillment of the law, thus
        achieving "the full measure" of that which the law requires.
        a.   The implication in this passage here is that if
             one cannot keep the second table of the ten
             commandments relating to human beings, then he
             certainly will not be able to keep the first table, which
             relates to obligations toward God. See I John 4:20
             where John says the same thing.
        b.   Paul's application here is to the commandments which
             prohibit adultery, murder, stealing, coveting and
             hurting one's neighbor. Love is practical.

c. An explanation
He is not speaking here about keeping the law as a legal basis for justification. We do not love in order to be saved. We love because we are saved and understand that the laws of God are given to us to keep us from getting hurt. The happy Christian is not a lawless person. Also note that 8 of the 10 commandments are negative.

3. Appendix: The relation of the law to the believer today must be discussed at this point.

a. Question #1: Why does Paul bring up the Ten Commandments, if the believer today is not under law but under grace? Being not under law today means being not under its obligations for our justification. However, being under grace means that grace has its duties also.
The background of the Hebrew word for Torah or law is the meaning of instruction. The law is God's teacher to tell us how to get the most out of life.

b. Question #2: In what sense was Paul speaking of law? He certainly did not mean the ceremonial law, which Christ fulfilled, nor did he refer to the civil law given to Israel as a nation. He meant the moral laws, summarized in the ten commandments, and even these he did not cite as a meritorious law code by which to earn justification before God. The laws of God were given to GUIDE life, not to GIVE it. As such, the laws of God serve a didactic function. They are like the fence around the child's playground. It is meant to keep the child from getting hurt and to help him get the most fun out of the "playground " of life.

c. Question #3: Are we under the Mosaic law today in any sense? Yes!

1.) Cause #1: We are human beings; and the moral laws were given to us as people. It would be just as foolish to ask whether we are under the law of gravity or the laws of electricity.

2.) Cause #2: The Mosaic moral law has been written into the fabric of God's created universe from the very beginning and we break it at our own peril.

3.) Cause #3: The Mosaic law did not make things right or wrong because it is apparent from Genesis 1 through Exodus 19 that the Mosaic law simply declared in clear form what was always right or wrong from the beginning of creation.

4.) Caused: All of the Ten Commandments but one are repeated in the New Testament and then they are even deepened. Jesus forbade, for example, even the hatred out of which murder comes and lust out of which adultery springs.

150

         5.) Cause #5: It is clear also that all of the ten commandments are summed up in the two greatest ones, wholehearted love for God and one's fellowman. See Matthew 22:34-40.

         6.) Cause #6: Finally, the commandments of the Lord, wherever they are found, fill love for the Lord full of content. Jesus said, "If you love me, you will keep my commandments" (John 14:15) See also 14:21,23,24.

  B. Romans 13:10 concern for one's neighbor and his welfare; and my neighbor is anyone in need.

VII. His Walk relative to this present age: The PRESENT (PERIOD)
Rom. 13:11-14

[11]And [as for] this also, know the season, that it is already the hour for you [pl] out of deep sleep to arise; for now is our salvation nearer than when we [first] believed. [12]The night has advanced [toward the dawn], and the day has come near. Let us, therefore, put away the works of the darkness, and let us put on the weapons of the light. [13]As in [the] day decently let us walk, not in revellings and drunkennesses, not in [unlawful] sexual intercourses and acts of shameless immorality, not in strife and envy; [14]but put on the Lord Jesus Christ and stop making provision for [fulfilling] the desires of the flesh.

What things are to characterize his walk relative to this Present Age?

  A. Wakefulness, spiritually speaking 13:11,12
There is to be no spiritual drowsiness. If a day with the Lord is as a thousand years and a thousand years as a day, then it has only been two days since the Lord was here as the Lord counts time. See II Peter 3:8. His coming back is soon so be alert.

  B. Decency/Propriety/Sobriety 13:13
There is to be no riotings or revelings.

    1. The revelries refer to things that disturb other people and are nuisances to others.

    2. The drunkennesses refer to things which were shameful in Paul's time, to say nothing of what they have become today.

  C. Purity/Chastity 13:13
There were to be no unlawful sexual intercourses, such as fornication, adultery, homosexuality, lesbianism, incest, or bestiality.

    1. Sexual intercourses refer to those kinds forbidden by God's Word.

    2. Shamelessnesses refer to immoral acts which are so filthy that most sinners commit them under the cover of darkness but not before the camera or on stage. This is the filthiest word in the Greek language.

  D. Peaceableness 13:13

There was to be no contentiousness or strife. Those guilty of such confrontation are ones who try to gain power and prestige illicitly.

E. Unselfishness/Contentment 13:13
There is to be no grudging envy or jealousy of others. This is the spirit of the person who is not satisfied with what he has and is always looking with envy on the blessings which someone else has and which have been denied to him.

F. Spirituality 13:14
Paul's last commands are that they are to put on once and for all the Lord Jesus Christ and to stop making provision for the flesh to gratify its desires. We are to put on the Lord like we would put on a long garment, so that He appears to our age when they see us. And then we are not to let our first thoughts be to gratify the desires of the Christless human nature. To put on Christ means that we are to be so intimately united to Christ that He, and not we, are seen by the contemporaries of our day.

VIII. The walk of the totally presented Christian relative to his fellow Christians: his PARTNERS in the Church. 14:1-15:4

¹But him who is being weak in the faith continue accepting [into your fellowship], [although] not for the purpose of quarrels over opinions. ²One continues having faith to eat all things, and he who is being weak continues eating [only] vegetables. ³Stop letting the one who is eating [the stronger] despise the one who is not eating [the weaker]; and stop letting the one who is not eating [the weaker] condemn the one who is eating [the stronger]; for God has accepted him. ⁴Who are you [s] yourself who are condemning another's servant? With reference to his own lord he stands or falls; and he will stand, for the Lord is having power to make him stand. ⁵For one regularly esteems one day better than another day, and another esteems every day; [but] let each one continue being fully convinced in his own mind. ⁶He who is observing the day [as sacred] is customarily observing it for the Lord, and he who is eating [the stronger] is customarily eating for the Lord, for he is giving thanks to God; and he who is not eating [the weaker] is not eating to the Lord, and [yet] he is giving thanks to God. ⁷For no one of us for himself is living, and no one for himself is dying; ⁸for if [3rd] we go on living, for the Lord we continue living; and if [3rd] we are dying, for the Lord we are dying. Therefore, whether we are living or whether we are dying, we are the Lord's. ⁹For because of this, Christ died and lived, in order that over both the dead and the living He might rule. ¹⁰But [as for] you [s] yourself, why are you [s] yourself [the weaker] condemning your [s] brother? Or, [as for] you [s] yourself [the stronger] also, why are your despising your [s] brother? For we all shall stand before the judgment seat of God. ¹¹For it stands written,

[As] I myself am living, says the Lord, to Me every knee will bow, And every tongue will give praise to God.

[12]So then each one of us concerning himself an account will give to God.

[13]Therefore, let us stop condemning one another any longer; but determine this thing rather, to stop giving an occasion for stumbling to the brother or a temptation to sin. [14]I know and stand persuaded in the Lord Jesus that nothing [amoral] is unclean by itself, except to the one continuing to regard something to be unclean; to that one [it is] unclean. [15]For if because of food your [s] brother is being caused grief, according to love you [s] are no longer walking. With your [s] food, stop destroying that one on behalf of whom Christ died. [16]Therefore, stop letting your [pl] goodness be evil spoken of. [17]For the kingdom of God is not eating and drinking but righteousness and peace and joy in [the] Holy Spirit. [18]For he who continues serving Christ in this [matter] is well-pleasing to God and approved by mankind. [19]So then, the things pertaining to peace let us continue pursuing, and the things pertaining to edification for one another.

[20]Stop tearing down because of food the work of God. All things [amoral] are indeed pure, but it is evil for the man who is eating with offense. [21]It is good not to eat meat or to drink wine or [to do anything] at which your [s] brother is going to take offense. [22][As for] you [s] yourself, the faith which you [s] are holding, continue holding in relation to yourself, [i.e., privately,] before God. Blessed is he who is not condemning himself for that which he is approving; [23]and he who is doubting, if he eats, stands condemned because [his eating] is not out of faith; and everything which is not out of faith is sin. [1]And we, ourselves, the strong ones, ought to continue bearing up the weaknesses of those without strength and to stop pleasing ourselves. [2]Let each one of us continue striving to please [his] neighbor for [his] good for [his] edification. [3]For even Christ did not please Himself; but just as it stands written, "The insults of those heaping insults on you [s] fell upon me." [4]For as many things as were written beforehand for our instruction were written, in order that, by means of endurance and by means of the consolation from the Scriptures, we might continue having hope.

A. Introductory matter: Romans 14:1 and 15:7 share somewhat the same idea.
   1. Romans 14:1 Continue accepting (into your fellowship) those weak in the faith, though not for the purpose of quarrelling over opinions.
   2. Romans 15:7 Continue accepting one another (into your fellowship), just as also Christ accepted us for (the advancement of the glory of God.)
B. The propositions (or categories) involved in Paul's instructions here:

1. Matters of indifference, those which are amoral (Paul is not speaking here about matters that are clearly moral (right) or immoral (wrong).
2. Matters regarding the observance of days (Paul is not speaking of Sabbath days or Lord's days for rest which God instituted at creation. Gen. 2:1,2. He is speaking here of the Jewish ceremonial days which, we can be sure, some Christians thought still should be observed.
3. Matters regarding clean and unclean foods (In order to avoid a problem here and to keep a clear conscience, some apparently had gone to eating only vegetables. See 14:2).
C. The principles which Paul states should be involved in making decisions about these amoral matters.
   1. 14:7-11 No one of us lives to himself and no one dies to himself, but we live and die to Christ. No one is "an island" but we are all connected to other people and, most importantly, to Christ.
   2. 14:10,12 All of us will have to give an account to Christ and to God of himself. Note the emphasis here on CHRISTIAN FREEDOM. The word used here for "the judgment seat (the Bema) of God is the same word used in II Cor. 5:10 where we are told that we must all appear before the judgment seat of Christ. This is not a judgment relative to our salvation but relative to rewards for faithful service as Christians. 14:13-15.
   3. None of us should put a stumbling block in a fellow Christian's way. Note the emphasis on CHRISTIAN LOVE. We must be careful that we do not bring grief to a weaker brother or, even worse, destroy his spiritual life. 14:15 See I Cor. 8 for additional dangers we must avoid.
   4. 14:8 All of us will gain, with a proper love, not only God's approval but man's also.
   5. 14:23 All that does not originate out of faith is sin. If we are not certain about the rightness of a certain action, it is not merely questionable, it is sinful. Consequently, if you are in doubt about the morality of something, don't do it.
      a. Some explanations of the above statement found in 14:23.
         1.) This sin is doing something which we are not certain is right.
         2.) This sin is doing something which we may suppose God has forbidden or which we are not certain He has allowed. (Hodge)
         3.) This sin is doing something we think may be wrong.
         4.) This sin is doing something which causes us to have a guilty conscience.
      b. Some quotations concerning the above statement

1.) Charles Hodge: "Whatever we do which we are not certain is right, to us is wrong." Charles Hodge. Commentary on the Epistle to the Romans, p. 428.
2.) R. St. John Parry: "When a man's faith either gives no answer to a question of conduct or condemns a particular line, this conduct is sinful." R. St. John Parry. Cambridge Greek Testament: Romans. Cambridge: at the University Press, 1921. p. 180
3.) James Stifler: "All that is not of faith is sin. Eating in doubt is not of faith. Therefore, it is sin and brings condemnation. A man's conduct must be limited by his faith." James M. Stifler, The Epistle to the Romans. Chicago: Moody Press, 1960. p. 231.
4.) Floyd Hamilton: "The person who does not know whether a thing is right or wrong must not do it until he is persuaded in his heart that it is right— for doing what we think to be wrong or what we are not certain to be right makes this thing wrong for us to do. We commit a sin if we do that which is doubtful or that which we do not believe to be right." Floyd E. Hamilton, The Epistle to the Romans. Philadelphia: The Presbyterian and Reformed Publishing Company, 1958. pp. 221, 222.
c. An explanation regarding the above statement
   1.) It is always wrong for one to do anything which he thinks to be wrong.
      a.) There can be sincere doubts about the rightfulness of a course of action, but one sins if he acts with such doubts in his mind.
      b.) There can also be sincere but ill-advised doubts regarding an action, and one sins if he acts with such doubts in his mind. (Regarding these, a person needs further instruction from the Bible since his doubts and the resultant condemnation of heart, should he act on them, are due to a lack of knowledge about Scriptural teaching. However, according to Romans 14:23, until such a time as those doubts are removed, he sins if he acts with these in mind.
   2.) It is not always right for one to do anything he thinks to be right.
      a.) There are legitimate certainties within the Scriptures, and no man sins when he acts in accord with these. (The Scriptures plainly command some things and prohibit others.)
      b.) However, there may be unwarranted certainties, which can still result in a sin if a man acts in accord with these. In other words,

all peace of mind following certain actions does not automatically mean the actions were right.

    i.) One's peace of mind may be caused by an ignorance of Scriptural teaching regarding a certain matter, in other words, a lack of light.

    ii.) It may be founded on a mistaken idea of what the Scriptures mean.

    iii.) It may be caused by a seared conscience which is not reacting properly to right and wrong (See I Timothy 4:2). One may foolishly and dangerously rationalize away the pain of conscience until he can no longer sense its guidance pertaining to right and wrong. As someone has said, "Quite often when a man thinks his mind is getting broader, it is only his conscience stretching."

    iv.) It may be caused by a deliberative and conscious suppression of the truth of God's Word as brought by the Holy Spirit. The result is that sinning can go on with no pains of conscience. (See Romans 1:18, where Paul speaks of people who "were holding down the truth in unrighteousness."

d. Some exhortations based on an understanding of the above statement:

    1.) Follow your conscience and you may or may not go right; disregard your conscience and you are bound to go wrong (See T. C. Hammond, Perfect Freedom, p. 61).

    2.) If you are sincerely interested in avoiding sin at all cost, your safest and only principle for action is the following: "IF YOU ARE IN DOUBT ABOUT A MATTER, DON'T DO IT."

    3.) If you do not have the time, the ability, and/or the tools to study the teaching of the Bible for yourself, be honest enough to recognize your lack and be willing to accept the teachings of those who have taken the time to dig into the text for themselves and to make their findings available to you. See Heb. 5:12-14.

    4.) Notice the supreme importance given to the commands of Jesus and our obedience to them in the Great Commission (Matt. 28:18-20). (We are "to make disciples of all nationalities, to continue baptizing them...and to continue teaching them to continue keeping all the things which Jesus commanded us." See also John 14:15, where Jesus said, "If you love me, you will obey me." Compare also John 14:21,23,24. See also John 14:31 and the connection that is made again between love and obedience. THE CHRISTIAN IS NOT A LAWLESS PERSON IN ANY WAY. GRACE HAS ITS OBLIGATIONS ALSO. A person cannot nourish, cherish, or favorably regard any sin in his heart without paying some severe consequences. See Psalm 66:18.

D. The prescriptions which Paul lists here to guide one in his relations with fellow Christians, be they weak or strong in the faith. Note that all but one are present tenses, stressing continuous activity.

1. We, the strong, are to continue receiving the weak with kindness and hospitality and not for purposes of endless disputation regarding the above matters.

2. We, the stronger, are to stop despising the weaker Christian who cannot eat. As we protect a hurting member of our bodies, we should do the same for a hurting member of the Body of Christ, the church. 14:3,10

3. We, the weaker, are to stop judging (or condemning) the stronger Christian. Note this very real temptation for the weaker brother who cannot do certain things which other stronger Christians can do. 14:3,4

4. Each Christian is to continue on being fully assured or convinced in his own mind of the rightness of what he is doing. 14:5

5. We are to stop passing judgment on one another in these clearly amoral areas. 14:13

6. We, the strong, must determine (Aorist tense) that we will not put a stumbling block in a brother's way, thus making it harder for him to be a Christian. 14:13

7. We must beware of destroying a brother. 14:15 (The Greek word used here is the regular word for eternal perishing.)

8. We must stop permitting our good actions to be evil spoken of by fellow church members or outsiders. 14:16

9. We must continue following after peace and edification for all. 14:19

10. We must stop destroying the work of God on account of our food. 14:20-33

11. We must continue having our faith to ourselves before God, but certainly not to flaunt this knowledge in the face of a weaker brother and thus running the risk of his destruction. 14:22

12. We must bear continuously the infirmities of the weak and stop striving to please ourselves. 15:1

13. We must continue striving to please our neighbor. 15:2 This means we will respect his scruples even though we may not share them. The illustration Paul uses is Christ who

157

suffered the reproaches and sufferings from others for their own good. If He had desired to please Himself, He never would have gone to the cross for us. Note that Paul does not say "please" your neighbor but "strive to please" him. It is impossible to please everyone but that does not mean that we should not try to do so.

E. Some proofs which Paul presents as evidence that one is living in relation to fellow Christians as a totally presented Christian should
1. love for others 14:7-15:4
2. concern for the welfare of others
3. carefulness not to hurt others
4. peaceableness with others
5. edification of others in their Christian walk
6. denial of self for others 14:21
7. humility in the presence of others
8. Appendix: Obviously, this does not mean that a church group may not officially discipline a deserving member. Such discipline needs to be done with firmness and with personal love for the sinning member.

F. Concluding remarks
1. AN EXPLANATION: A weak Christian is one whom some amoral matters in the immoral category and consequently he cannot do them with the firm conviction they are right. See Romans 14:23b. In addition, he is usually very critical of those who do not agree with him on his stance regarding these matters. The strong Christian, in this context, is one who has studied the Bible thoroughly and has moral, immoral, and amoral matters biblically identified. In addition to this, he is willing to give up some perfectly legitimate right he has in order to help a weak Christian who does not agree with him. The "meat offered to idols" issue discussed in I Corinthian 8:1-11:1 is a case in point. Paul says there he would not eat meat at all if such would make his weaker Christian friend to stumble (I Cor. 8:13). Finally, this matter of weaker and stronger Christians is not a differentiation between carnal and Spirit-filled Christians.
2. AN EXHORTATION: Continue striving to keep on having a conscience void of offense toward God and toward mankind always. See Acts 24:16. Or as Paul puts it another place, continue becoming void of offense to Jews, and to Greeks, and to the church of God (I Cor. 10:32). One will never have a ministry to people if, in these amoral issues, he does not try to carry on his ministry as Paul did. We Christians dare not say that we do not care what other people think of us. If they do not like us, they will not want our Christ.
3. TWO EXTREMES: In any Christian group, there are always two extremes evident with regard to the amoral matters under discussion here. One is the LIBERTINE tendency which manifests itself in an attitude which does not care

what other people believe. Such a person says, "It doesn't bother my conscience so who cares what other people think." The other extreme is the LEGALISTIC tendency which demonstrates itself in a kind of rigid bondage to the thinking of other people and a terrible fear of hurting others that almost paralyzes any activity at all. Three things need to be remembered here. 1. There is a third alternative in between and that is LOVE. It enables one to try to keep a balance between the other two. 2. If one has to make a choice between libertinism and legalism, it is generally safer to lean a little heavier on the legalistic side than the other. You will hurt fewer people if you do. 3. Remember that what we are talking about here is a BONDAGE of sorts; however, it is a self-imposed one. See I Corinthians 9:19 where Paul says that although he is free, he has brought himself into bondage to all in order that he might gain more converts for Christ. He than adds, "To all I have become all things in order that by all means I may save some" (I Cor. 9:22).

4. AN EMERGENCY: Too many groups of Christians do not know where their leaders stand on many of these kinds of amoral issues. Also, it is very scary but, to the degree that one's followers have confidence in their leader's exegesis, the more his convictions will become their own. The leader's moral, immoral, and amoral judgments will become those of his people. Although it is a fearful and awesome responsibility, the people should be able to imitate their leader SAFELY. See I Cor. 11:1, which is the last verse of the section in I Corinthians dealing with the weaker brother and the amoral matter of eating the meat offered to idols. In other words, Christian leaders should be mature Christians who are able to partake of solid food and who, because of practice, have their senses trained for the discerning of moral, immoral, and hence also amoral practices. See Hebrews 5:14.

5. AN ELIMINATION: Some have seen a kind of hypocrisy in the teaching here, since on some occasions, under certain circumstances, a person will live one way and on other occasions, another way. It is important here to eliminate this charge of hypocrisy by pointing out that the only actions to which reference is made here are those which are clearly amoral. The motive of the strong Christian acting thusly is not to hide but to help the weak Christian, not to deceive him but to edify him. See I Corinthians 10:27-29 where Paul says on one occasion he will eat meat that has been offered to idols and on another he will not because a weaker brother is present. Note he would rather hurt an unbelieving host by refusing his food than to hurt a weaker Christian who is there with him. Also remember, however, that when it was a matter of moral principle or a clearly immoral issue, Paul and other faithful Christians took their

159

stand for the right, no matter what the conditions around them were. To do otherwise in those instances would have been hypocrisy and deception. In conclusion, certain actions may be right under certain circumstances and wrong under others but only in the clearly amoral realm. In addition, if you have to make a choice regarding whom to hurt, hurt first of all the non-Christian. If it is the choice of two Christians, hurt the stronger since he supposedly can take the pain with fewer dire consequences.

6. AN EQUANIMITY (or composure and patience of mind): Finally, we must remember that new believers must be dealt with carefully and considerately. We dare not try to force them into an adult Christian life-style. We must give them time, with good and careful teaching, to grow up. We do not expect a two-year old to walk like a twenty-year old in the physical realm. Neither should we expect this in the spiritual realm. And let's remember that not all weak Christians with reference to certain amoral matters are new-born Christians. Some have been Christians a long while and still have wrong convictions about some amoral matters.

G. Appendix: The following are "ten commandments" for one to use in trying to determine the morality, the immorality, or the amorality of matters about which the Bible is silent:

1. You shall glorify God and protect your fellowship with Him at all costs. (I Cor. 10:31)
2. You shall obey the commandments of God's Word. (John 14:15,21,23,24)
3. You shall maintain a pure conscience before God and mankind always. (Acts 24:16)
4. You shall do nothing which you could not desire everyone to do. (Matthew 7:12,1 Cor. 11:1)
5. You shall not bring shame upon your parents. (Exodus 20:12; Matt. 15:4)
6. You shall take care of your body. (I Cor. 6:19,20)
7. You shall not waste time, talents, effort or money. (Matt. 6:19,20; Eph. 5:16)
8. You shall not hurt a weaker brother. (Romans 14:1-15:4; I Cor. 8:1-11:1)
9. You shall not bring comfort or aid to your enemy, the Devil. (Romans 6:13; cf. II Chr. 19:2)
10. You shall not do anything about which you have doubts as to its rightness or wrongness. (Romans 14:23b)
11. Appendix: In all circumstances, ask yourself, "WHAT WOULD JESUS DO IN THIS SITUATION???????????" and then DO IT!

A Weak Christian is: one who has clearly amoral matters in the immoral category; and he is generally critical and condemnatory of those who don't agree with him. He can be Spirit-filled and have been a Christian for a long time.

A Strong Christian is: one who has his moral, immoral and amoral matters biblically located and can define his position biblically; and, he is willing cheerfully and readily to give up a perfect right he has for the sake of a weaker Christian.

Note: An excellent book on the rights of a spirit-controlled Christian is the following: *Have We No Rights?* by Mabel Williamson, Chicago: Moody Press, 1957. See especially the end of chapter four (p. 37).

Chapter Ten

Paul's Termination of the Epistle to the Romans
Romans 15:5-16:27

I. Paul's encouragement to unity 15:5-13

⁵And may the God of endurance and of consolation grant you [pl] to continue agreeing with one another according to Christ Jesus, ⁶in order that with one accord with one mouth you may continue glorifying the God and Father of our Lord Jesus Christ.

⁷Wherefore continue accepting one another [into your fellowship], just as also Christ accepted us for [the advancement of] the glory of God. ⁸For I am saying that Christ has become a minister of the circumcision on behalf of [the] truth of God, in order that He might confirm the promises belonging to the fathers ⁹and that the Gentiles on behalf of [His] mercy might glorify God even as it stands written,

> *Because of this I shall praise you [s] among the Gentiles and to your [s] name I shall sing.*

¹⁰And again it is saying,

> *Rejoice, O Gentiles, with His people.*

¹¹And again,

> *Continue praising the Lord, all you [pl] Gentiles,*
> *And let all the peoples praise Him.*

¹²And again Isaiah is saying,

> *The root of Jesse will exist,*
> *And He who is rising up to be ruling over [the] Gentiles;*
> *On Him will [the] Gentiles hope.*

¹³And may the God of hope fill you with all joy and peace while you are believing, in order that you may continue increasing in hope by [the] power of the Holy Spirit.

A. Plea #1 is Paul's entreaty to unity.
    1. The expressions emphasizing unity in these verses are
        a. Continue agreeing with one another.
        b. Continue glorifying God with one accord.
        c. Continue doing it with one mouth.

     2.   Old Testament passages stressing unity: Note that the following references, which are quoted by Paul in the epistle, all stress the fact that Christ did not come only for Jews but also for Gentiles. Note also that the references cited come from every part of the Jewish Old Testament, viz., the law, the prophets and the writings.
- a. Psa. 18:49,50
- b. Deut. 32:43
- c. Psa. 117:1
- d. Isa. 11:10

- B. Plea #2 is an exhortation to love one another. 15:7
- C. Plea #3 is a plea for joyfulness.
- D. Plea #4 is a plea for peace, a lack of inner tension and worrying.
- E. Plea #5 is a desire for them to have hope. Note that there are no situations which are hopeless with God in the picture, only people who have become hopeless over situations.
- F. Plea #6 is that they may exhibit the power of the Holy Spirit.
- G. Appendix #1: All of the above are sources from which UNITY stems.
- H. Appendix #2: The emphasis here is on the one thing that could have caused disunity in the early church, the bringing in of the Gentiles. See the many references to the Gentiles: 15:9,10,11,12,16,18,21,27.
- I. Appendix #3: From the list above [B-F], it seems possible that Paul might have had in mind the fruit of the Spirit. See Gal. 5:22,23.

II. Paul's explanation of his task 15:14-21 Note how he identifies himself.

[14]And I myself also stand persuaded concerning you [pl], my brothers, that you yourselves also are full of goodness, having been filled with all knowledge, being able also to continue admonishing one another. [15]But the more boldly I have written to you [pl] in part, as one reminding you [pl] again because of the grace which has been given to me from God, [16]in order that I may be a minister of Christ Jesus unto the Gentiles, continuing to serve the gospel of God as a priest, in order that the offering of the Gentiles may become acceptable because it has been sanctified by [the] Holy Spirit. [17]Therefore, I am having [my] boast in Christ Jesus in reference to the things pertaining to God; [18]for I will not dare to speak of any thing [except] those which Christ accomplished by means of me for [the] obedience of [the] Gentiles, by word and deed, [19]by [the] power of signs and wonders, by [the] power of [the] Spirit; so that I have from Jerusalem and roundabout to Illyricum caused the gospel of Christ to be fully known. [20]And thus [I am] earnestly striving to continue preaching the gospel where Christ has not been named, lest upon another's foundation I continue building; [21]but just as it stands written,

> *They will see to whom it was not announced concerning Him,*
> *And the ones who have not heard will understand.*

A. He claims to be a receiver of grace to be a minister of Christ to the Gentiles. 15:15,16
B. He is a minister belonging to Jesus Christ. 15:16
C. He is a servant of the Gospel of God. 15:16
D. He is a priest offering up as his sacrifice the Gentiles who are accepting Christ. 15:16
E. He is one who rejoices greatly in Christ Jesus. 15:17
*F. He is an instrument whom Christ uses to carry out His work. Note that he stresses not what he did but what Christ did through him. 15:18
G. He is a traveler from Jerusalem to Illyricum and a missionary in these same regions. Note he says he has fully preached the Gospel throughout these areas. 15:19b,20a
H. He is a pioneer preacher heralding Christ where He has not been named before. 15:20a
I. He is an initiator or founder of churches everywhere he goes. He did not like to build on the foundations laid by others. 15:20b

III. **Paul's explanation of his personal plans** 15:22-29

22Wherefore also I was repeatedly hindered these many times from coming to you [pl] 23but now, because I am no longer having place in these regions and because I have been having a longing to come to you [pl] for many years, 24as soon I am going to Spain, [I shall come]. For I am hoping, while I am passing by, to see you [pl] and by you [pl] to be helped on my journey there, if from you [pl] [i.e., from your company] first of all in some measure I may be satisfied; 25but now I am going to Jerusalem in order to be ministering to the saints; 26for Macedonia and Achaia resolved a certain contribution to make for the poor ones of the saints which are in Jerusalem. 27For they resolved and they are their debtors; for if [1st] in their spiritual things the Gentiles fellowshipped, they ought also in fleshly things to minister to them. 28Therefore, after I have accomplished this, and after I have sealed for them this fruit, I shall go away through you [pl] [i.e., through your city], to Spain; 29and I know that, while I am coming to you [pl], in the fullness of the blessing of Christ I shall come.

Since he had no more places for pioneer preaching in the regions from Jerusalem to Illyricum, he states his further goals:
A. He refers to his strong desire many times to come to Rome for a visit, although he has been hindered up to this time.
B. He describes his hope and trust that he can go on to Spain with the gospel.
1. The early writers. Clement of Rome and the writer of the Muratorian Canon, seem to indicate that he finally did get to Spain.
2. Acts closes with Paul still preaching in his own hired house in Rome, without mentioning his death. See Acts 28.

3. The Prison Epistles, which seemingly were written from the 1st Roman imprisonment (Acts 28), have a very different character than II Timothy. Philippians implies an imminent release of Paul while II Timothy seems to describe a much worse imprisonment, a second one from which Paul never came out alive. Compare Phil. 2:23, 24 with II Tim. 1:15-17; 4:6-9.

4. II Timothy 4:6-9 seems to indicate an expectation on his part of death at any time.

5. Conclusion: Apparently, Paul suffered two imprisonments in Rome with some more preaching missions in between. The first imprisonment in his own hired house is described in Acts 28, where Luke ends his account of Paul's career. Had he written additional chapters of Acts, he certainly would have given us additional preaching missions and the second imprisonment in Rome and his death at the hands of Nero.

C. His stated intention, first, was to visit Jerusalem to deliver personally the offering for the poor at Jerusalem which he had been collecting in Macedonia and Achaia on his third missionary journey. See I Corinthians 8 and 9 where he instructs the Corinthians to have their offering for Jerusalem ready for him when he arrives.

D. Appendix: What actually happened was that he was arrested in Jerusalem when he arrived, jailed and later imprisoned for two years in Caesarea while Felix and Festus mishandled his case. Later, because he appealed to appear before Caesar, he was sent on to Rome as Luke describes it in Acts 27 and 28.

IV. **Paul's exhortation to prayer** 15:30-33 Note Paul's misgivings about his trip to Jerusalem.

30But I am beseeching you [pl], brothers, by means of our Lord Jesus Christ and by means of the love of the Spirit, to strive together with me in [your] prayers on behalf of me to God 31in order that I may be delivered from those who are not believing in Judea and [in order that] my ministry for Jerusalem may become acceptable to the saints, 32in order that, with joy having come to you [pl] through the will of God, I may find rest in company with you [pl]. 33May the God of peace [be] with all of you [pl]. Amen.

A. Request #1: He wants the Roman Christians to pray that he will be delivered from the unbelieving Jews in Judea.

B. Request #2: He wants them to pray that his financial ministration in Jerusalem will be accepted by the church in Jerusalem. He was afraid apparently that Jewish pride and prejudice might cause them to reject this Gentile money from the "mission field." Often gifts of money are considered to come from superiors to inferiors. Here was a case where mission churches were giving help to the home base; and that could hurt self-esteem, no matter how badly the money was needed.

165

C. Request #3: He desires to come to them in joy through the will of God. Note that Paul is now willing to come to them if God is willing.
D. Request #4: He is apparently in need of rest and wants them to pray that he will find rest in their fellowship. Apparently, God knew he needed rest before that time and gave him rest for two years in a Caesarean jail.
E. Another benediction:
There are five benedictions which close out this epistle. This is the third of the five. See Romans 15:5, 13, 33; 16:20b and 25-27. Paul leaves them his blessing and his prayers as he closes.

V. **Paul's expression of greetings (saluting) 16:1-16**

¹And I am commending to you Phoebe, our sister, who is also a servant of the church which is in Cenchrea, ²in order that you may welcome her in [the] Lord worthily of the saints and you may assist her in whatever matter she may be having need of you [pl], for she herself also a helper of many became and of me myself [also].

³Greet Priscilla and Aquila, my fellow-workers in Christ Jesus, ⁴who on behalf of my life their own necks [s] laid down for whom not only I myself am giving thanks but also all the churches of the Gentiles, ⁵and [greet] the church in their house. Greet Epaenetus, my beloved, who is the first fruits of Asia for Christ. ⁶Greet Mary, who labored much for you [pl]. ⁷Greet Andronicus and Junias, my fellow-countrymen and fellow-prisoners, who are of note among the apostles, who also before me have become in Christ. ⁸Greet Ampliatus, my beloved, in [the] Lord. ⁹Greet Urbanus, our fellow-worker in Christ, and Stachys, my beloved. ¹⁰Greet Apelles, the approved one in Christ. Greet those [of the household] of Aristobulus. ¹¹Greet Herodion, my kinsman. Greet those [of the household] of Narcissus, who are being in the Lord. Greet Tryphaena and Tryphosa, who have labored in [the] Lord. ¹²Greet Persis, the beloved, who labored much in [the] Lord. ¹³Greet Rufus, the elect one in [the] Lord, and his mother and mine. ¹⁴Greet Asyncritus, Phlegon, Hermes, Patrobas, Hermas, and the brothers together with them. ¹⁵Greet Philologus and Julia, Nereus and his sister, and Olympas and all the saints together with them. ¹⁶Greet one another with a holy kiss. All the churches of Christ continue to greet you.

A. The reasons for the list of names which Paul presents in Romans 16
1. The list is a sincere salutation to friends whom he had in Rome.
   a. Travel was very common in that day and he could have met many of them elsewhere on his travels within the Empire.
   b. It was extremely easy on the part of a Roman citizen.
   c. It was forced on some, such as Priscilla and Aquila who were expelled from Rome under Claudius during the A.D. 40's. See Acts 18:2.

166

2. This list was also a point of contact with a church he had not founded or visited before. For this reason he apparently tried to think of everyone whom he had met before who were in Rome.
3. This list of names is a very personal ending to an otherwise very impersonal epistle. Exclude Romans 1:1-17 and 15:5 to the end and this letter reads like an essay on justification by faith.
4. Appendix: There may have been other reasons why this list of names was added; however, the above are probably the main ones.

B. Some individuals in the list
1. Phoebe
   a. She was probably the carrier of the letter to Rome and the letter served as a commendation of her to the Roman church.
   b. She was a sister in Christ, a Christian.
   c. She was a servant (or a deaconess) in the church at Cenchrea, the port of Corinth on the Saronic Gulf.
   d. She was a helper of many and of Paul in particular. Paul does not say how.
2. Priscilla and Aquila
   a. They were believers who apparently had returned to Rome from their former home in Corinth.
   b. They were fellow-workers with Paul in tent-making in Corinth on his second missionary journey.
   c. They were fellow-workers with Paul in Christ.
   d. They were associates with Paul in Ephesus. See Acts 18:2, 18, 26.
   e. They were people who risked their lives for Paul, although we are not told how.
   f. They were people who had a church in their house in Rome. Apparently wherever they went, their home became a center of Christian worship. Their pilgrimage took them from Rome originally, to Corinth, to Ephesus, back to Rome and then to Ephesus again. See II Tim. 4:19.
3. Andronicus and Junius v. 7
   a. One view: They were men of note among the apostles, with the word "apostles" being used in a very broad sense. It would seem that Paul's use of this word elsewhere, however, was in a narrower sense, not wider.
   b. A more probable view: They were men known well by the apostles, although they themselves were not apostles.
4. Appendix

    a. The salutation or greeting which Paul extends in the ending of his epistle means to bid someone welcome or to wish them well. At the time and in that location it was not a mere slight gesture of a few words but generally included an embrace and a kiss.

    b. The holy kiss

        1.) This was token of love for the recipient.

        2.) At the time it was part of public worship.

        3.) It may have been a carryover from the Jewish synagogue worship.

        4.) It was a practice involving men with men and women with women.

        5.) Appendix: Note the remark of Athenagoras in his "Plea for the Christians, Section XXXII: "On behalf of those, then, to whom we apply the names of brothers and sisters, and other designations of relationship, we exercise the greatest care that their bodies should remain undefiled and uncorrupted; for the Logos again says to us, 'If any one kiss a second time because it has given him pleasure, (he sins);'" adding. therefore the kiss, or rather the salutation, should be given with the greatest care, since, if there be mixed with it the least defilement of thought, it excludes us from eternal life.'"

VI. **Paul's enlightenment of them with regard to dissension and apostasy (warning) 16:17-20a,**

¹⁷I continue begging you, brothers, to continue looking out for those causing divisions and occasions for stumbling contrary to the teaching which you yourselves learned, and continue turning away from them; ¹⁸for such ones are not serving our Lord Jesus Christ but their own belly, and by means of smooth and fair speech they are deceiving the hearts of the innocent. ¹⁹For your [pl] obedience has come to [the knowledge of] all; over you, therefore, I continue rejoicing, but I continue desiring you to be wise with reference to goodness and innocent with reference to evil. ²⁰ᵃAnd the God of peace will crush Satan under your [pl] feet shortly.

KEEP YOUR EYE ON TEACHERS WHO ARE CHARACTERIZED BY THE FOLLOWING:

A. Dissension and division

B. Placing occasions to stumble or stumbling blocks in people's ways

C. Heresy with reference to their doctrinal beliefs

D. Lack of service to Christ

E. Service to their own bellies with selfish gluttony

F. Deception

G. Appendix:

    1. Command #1: Continue looking out for such.

2. Command #2: Continue turning away from such.
3. Command #3: Continue being wise with reference to goodness. Know everything you can about that which is good and right.
4. Command #4: Continue being simple with regard to evil. See I Cor. 14:20. Be innocent with regard to all that is evil. In other words, "Personal experience with evil adds nothing to your usefulness in the Lord's service. God often uses in a mighty way the testimony of those who have been saved out of flagrant sinfulness, but He would have His people be simple concerning evil." Paul wrote in I Cor. 14:20, "Brothers, stop becoming little children in your minds; but with reference to wickedness continue being infants and in your minds continue becoming mature."

VII. Paul's ending of the epistle 16:20b-27

20bMay the grace of our Lord Jesus [be] with you [pl].

21Timothy, my fellow-worker, is greeting you, and Lucius and Jason and Sosipater, my fellow-countrymen. 22I myself, Tertius, who has written the epistle, am greeting you in [the] Lord. 23Gaius, my host and [host] of the whole church, is greeting you. Erastus, the treasurer of the city, is greeting you, and Quartos, the brother. (Verse 24 is missing in our best Greek manuscripts.)

25Now to the One who is being able to establish you according to my gospel and the message concerning Jesus Christ, according to [the] revelation of [the] mystery which for eternal times has been concealed 26but now which has been manifested and which by means of [the] prophetic writings according to the commandment of the eternal God, has been made known for the obedience [stemming] from faith among all the Gentiles, 27to the only wise God, by means of Jesus Christ, be the glory unto the ages of the ages. Amen.

A. The signatures
   1. Timothy, called here Paul's fellow worker
   2. Lucius, a Christian from Cyrene in North Africa, a teacher in the church at Antioch, and a companion of Paul's now
   3. Jason, a Christian of Thessalonica, now a companion of Paul's and apparently a kinsman.
   4. Sosipater, also a companion and a Christian kinsman
   5. Tertius, the amanuensis or scribe who took down the notes for the epistle
   6 Gaius, Paul's host and the host of the church which met in his house
   7. Erastus, the treasurer of the city of Corinth
   8. Quartus, the brother

B. The final benediction of the epistle — 16:25-27 (The last of five benedictions: See Rom. 15:5,13,33; and 16:20b for the other four.

"Now to the One who is able to establish you according to my gospel and the message concerning Jesus Christ, according to the revelation of the mystery which has been concealed for eternal times but which has been manifested now and which, by means of the prophetic writings according to the commandment of the eternal God, has been made known for the obedience which comes from faith among all Gentiles, to the only wise God, by means of Jesus Christ, be glory unto the ages of the ages. Amen."

A Skeleton Outline of the Epistle to the Romans

I.   The Salutation 1:1-7
  A.   Paul's introduction of himself
  B.   Paul's introduction of the Gospel of God
  C.   Paul's introduction of Christ, the Core of the Gospel
  D.   Paul's introduction of his addressees, the Roman Christians
  E.   Paul's introduction of his desires for his readers, grace and peace

II. The Information which Paul gives them 1:8-15
  A.   Paul's praise for the Roman Christians' faith
  B.   Paul's prayers for them unceasingly
  C.   Paul's purposes in wanting to come to see them

III. The Summarization of the epistle: THE KEY VERSES OF THE EPISTLE 1:16,17
  A.   Paul's confidence in the Gospel: "I am not ashamed of the Gospel"
  B.   The characterization of the Gospel: "the power of God"
  C.   The concern of the Gospel: "Salvation for everyone"
  D.   The condition for receiving the Gospel: "everyone who is believing"
  E.   The consecution in preaching the Gospel: "to the Jew first, and also to the Greek"
  F.   The content of the Gospel: "a revelation of a righteousness from God, a revelation by faith unto faith"
  G.   The confirmation of this Gospel from the Old Testament: Habakkuk 2:4 "And the one who is righteous by faith will live."

IV. The CONDEMNATION of everyone based on their own works
  A.   The Gentiles 1:18-32
  B.   The principles of God's judgment based on works 2:1-16
  C.   The Jews 2:17-3:9
  D.   The whole world 3:9-20

V.   The JUSTIFICATION based on personal faith in Christ
  A.   The characterization of that righteousness 3:21-31
  B.   The illustrations of it from the Old Testament: Abraham and David 4:1-17a
  C.   The characterization of Abraham's faith reckoned for righteousness 4:17b-25
  D.   The blessings of it 5:1-11

VI. The IMPUTATION of Adam's sin to all in Adam and of Christ's righteousness to all in Christ 5:12-21

VII. THE SANCTIFICATION possible for all justified by faith 6-8
  A.   Our deliverance from a life of sin 6:1-14
  B.   Our deliverance from individual acts of sin 6:15-23
  C.   Our deliverance from law as a legalistic means of holiness 7:1-7

D. The conflict between the law and indwelling sin in the carnal Christian 7:8-25
E. The blessings of the Spirit-led life 8:1-39
VIII. The RENUNCIATION by Israel of justification by faith but Israel's ultimate SALVATION 9-11
A. The sovereignty of God in relation to it 9:1-24
B. The responsibility and free will of Israel in rejecting it 9:25-10:21
C. The rejection of Israel as not total or permanent 11:1-36 (The olive tree analogy & Israel's ultimate salvation)
IX. The CONVERSATION (Conduct) of the totally consecrated Christian in various relationships: 12:1-15:4
A. Introduction 12:1,2
B. His partners in the church 12:3-8
C. His pursuit of the work of Christ 12:9-13
D. The people around him in general 12:14-16
E. His persecutors 12:17-21
F. The powers over him, viz.. his government 13:1-7
G. The prescriptions found in the laws of God 13:8-10
H. The present period, i.e. the age in which he lives 13:11-14
I. His partners in the church, those weaker and those stronger 14:1-15:4
X. TERMINATION 15:5-16:27
A. Paul's encouragement to unity 15:5-13
B. Paul's explanation of his task as completed 15:14-21
C. Paul's explanation of his personal plans for the future 15:22-29
D. Paul's exhortation to prayer for his ministry in Jerusalem 15:30-33
E. Paul's expression of greetings (salutations) to his friends 16:1-16
F. Paul's enlightenment of them with regard to a dissension and apostasy (warning) 16:17-20a
G. Paul's ending of the epistle with signatures and a benediction 16:20b-27

A Translation of Paul's Epistle to the Romans
by Dr. Wesley L. Gerig

ROMANS 1

1:1-7   THE SALUTATION of the epistle

[1]Paul, a bond-servant belonging to Christ Jesus, a called apostle, who has been set apart for the gospel of God, [2]which was promised beforehand through His prophets in the holy Scriptures [3]concerning His Son, the One who came into being from the seed of David according to the flesh, [4]the One who has been marked out the Son of God with power according to the spirit of holiness by the resurrection from the dead, Jesus Christ, our Lord, [5]through whom we received grace and apostleship for obedience [stemming] from faith among all the Gentiles on behalf of His name, [6]among whom you yourselves also are called ones belonging to Jesus Christ, [7]to all the ones being in Rome, beloved ones of God, called saints: Grace be to you and peace from God our Father and the Lord Jesus Christ.

1:8-15   INFORMATION about Paul

[8]First of all, I continue giving thanks to my God through Jesus Christ concerning all of you [pl] because your [pl] faith is being proclaimed in the whole world. [9]For God is my witness, whom I continue serving with my spirit in the gospel of His Son, that unceasingly I continue making mention of you [pl] always in my prayers, [10]praying if somehow now at last I shall succeed in the will of God to come to you [pl]. [11]For I am fervently longing to see you [pl] in order that I may impart some spiritual gift to you [pl] in order that you [pl] may be established, [12]that is [in order that I] may receive encouragement among you through [our] mutual faith, both yours and mine. [13]And I am not wanting you [pl] to continue being ignorant, brothers, that many times I determined to come to you, but I was prevented until now, in order that I might have some fruit also among you [pl], just as also among the

remaining Gentiles. [14]For both to the Greeks and to the barbarians, both to wise ones and to foolish ones, I am a debtor; [15]thus my eagerness is to preach the gospel also to you [pl], the ones who are in Rome.

1:16-17 THE SUMMARIZATION of the epistle

[16]For I am not being ashamed of the gospel. For it is power from God for salvation for every one who is believing, for the Jew first and for the Greek. [17]For a righteousness from God in it is being revealed by faith unto faith, just as it stands written, "But the one who is righteous by faith will live."

1:18-25 CONDEMNATION of the Gentile world on the basis of evil works

[18]For wrath from God is going to be revealed from heaven against all ungodliness and unrighteousness of mankind, those who continue holding down the truth in unrighteousness; [19]because that which is known concerning God is clear among them; for God has made it known to them. [20]For His invisible [attributes] from the [time of] the creation of the world by means of [His] created things being perceived, are being clearly seen, namely His eternal power and godhead, so that they are without excuse; [21]because although they had known God, as God they did not glorify [Him] nor did they give thanks, but they were given over to worthless things in their thoughts and their foolish heart was darkened. [22]Although they were claiming to be wise ones, they became fools; [23]and they exchanged the glory of the immortal God for the likeness of an image of mortal man and of birds and of four-footed animals and of creeping things. [24]Wherefore God delivered them over in the lusts of their hearts unto uncleanness in order to continue dishonoring their bodies among them, [25]since indeed they exchanged the truth of God for the lie, and they worshipped and served the creature rather than the One who created [it], who is blessed forever. Amen.

1:26-27

²⁶Because of this God delivered them over unto dishonorable emotions; for, on the one hand, their females exchanged the natural [sexual] use for that contrary to nature; ²⁷and likewise, on the other hand, the males, because they had left the natural [sexual] use of the female, burned with their lust for one another, males with males continuing to commit this shameful act and continuing to receive back in themselves the penalty of their error which was unavoidable.

1:28-32

²⁸And just as they did not approve of having God in their knowledge, God delivered them over to an unapproved mind, to continue practicing the things not proper, ²⁹[those] who are filled with all unrighteousness, maliciousness, covetousness, badness; full of envy, murder, strife, deceit, depravity; tale-bearers, ³⁰slanderers, haters of God, insolent persons, proud, boasters, inventors of evil things, to parents disobedient, ³¹without understanding, covenant-breaking, without natural affection, merciless; ³²who, although the righteous requirement of God they have fully known, that those who are practicing such things are worthy of death, not only continue practicing them but also continue giving approval to those who are practicing [them].

ROMANS 2

2:1-11   CONDEMNATION: Principles of God's judgment for all depending on their own works for their justification

¹Therefore you [s] are without excuse, every man who is judging; for wherein you [s] are judging the other [person] you yourself are condemning; for the same things you [s] who are judging are practicing. ²But we know that the judgment of God is according to truth against the ones practicing such things. ³And are you [s] thinking this, O

man who is judging the ones practicing such things and doing [the] same things, that you yourself will escape the judgment of God? ⁴Or the riches of His goodness and forbearance and longsuffering are you [s] despising, being ignorant that the goodness of God is bringing you [s] to repentance? ⁵But according to your [s] hardness and impenitent heart you [s] are continuing to treasure up for yourself wrath on the day of wrath and revelation of the righteous judgment of God, ⁶who will pay back to each one according to his works; ⁷on the one hand, to the ones who continue seeking for glory and honor and immortality on the basis of endurance in good work, [He will pay back] eternal life; ⁸but, on the other hand, to those who both continue disobeying the truth out of selfishness and who continue obeying unrighteousness [will be] wrath and anger--⁹tribulation and anguish against every soul of man who continues working evil, both of [the] Jew first and [the] Greek; ¹⁰but glory and honor and peace [will be given] to every one continuing to work goodness, both to [the] Jew first and to [the] Greek. ¹¹For there is no respect of persons with God.

2:12-16

¹²For as many as sinned without law, without law also will perish; and as many as sinned with law, by means of law will be judged, ¹³for the hearers of law are not just before God, but the doers of law will be justified; ¹⁴(for whenever Gentiles, those not having the law, by nature continue practicing the things of the law, these, although they are not having the law, are for themselves a law ¹⁵because they are showing the work of the law written on their hearts, while their conscience is bearing witness in support [of the fact] and their thoughts among themselves are repeatedly condemning or even defending [them]) ¹⁶on the day when God is going to judge the hidden things of men according to my gospel by means of Jesus Christ.

2:17-24   CONDEMNATION of the Jewish world on the basis of evil works

[17]But if [1st] you yourself continue bearing the name "Jew" and continue trusting in [the] law and continue glorying in God [18]and continue knowing [His] will and continue approving the things which are excellent because you [s] are being taught from the law, [19]and you [s] stand persuaded that you yourself are a guide of blind ones, a light of those in darkness, [20]an instructor of foolish ones, a teacher of babies, who is having the form of knowledge and of truth in the law-- [21]as for you [s], the one teaching another, you [s] are teaching yourself, are you [s] not? As for you [s], the one preaching not to be stealing, are you [s] stealing? [22]As for you [s], the one claiming not to be committing adultery, are you [s] committing adultery? As for you [s], the one detesting idols, are you [s] robbing temples? [23]You [s] who are boasting in the law, through the transgression of the law are you [s] continuing to dishonor God? [24]For the name of God because of you [pl] is continually being blasphemed among the Gentiles just as it stands written.

2:25-29

[25]For, on the one hand, circumcision is profitable if [3rd] you [s] are practicing the law; but if [3rd] a transgressor of the law you are, your [s] circumcision has become uncircumcision. [26]If [3rd] therefore the uncircumcision the righteous ordinances of the law continues keeping, his uncircumcision for circumcision will be reckoned, will it not? [27]And the uncircumcision by nature, if [partc.] it is fulfilling the law, will judge you [s], the transgressor of the law, by means of [your] written code and circumcision. [28]For the Jew who is one outwardly is not [the true Jew], nor is the circumcision which is outwardly in the flesh [true circumcision], [29]but the Jew who is one inwardly is [the true Jew] and circumcision of the heart, in [the] spirit, not in [the] letter [of the law], is [the true circumcision], whose praise is not from men but from God.

ROMANS 3

3:1-4

¹What therefore is the advantage of the Jew, or what is the profit of circumcision? ²Much in every way. For first, they were entrusted with the oracles of God. ³For what if [1st] certain ones were not faithful, their unfaithfulness will not put the faithfulness of God out of business, will it? ⁴May it not be so! But let God continue becoming true, and every man a liar, even as it stands written,

> In order that you [s] may be justified by your [s] words
> And may win [the case] while you [s] are being judged.

3:5-9a

⁵But if [1st] our unrighteousness continues enhancing [the] righteousness of God, what shall we say? God, the One who is going to inflict wrath, is not unrighteous, is He? I am speaking according to men. ⁶May it not be so! Since how [then] will God judge the world? ⁷But if [1st] the truthfulness of God by means of my lie is made supremely great for His glory, why am I myself also still being judged as a sinner? ⁸[And why not] (even as we are being blasphemously reported and even as certain ones are saying that we are speaking) let us do evil things in order that good things may come? (whose condemnation is just). ⁹What therefore? Are we being in a worse position [than they]? Not in every respect;

3:9b-20   CONDEMNATION of the entire world on the basis of evil works

for we previously brought a charge against both Jews and Greeks that all are under sin, ¹⁰even as it stands written,

> There is **none** righteous, **not even one;**
> ¹¹There is none who is understanding;
> There is none who is seeking God;

¹²**All** have turned aside, together **they** have become unprofitable;
There is **none practicing** goodness, there is **not even one;**

¹³Their throat is a grave which has been opened;
With their tongues they were deceiving;
The poison of asps is under their lips,
¹⁴Whose mouth is continually full of cursing and bitter hatred;
¹⁵Their feet are quick to shed blood;
¹⁶Destruction and misery are in their ways,
¹⁷And the way of peace they have not known;
¹⁸There is no fear of God before their eyes.

¹⁹And we know that as many things as the law is speaking, it is speaking to those with the law, in order that every mouth may be put to silence and all the world may become liable to judgment with reference to God. ²⁰Wherefore by the works of law, no flesh will be justified before Him; for by means of law is the full knowledge of sin.

3:21-26   JUSTIFICATION: A characterization of a justification available by faith

²¹But now, apart from law a righteousness from God has been manifested, being witnessed by the law and the prophets, ²²even a righteousness from God by means of faith in Jesus Christ, for all the ones believing, (for there is no distinction, ²³for all have sinned and are continuing to come short of the glory of God), ²⁴who are being justified as a gift by His grace by means of the redemption which is in Christ Jesus, ²⁵whom God set forth [as] a propitiation, by means of faith, by His blood, for a manifestation of His righteousness, because of [His] passing over of the sins having happened before in the forbearance of God, ²⁶for a manifestation, [I say,] of His righteousness in the present season in order that He may continue being just and justifying the one [who is having] faith in Jesus.

[27]Where therefore is the boasting? It has been excluded. By means of what sort of principle? Of works? No, by means of the principle of faith. [28]For we continue reckoning that a man is being justified by means of faith apart from works of law. [29]Or does God belong to Jews only? [He belongs] also to Gentiles, does He not? Yes, also to Gentiles, [30]if [1st] indeed God is One who will justify [the] circumcision by faith and [the] uncircumcision by means of faith. [31]Are we therefore putting law out of business by means of faith? May it not be so! but we are [really] establishing law.

ROMANS 4

4:1-13   JUSTIFICATION: Two illustrations of justification by faith

[1]What therefore shall we say that Abraham, our forefather according to the flesh, has found? [2]For if [1st] Abraham out of works was justified, he is having grounds for boasting, but not before God [does he have grounds for boasting]. [3]For what is the Scripture saying? "And Abraham believed God, and it was reckoned to him for righteousness." [4]But to the one who is working, the reward is not reckoned according to grace but according to debt; [5]but to the one who is not working but believing on the One who is justifying the ungodly [person], his faith is reckoned for righteousness; [6]just as David also is saying regarding the blessedness of the man to whom God is reckoning righteousness apart from works:

> [7]Blessed are [the ones] whose lawless acts have been forgiven and whose sins have been covered.
> [8]Blessed is a man whose sin the Lord will never reckon [to him].

⁹Was this blessedness [pronounced] therefore at [the time of] his circumcision or at [the time of] his uncircumcision? For we are saying, "Faith was reckoned to Abraham for righteousness." ¹⁰How therefore was it reckoned, while he was in circumcision or in uncircumcision? [It was] not in circumcision but in uncircumcision; ¹¹and [the] sign of circumcision he received [as] a seal of the righteousness of faith, that [which he had in a state] of uncircumcision, in order that he might continue being father of all the ones believing through [a state of] uncircumcision, in order that righteousness might be reckoned to them; ¹²and the father of circumcision to those not only from the circumcision [group] but also to those continuing to march in the footsteps of the faith of our father, Abraham, [which he had] in uncircumcision. ¹³For not by means of law was the promise to Abraham or to his seed [viz.,] that he was to be the heir of the world, but by means of a righteousness (stemming) from faith.

4:14-22   JUSTIFICATION: A characterization of Abraham's faith   (4:17b-25)

¹⁴For if [1st] those out of law [are] heirs, faith has been emptied of meaning and the promise has been put out of business; ¹⁵for the law produces wrath; but where there is no law, neither is there transgression. ¹⁶Because of this it is by faith, in order that it may be according to grace, in order that the promise may continue being sure for all the seed, not only for the one [who is] of the law but also for the one [who is] of the faith of Abraham, who is father of all of us, ¹⁷even as it stands written, "A father of many nations I have appointed you (s)" before [the] God in whom he believed, who is the One giving life to the dead and calling the things which are not existing as though they are existing; ¹⁸who contrary to hope, on the basis of hope believed so that he became a father of many nations according to that which had been spoken, "Thus your (s) seed will be." ¹⁹And because he did not weaken in faith, he considered his own body as having become dead, because it was about a hundred years old, and the deadness of the womb of Sarah; ²⁰but at the promise of God, he did

not waver with unbelief, but he became strengthened in faith, having given glory to God [21]and having been fully convinced that what He has promised, He is also able to perform. [22]Therefore, also, it was reckoned to him for righteousness.

4:23-25

[23]But it was not written on account of him alone, [viz.,] that it was reckoned to him [24]but also on account of us, to whom it is about to be reckoned, to those who continue believing on the One who raised Jesus, our Lord, from the dead, [Jesus] [25]who was delivered over on account of our transgressions and was raised on account of our justification.

ROMANS 5

5:1-11   JUSTIFICATION: The effectuation of justification by faith

[1]Because, therefore, we have been justified by faith, we continue having peace with God by means of our Lord Jesus Christ, [2]by means of whom also we have had the introduction by faith into this grace in which we have come to stand; and we continue glorying because of the hope of the glory of God. [3]And not only [this], but we also continue glorying in tribulations, because we know that tribulation continues producing endurance, [4]and endurance [produces] approved character, and approved character [produces] hope; [5]and hope is not disappointing [us], because the love of God has been poured out in our hearts by means of [the] Holy Spirit who has been given to us. [6]Indeed, while we were yet weak, Christ died at the proper season on behalf of the ungodly. [7]For [the fact is that] only rarely on behalf of a righteous [person] will someone die; for on behalf of the good person someone might even dare to die; [8]but God is exhibiting His own love for us because, while we were yet sinners, Christ died on behalf of us. [9]Therefore, how much more rather, because
182

we have been justified now by His blood, shall we be saved by means of Him from wrath. [10]For if [1st] while we were enemies, we were reconciled, shall we be saved by His life; [11]and not only [this], but (we are) also glorying in God by means of our Lord Jesus Christ, by means of whom now we have received the reconciliation.

5:12-21   IMPUTATION: The imputation of Adam's sin and Christ's righteousness

[12]Because of this, just as by means of one man sin entered into the world, and by means of sin, death, and thus death permeated all men, because all sinned-- [13]for until [the] law, sin was in [the] world, but sin is not reckoned while law is not existing; [14]but death reigned from Adam until Moses even over those who had not sinned after the likeness of the transgression of Adam, who is a type of the One coming. [15]But not as the transgression, so also [is] the free gift; for if [1st] by the transgression of the one, the many died, how much more rather did the grace of God and the gift by grace, that of the one Man, Jesus Christ, for the many become available in abundance. [16]And not as by means of one who sinned [is] the gift; for, on the one hand, judgment [was] from one [transgression] unto condemnation; but, on the other hand, the free gift [was] from many transgressions unto justification. [17]For if [1st] by the transgression of the one, death reigned by means of the one, how much more rather will the ones receiving the abundance of grace and the gift of righteousness reign in life by means of One, Jesus Christ. [18]Consequently therefore, as by means of one transgression [the judgment came] unto all mankind for condemnation, in the same manner also by means of one righteous act [the gift came] unto all mankind for a justification [characterized by] life. [19]For just as by means of the disobedience of the one man, the many were put down [on the books] as sinners, in the same manner also by means of the obedience of the One, the many will be put down [as] righteous. [20]But law entered in alongside in order that the transgression might become greater; but where sin became greater, grace became present in greater abundance; [21]in order that, just as sin reigned

by death, in the same manner also grace might reign by means of righteousness unto eternal life by means of Jesus Christ, our Lord.

ROMANS 6

6:1-11   SANCTIFICATION: Freedom from living a life of sin

[1]What, therefore, shall we say? Shall we continue remaining in sin in order that grace may become greater? [2]May it not be so! Since we indeed died to sin, how shall we any longer continue living in it? [3]Or are you ignorant that as many of us as were baptized into Christ Jesus into His death were baptized? [4]We were buried together, therefore, with Him by means of baptism unto [His] death in order that, just as Christ was raised from the dead by means of the glory of the Father, so also we ourselves in newness of life might walk. [5]For if we have become planted together in the likeness of His death, yet also [in the likeness] of (His) resurrection we shall be; [6]Because we are knowing this, that our old man was crucified together with (Him) in order that the body of sin might be put out of business, in order that we might no longer continue being a bond servant to sin; [7]for the one who has died has been freed from sin. [8]But if we died together with Christ, we are believing that we also shall live together with Him, [9]because we know that Christ, because He has been raised from the dead, no longer is going to die, death no longer is lording it over Him. [10]For [the death] which He died, to sin He died once for all; but [the life] which He is living, he continues living to God. [11]So also you yourselves, continue reckoning yourselves being dead indeed to sin but living to God in Christ Jesus.

6:12-14

[12]Therefore stop letting sin reign in your [pl] mortal body in order that you should continue obeying its desires, [13]and stop presenting your [pl] members [as] weapons of

184

unrighteousness to sin, but present yourselves to God as if living from [the] dead and your [pl] members [as] weapons of righteousness to God, [14]for sin will not lord it over you [pl]; for you [pl] are not under law but under grace.

6:15-23 SANCTIFICATION: Freedom from committing occasional acts of sin

[15]What therefore? Shall we commit an act of sin because we are not under law but under grace? May it not be so! [16]You [pl] know, do you [pl] not, that to whom you [pl] continue presenting yourselves [as] bond servants unto obedience, [his] bond servants you are whom you continue obeying, whether of sin unto death or of obedience unto righteousness? [17]But thanks [be] to God that you used to be bond servants of sin, but you [pl] obeyed from [the] heart the pattern of teaching unto which you [pl] were delivered; [18]and because you [pl] were made free from sin, you [pl] became bond servants to righteousness. [19]I am speaking humanly because of the weakness of your [pl] flesh. For just as you [pl] presented your [pl] members subject to uncleanness and lawlessness for lawlessness, even so now present your [pl] members subject to righteousness for holiness. [20]For when you [pl] used to be bond servants of sin, you [pl] were free with reference to righteousness. [21]Therefore, what fruit did you used to have then [in the things] of which you are now being ashamed? For the end of those things is death. [22]But now, because you [pl] have become free from sin and have become bond servants to God, you [pl] are continuing to have your [pl] fruit unto holiness, and the end, eternal life. [23]For the wages of sin is death, but the free gift of God is life eternal in Christ Jesus, our Lord.

ROMANS 7

7:1-6   SANCTIFICATION: Freedom from law as a legalistic means to holiness

[1]Or are you continuing to be ignorant, brothers, (for I am speaking to ones who are knowing law) that the law lords it over man for as long a time as he is living? [2]For the married woman has been bound by law to her husband while he is living; but if her husband dies, she has been discharged from the law relative to her husband. [3]So then, while her husband is living, an adulteress she will be called, if she becomes another man's (wife); but if her husband dies, she is free from the law so that she is not an adulteress, although she becomes another man's [wife]. [4]So then, my brothers, you yourselves also were made dead to the law by means of the body of Christ, in order that you might become another's [wife], the One who was raised from the dead, in order that we might produce fruit for God. [5]For when we were in the flesh, the passions of sins, those which were by means of the law, kept on working in our members in order to produce fruit for death, [6]But now we have become discharged from the law, because we died [to that] by which we were being bound, so that we continue being bond servants in newness of spirit and not in oldness of letter.

7:7-12   SANCTIFICATION: The conflict between the law and indwelling sin in our bodily members

[7]What, therefore, shall we say? Is the law sin? May it not be so! But sin I did not know except by means of law. For I had not known about coveting except the law kept saying, "You [s] shall not covet"; [8]but having taken [the] opportunity, sin by means of the commandment produced in me all [manner of] coveting; for apart from law, sin is dead. [9]But I myself was living apart from law then; but, after the commandment came, sin came to life, and I myself died; [10]and the commandment which was

186

[to be] unto life, this was found by me [to be] unto death; ¹¹for sin having taken [the] opportunity by means of the commandment deceived me and by means of it killed [me]. ¹²So then, the law is indeed holy, and the commandment is holy and righteous and good.

7:13-25

¹³Did, therefore, that which is good become death for me? May it not be so! But sin [has become death for me], in order that it may appear sin, continuing to work death in me by means of that which is good, in order that sin by means of the commandment may become exceedingly sinful. ¹⁴For we know that the law is spiritual; but I myself am carnal, (I) who have been sold under sin. ¹⁵For what I continue doing, I am not [really] knowing; for not what I am desiring, this am I practicing; but what I am hating, this I am practicing. ¹⁶But if [1st] what I am not desiring, this I am practicing, I am consenting to the law that it is good. ¹⁷But now no longer am I myself doing it but [it is] sin which is dwelling in me. ¹⁸For I know that [there is] not dwelling in me, that is in my flesh, [any] good thing; for to be desiring continues to be present with me, but to continue doing the good is not: ¹⁹for not good which I am desiring am I practicing, but evil which I am not desiring, this I am practicing. ²⁰But if [1st] what I myself am not desiring, this I myself am practicing, no longer am I myself doing it but sin which is dwelling in me. ²¹I am finding then the principle in me, the one who is desiring to be practicing good, that in me evil is continually present; ²²for I continue taking delight in the law of God with respect to the inner man, ²³but I continue seeing another law among my members which is continuing to war with the law of my mind and which is continually making me a prisoner to the law of sin which is among my members. ²⁴I am a miserable man; who will deliver me from the body of this death? ²⁵But thanks be to God, [deliverance is] through Jesus Christ, our Lord. So then, on the one hand, I myself with my mind am continuing to serve [the] law of God, but, on the other hand, with my flesh [the] law of sin.

ROMANS 8

8:1-11   SANCTIFICATION: The blessings of the Spirit-led life

[1]There is, therefore, now no condemnation to those who are in Christ Jesus. [2]For the law of the Spirit of life in Christ Jesus has freed you [s] from the law of sin and death. [3]As for that which was impossible for the law because it was being weakened by means of the flesh, God, who sent His own Son in the likeness of flesh of sin and for a sin offering, condemned sin the flesh, [4]in order that the righteous requirement of the law might be fulfilled in us who are not continuing to walk according to the flesh but according to the Spirit. [5]For those who are according to the flesh continue setting their minds on the things of the flesh, but those who are according to the Spirit [continue setting their minds] on the things of the Spirit. [6]For the manner of thinking belonging to the flesh is death, but the manner of thinking belonging to the Spirit is life and peace. [7]Therefore, the manner of thinking belonging to the flesh is hostile toward God; for to the law of God it is not subjecting itself for neither is it able [to be subjecting.] [8]But those who are in the flesh are not being able to please God. [9]But you, yourselves, are not in [the] flesh but in [the] Spirit, if [1st] indeed [the] Spirit of God is dwelling you. But if [1st] anyone is not possessing [the] Spirit of Christ, this one is not His. [10]But if [1st] Christ is in you [pl], on the one hand, your body is dead because of sin, but, on the other hand, your spirit is life because of righteousness. [11]And if [1st] the Spirit of the One who raised Jesus from [the] dead is dwelling in you [pl], the One who raised Christ Jesus from [the] dead will also quicken your [pl] mortal bodies by means of His Spirit who continues dwelling in you [pl].

8:12-17

[12]So then, brothers, we are debtors, not to the flesh in order to continue living according to [the] flesh; [13]for if [1st] according to [the] flesh you continue living, you [pl] are about to be dying; but if [1st] by [the] Spirit, the practices

188

of the body you [pl] continue putting to death, you [pl] will live. ¹⁴For as many as are continuing to be led by [the] Spirit of God, these are sons of God. ¹⁵For you [pl] did not receive again [the] spirit of bondage unto fear, but you [pl] received [the] Spirit of adoption, by whom we continue crying out, "Abba, Father." ¹⁶(And) the Spirit Himself continues bearing witness together with our spirit that we are children of God. ¹⁷And since [we are] children, [we are] also heirs, on the one hand, heirs of God, and, on the other hand, fellow heirs together with Christ, if [1st] indeed we continue suffering together with Him that we may also be glorified together with Him.

8:18-25

¹⁸For I am reckoning that the sufferings of the present season are not worthy [to be compared] with the coming glory to be revealed unto us. ¹⁹For the eager expectation of the creation is waiting eagerly for the revelation of the sons of God. ²⁰For the creation was subjected to frustration, not willingly but because of the One who subjected [it], on the basis of hope ²¹because the creation itself also will be freed from the bondage of the corruption unto the freedom of the glory of the children of God. ²²For we know that all the creation continues groaning together and travailing together until the present, ²³and not only [this], but we ourselves also, who continue having the first-fruits of the Spirit, even we, ourselves, in ourselves are groaning, while we are waiting for the adoption, the redemption of our body. ²⁴For hope we were saved; but hope which is being seen is not hope; for, who continues hoping for what he is seeing; ²⁵But if for what we are not seeing we continue hoping for, [then] by means of endurance we continue waiting [for it].

8:26-30

²⁶And likewise also the Spirit continues helping [us] together in our weakness; for we do not know for what we should pray as is proper, but the Spirit Himself continues interceding on our behalf with indescribable groanings;

²⁷and the One who continually searches the hearts knows what the Spirit's manner of thinking is, because according to [the will of] God He continues making intercession on behalf of the saints. ²⁸And we know that, for those who are continuing to love God, all things He continues working together for good, for those who are according to [His] purpose being called. ²⁹Because those whom He foreknew, He also foreordained [to be] conformed together to the image of His Son, in order that He might be firstborn among many brothers; ³⁰and those whom He foreordained, these also He called; and those whom He called, these also He justified; and those whom He justified, these He also glorified.

8:31-39

³¹What then shall we say to these things? Since God is on our side, who [is] against us? ³²He, who indeed His own Son did not spare but on behalf of us all delivered Him up, how will He not together with Him all things freely offer us? ³³Who will bring a charge against [the] elect of God? He who is justifying is God. ³⁴Who is the One condemning? [It is] Christ Jesus, who died, but more, who was raised, who is also at [the] right hand of God, who is also interceding on behalf of us. ³⁵Who will separate us from Christ's love? [Will] tribulation or distress or persecution or famine or lack of clothing or peril or sword? ³⁶Even as it stands written,

> On account of you [s], we continue being put to death all the day;
> We were reckoned as sheep for butchering.

³⁷But in all these things we continue being more than [merely] conquering by means of the One who loved us. ³⁸For I stand persuaded that neither death nor life nor angels nor rulers nor things present nor things future nor powers ³⁹nor height nor depth nor any other created thing will be able to separate us from God's love, which is in Christ Jesus, our Lord.

190

CHAPTERS 9-11 RENUNCIATION BUT ULTIMATE SALVATION

ROMANS 9

9:1-5   Israel's renunciation of justification by faith and God's sovereignty in relation to it (9:1-29)

[1]I am speaking truth in Christ, I am not lying, because my conscience is bearing witness to me by the Holy Spirit, [2]that [there] is for me great grief and unceasing sorrow in my heart. [3]For I could wish that I myself would be accursed from Christ on behalf of my brothers, my kinsmen according to [the] flesh, [4]who are Israelites, whose are the adoption and the glory and the covenants and the giving of the law and the service and the promises, [5]whose are the fathers, and from whom [is] the Christ according to the flesh, God, the One being over all things blessed forever. Amen

9:6-13

[6]But by no means has the word of God failed. For [as for] all those from Israel, these are not Israel, [7]neither because they are seed of Abraham, [are they] all children, but "in Isaac will your [s] seed be called." [8]That is, [as for] the children of the flesh, these are not children of God, but the children of the promise are being reckoned for seed. [9]For the word of promise is this, "At this season I shall come and [there] will be a son for Sarah." [10]And not only [this], but also Rebecca, while by one [man] she was conceiving, Isaac, our father-- [11]([for the children], although they were not yet born nor had done anything good or foolish, in order that the purpose of God might continue remaining according to [the principle] of election, not by works, but by the One calling) -- [12]it was said to her, "The elder will serve the younger"; [13]even as it stands written, "Jacob I loved, but Esau I hated."

9:14-18

¹⁴What then shall we say? [There] is no unrighteousness with God, is there? May it not be so! ¹⁵For to Moses, He is saying, "I will have mercy on whomever I am having mercy, and I will have compassion on whomever I am having compassion." ¹⁶So then [it is] not of the one willing nor of the one running but of the One showing mercy, [viz.], God. ¹⁷For the Scripture is saying to Pharaoh, "For this very [purpose] I raised you [s] up, in order that I might show forth in you [s] My power, and in order that My name might be spread abroad in all the land." ¹⁸So then He is having mercy on whom He is willing, and whom He is willing He is hardening.

9:19-29

¹⁹You [s] will say to me then, "Why is He still finding fault? For who has resisted His will?" ²⁰O man, on the contrary, who are you [s], the one answering back to God? The thing formed will not say to the one who has formed it, "Why did you [s] make me this way," will it? ²¹The potter is having authority over the clay, does he not, to make out of the same lump, this one a vessel for honor and that one [a vessel] for dishonor? ²²But, [what will you say then] if God, although He was desiring to show forth wrath and to make known His power, endured with much longsuffering vessels [deserving] of wrath which prepared themselves for destruction, ²³and [that] in order that He might make known the riches of His glory upon vessels [deserving] of mercy, which He prepared beforehand for glory, ²⁴even us whom He called not only from Jews but also from Gentiles? ²⁵As also in Hosea He is saying,

> I will call that which is not my people "my people,"
> And her who is not beloved "beloved."
> ²⁶And it will be in the place where it was said to them,
> "You yourselves are not my people,"
> There they will be called sons of [the] living God.

²⁷And Isaiah is crying on behalf of Israel:

> If the number of the sons of Israel should be as the sand of the sea, the remnant (only) will be saved.
>
> ²⁸For [His] word [the] Lord will perform upon the earth, accomplishing it and executing it quickly.

²⁹And, just as Isaiah has foretold,

> Except [the] Lord of Hosts had left behind a seed for us, As Sodom we would have become and we would have become like Gomorrah.

9:30-33 Israel's renunciation of justification by faith by her own free will (9:30-10:21)

³⁰What then shall we say? [It is this], that [the] Gentiles, who were not pursuing righteousness, overtook righteousness, but a righteousness which is by faith; ³¹and Israel, who was pursuing a law [which was to produce] righteousness did not reach [that] law. ³²Because of what? Because [they pursued] not by faith but, as it were, by works; for they stumbled over the stone of stumbling, ³³even as it stands written:

> Behold, I am going to lay in Zion a stone of stumbling and a rock of offense; But everyone continuing to believe on Him will not be disappointed.

ROMANS 10

10:1-13

¹Brothers, really the good will of my heart and [my] supplication to God on behalf of them is for [their] salvation. ²For I continue bearing witness with reference to them that they continue to have a zeal for God, but not according to knowledge; ³for, because they were ignorant of the righteousness from God and because they were seeking

193

their own [righteousness] to establish, to the righteousness from God they were not subjected. ⁴For Christ is the termination of law for righteousness to everyone who is believing. ⁵For Moses writes that the man who has done the righteousness which is out of law will live by it; ⁶but the righteousness which is out of faith is speaking in this manner: Do not say in your [s] heart, "Who will go up into the heaven?" that is in order to bring Christ down; ⁷or "Who will descend into the abyss?" that is, in order to bring Christ up from the dead. ⁸But what is it saying? "The spoken word is near you [s], in your [s] mouth and in your [s] heart, that is, the spoken word concerning faith which we are preaching, ⁹[viz.] that if [3rd] you [s] confess with your [s] mouth Jesus [to be] Lord and you [s] believe with your [s] heart that God raised Him from the dead, you [s] will be saved; ¹⁰for with [the] heart one continues believing for righteousness and with [the] mouth confession is being made for salvation." ¹¹For the Scripture is saying "Everyone who is believing on Him will not be disappointed." ¹²For there is no distinction between Jew and Greek. For the same Lord is [Lord] of all, He who is being rich toward all the ones who continue calling upon Him; ¹³for everyone who calls upon the name of the Lord will be saved.

10:14-21

¹⁴How then will they call [on Him] in whom they have not believed? And how shall they believe [on Him] of whom they have not heard? And how shall they hear without [someone] preaching? ¹⁵And how shall they preach if [3rd] they are not sent forth? Even as it stands written, "How beautiful are the feet of those who are preaching the gospel of good things." ¹⁶But not all hearkened to the gospel. For Isaiah is saying, "Lord who believed our report?" ¹⁷So then faith is from hearing, and hearing is by means of the spoken word concerning Christ. ¹⁸But I am saying they all have heard, have they not? Indeed,

> Into all the earth their sound went out,
> And unto the ends of the inhabited earth their
> spoken words.

194

¹⁹But I am saying, Israel knew, did she not? First of all, Moses is saying,

> I myself will make you jealous with [that which is] not a nation,
> And with a senseless nation I will make you angry.

²⁰And Isaiah is being bold and is saying,

> I was found by those who were not seeking me,
> I became manifest to those who were not inquiring after me.

²¹But to Israel, he is saying "During the whole day, I stretched out my hands to a people who continue being disobedient and obstinate."

ROMANS 11

Israel's renunciation of justification by faith: not total or permanent as illustrated by the olive tree analogy (chapter 11)

11:1-10

¹I am saying, therefore, "God did not reject His people, did He?" May it not be so! For I myself also am an Israelite, out from the seed of Abraham, from the tribe of Benjamin. ²God did not reject His people whom he foreknew. Or, you [pl] know, do you not, in [the passage referring to] Elijah, what the Scripture is saying, how he continues pleading to God against Israel? ³"Lord, your [s] prophets they killed, your [s] altars they destroyed, and I myself have been left alone and they continue seeking my life." ⁴But what does the divine answer say to him? "I have kept for Myself seven thousand men who did not bow [the] knee to Baal." ⁵In this manner, therefore, also at the present time a remnant according to the election of grace has come into being; ⁶but since it is by grace, it is no longer by works;

for otherwise grace becomes no longer grace. [7]What then? That for which Israel is seeking, this she did not obtain, but the election obtained [it]; but the remaining ones were hardened; [8]just as it stands written,

> God gave to them a spirit of [spiritual] insensibility, eyes in order that they might stop seeing and ears in order that they might stop hearing, until this very day.

[9]And David is saying,

> Let their table become a snare and a trap
> and a stumbling block and a recompense to them;
> [10]Let their eyes be darkened in order that they may stop seeing, and bow down their back continually.

11:11-16

[11]I am saying, therefore, "They did not stumble in order that they might fall [into ruin], did they?" May it not be so! But by their transgression, salvation [came] to the Gentiles in order that it might make them jealous. [12]But if [1st] their transgression is riches for the world and their defeat is riches for the Gentiles, how much more [will be] their completed number. [13]But I am speaking to you [pl], the Gentiles. Because I myself am, therefore, an apostle of the Gentiles, my ministry I am glorifying, [14]if [1st] somehow I may make my flesh, [i.e., my fellow countrymen], jealous and may save some of them. [15]For if [1st] the casting away of them is the reconciliation of the world, what will the acceptance [of them by God] be except life from the dead? [16]And if [1st] the first fruits are holy, [so] also is the lump; and if [1st] the root is holy, [so] also are the branches.

11:17-24

[17]But if [1st] certain ones of the branches were broken off, and you [s] yourself, although you [s] belonged to a wild olive tree, were grafted in among them and became a fellow-partaker [with them] of the root of the fatness of

the olive tree, ¹⁸stop boasting over the branches; but if [1st] you [s] are boasting, you [s] yourself are not bearing the root but the root [is bearing] you [s]. ¹⁹Therefore, you [s] will say, "Branches were broken off in order that I myself might be grafted in." ²⁰Well, because of unbelief they were broken off, but you [s] yourself have come to stand because of faith. Stop being proud, but continue fearing; ²¹for if [1st] God the natural branches did not spare, neither will He spare you [s]. ²²Behold, therefore, the goodness and the severity of God; on the one hand, toward those who have fallen, severity, but toward you [s], the goodness of God, if [3rd] you [s] continue on remaining in His goodness; otherwise, you yourself also will be cut out. ²³And those also, if [3rd] they do not continue remaining in unbelief, will be grafted in; for God is able to graft them in again. ²⁴For if [1st] you [s] yourself were cut out of that which was naturally a wild olive tree, and, contrary to nature, were grafted into a cultivated olive tree, how much more rather will these which are the natural [branches] be grafted back into their own olive tree?

11:25-32

²⁵For I am not desiring you [pl] to continue being ignorant, brothers, with reference to this mystery, lest you [pl] continue being wise in yourselves, that a hardening in part has come to pass for Israel until the full number of the Gentiles enter; ²⁶and in like manner all Israel will be saved, even as it stands written,

> The Deliverer will come out of Zion;
> He will take away ungodliness from Jacob.
> ²⁷And this is for them the covenant from Me,
> Whenever I shall take away their sins.

²⁸On the one hand, according to the gospel, [they are] enemies on account of you [pl]; but, on the other hand, according to the election, [they are] beloved on account of the fathers. ²⁹For irrevocable [i.e. lit. without regret] are the free gifts and the calling of God. ³⁰For just as you yourselves formerly were disobedient to God, but now have

been shown mercy because of the disobedience of these, [31]so also have these now been disobedient in order that by the [same] mercy [shown to] you they themselves also now may be shown mercy. [32]For God has imprisoned them all unto disobedience in order that upon all He might have mercy.

11:33-36

> [33]O, the depth of the riches and wisdom and knowledge of God; how unsearchable are His decrees and how incomprehensible are His ways! [34]For who has known [the] mind of [the] Lord? Or who has become His counselor? [35]Or who gave to Him first, and it will be paid back to Him?

[36]Because out from Him, and by means of Him, and for Him are all things; to Him be the glory forever. Amen.

CONVERSATION: The totally presented Christian's walk in various relationships (12:1-15:5)

ROMANS 12

12:1-2   Introductory Pleas

[1]I am beseeching you [pl], therefore, brothers, in view of the mercies of God, to present your [pl] bodies [as] a sacrifice, [which is] living, holy, well-pleasing to God, your [pl] reasonable service; [2]and stop conforming yourselves to this age but continue permitting yourselves to be transformed by the renewing of [your] mind, in order that you [pl] may continue discovering what the will of God is, that [will] which is good and well-pleasing and perfect.

12:3-8   Our relationship to our PARTNERS in the church

198

³For I am saying, by means of the grace which has been given to me, to everyone who is among you [pl] not to be thinking more highly [of himself] than what he ought to be thinking; but to continue thinking soberly, as to each one God has assigned a measure of faith. ⁴For just as in one body, we customarily have many members but all the members are not having the same function, ⁵so we, the many, are one body in Christ and everyone members one of another. ⁶And because [we are] having free gifts [which are] different according to the grace which has been given to us--whether prophecy, [let us prophesy] according to the proportion of [our] faith; ⁷or ministry, [let us give ourselves] to [our] ministry; or the one teaching, to his teaching; ⁸or the one exhorting, to his exhortation; [as for] that one who is sharing with [someone], [let him do it] with sincerity; [as for] that one who is superintending, [let him do it] with diligence; [as for] that one who is showing mercy, [let him do it] with gladness.

12:9-13   Our relationship to our PURSUIT of Christ's work

⁹[Let] love be without hypocrisy. Continue abhorring that which is evil; continue cleaving to that which is good. ¹⁰With brotherly love, [be] loving tenderly; with reference to honor, continue regarding one another more highly [than oneself]; ¹¹in diligence, not being lazy; in spirit being zealous; continuing to serve the Lord; ¹²in hope continuing to rejoice; in tribulation continuing to endure, in prayer continuing to persevere; ¹³in the needs of the saints continuing to become a partner; [and] hospitality continuing to pursue.

12:14-21   Our relationship to PEOPLE in general and PERSECUTORS in particular

¹⁴Continue speaking well of those who are persecuting; continue speaking well and stop cursing. ¹⁵Continue rejoicing with ones who are rejoicing; continue weeping with ones who are weeping. ¹⁶The same thing

with reference to one another continue thinking,
not continuing to think high things but continually
allowing yourselves to be occupied with lowly things.
Stop becoming wise among yourselves, [i.e., in your own
estimation].

[17]Stop paying back to anyone evil for evil; continue
taking thought for things that are good in the sight of all
mankind; [18]if it is possible, as far as you [are concerned],
with all mankind continue living at peace; [19]stop avenging
yourselves, beloved, but make room for the wrath [of God],
for it stands written,

> To me vengeance belongs, I myself will pay back, the
> Lord is saying.

[20]But if [3rd] your [s] enemy is hungering, continue
feeding him; if [3rd] he is thirsting, continue giving him
[something] to drink; for by doing this coals of fire [s] you
will heap upon his head. [21]Stop being overcome by evil
[done to you], but continually overcome by goodness that
evil.

ROMANS 13

13:1-7   **Our relationship to the POWERS THAT BE**

[1]Let every soul to the authorities who are over him
continue subjecting himself; for there is no authority
except by God and those which by God stand appointed.
[2]So then he who continues resisting the authority, against
the ordinance of God he has set himself; and those
who have set themselves against [this] will receive for
themselves [penal] judgment. [3]For those who are ruling are
not a cause for fear to the good work but to the evil. You [s]
do not want to continue fearing the authority, do you [s]?
[Then] goodness continue practicing, and you [s] will have
praise from it [i.e., the authority]; [4]for a minister of God

200

it is for you [s] for good. But if [3rd] you continue doing that which is evil, keep on fearing; for it is not without just cause wearing the sword. For a minister of God it is, a punisher for [the execution of] wrath on the one who is practicing evil. 5Therefore, it is necessary to continue subjecting one's self, not only because of [a fear of] wrath but also because of conscience. 6For because of this also tribute continue paying; for ministers of God they are who are busily engaging [themselves] with this very thing. 7Pay back to all their dues: tribute to the one [entitled to receive] tribute, custom to whom custom, fear to whom fear, and honor to whom honor.

13:8-10   Our relationship to the PRESCRIPTIONS of God

8Do not continue owing anyone anything except to continue loving one another; for the one who is loving the other has fulfilled the law. 9For [as for] this, you [s] shall not commit adultery, you [s] shall not commit murder, you [s] shall not steal, you [s] shall not covet, and if there is any other commandment, in this saying it is customarily summed up, in this, you [s] shall love your [s] neighbor as yourself. 10Love does not work evil for its neighbor; therefore, love is the fulfillment of the law.

13:11-14   Our relationship to the PRESENT PERIOD ("this age")

11And [as for] this also, know the season, that it is already the hour for you [pl] out of deep sleep to arise; for now is our salvation nearer than when we [first] believed. 12The night has advanced [toward the dawn], and the day has come near. Let us, therefore, put away the works of the darkness, and let us put on the weapons of the light. 13As in [the] day decently let us walk, not in revelings and drunkennesses, not in [unlawful] sexual intercourses and acts of shameless immorality, not in strife and envy; 14but put on the Lord Jesus Christ and stop making provision for [fulfilling] the desires of the flesh.

ROMANS 14:1-15:4

14:1-15:4 Our relationship to our PARTNERS in the church (weaker and stronger Christians)

[1]But him who is being weak in the faith continue accepting [into your fellowship], [although] not for the purpose of quarrels over opinions. [2]One continues having faith to eat all things, and he who is being weak continues eating [only] vegetables. [3]Stop letting the one who is eating [the stronger] despise the one who is not eating [the weaker]; and stop letting the one who is not eating [the weaker] condemn the one who is eating [the stronger]; for God has accepted him. [4]Who are you [s] yourself who are condemning another's servant? With reference to his own lord he stands or falls; and he will stand, for the Lord is having power to make him stand. [5]For one regularly esteems one day better than another day, and another esteems every day; [but] let each one continue being fully convinced in his own mind. [6]He who is observing the day [as sacred] is customarily observing it for the Lord, and he who is eating [the stronger] is customarily eating for the Lord, for he is giving thanks to God; and he who is not eating [the weaker] is not eating to the Lord, and [yet] he is giving thanks to God. [7]For no one of us for himself is living, and no one for himself is dying; [8]for if [3rd] we go on living, for the Lord we continue living; and if [3rd] we are dying, for the Lord we are dying. Therefore, whether we are living or whether we are dying, we are the Lord's. [9]For because of this, Christ died and lived, in order that over both the dead and the living He might rule. [10]But [as for] you [s] yourself, why are you [s] yourself [the weaker] condemning your [s] brother? Or, [as for] you [s] yourself [the stronger] also, why are your despising your [s] brother? For we all shall stand before the judgment seat of God. [11]For it stands written,

[As] I myself am living, says the Lord, to Me every knee will bow,
And every tongue will give praise to God.

[12]So then each one of us concerning himself an account will give to God.

14:13-20

[13]Therefore, let us stop condemning one another any longer; but determine this thing rather, to stop giving an occasion for stumbling to the brother or a temptation to sin. [14]I know and stand persuaded in the Lord Jesus that nothing [amoral] is unclean by itself, except to the one continuing to regard something to be unclean; to that one [it is] unclean. [15]For if because of food your [s] brother is being caused grief, according to love you [s] are no longer walking. With your [s] food, stop destroying that one on behalf of whom Christ died. [16]Therefore, stop letting your [pl] goodness be evil spoken of. [17]For the kingdom of God is not eating and drinking but righteousness and peace and joy in [the] Holy Spirit. [18]For he who continues serving Christ in this [matter] is well-pleasing to God and approved by mankind. [19]So then, the things pertaining to peace let us continue pursuing, and the things pertaining to edification for one another.

14:21-23

[20]Stop tearing down because of food the work of God. All things [amoral] are indeed pure, but it is evil for the man who is eating with offense. [21]It is good not to eat meat or to drink wine or [to do anything] at which your [s] brother is going to take offense. [22][As for] you [s] yourself, the faith which you [s] are holding, continue holding in relation to yourself, [i.e., privately,] before God. Blessed is he who is not condemning himself for that which he is approving; [23]and he who is doubting, if he eats, stands condemned because [his eating] is not out of faith; and everything which is not out of faith is sin.

15:1-4

[1]And we, ourselves, the strong ones, ought to continue bearing up the weaknesses of those without strength and to stop pleasing ourselves. [2]Let each one of us continue striving to please [his] neighbor for [his] good for [his] edification. [3]For even Christ did not please Himself; but just as it stands written, "The insults of those heaping insults on you [s] fell upon me." [4]For as many things as were written beforehand for our instruction were written, in order that, by means of endurance and by means of the consolation from the Scriptures, we might continue having hope.

ROMANS 15:5-16:27

15:5-16:27   TERMINATION

15:5-13   Paul's encouragement to unity

[5]And may the God of endurance and of consolation grant you [pl] to continue agreeing with one another according to Christ Jesus, [6]in order that with one accord with one mouth you may continue glorifying the God and Father of our Lord Jesus Christ.

[7]Wherefore continue accepting one another [into your fellowship], just as also Christ accepted us for [the advancement of] the glory of God. [8]For I am saying that Christ has become a minister of the circumcision on behalf of [the] truth of God, in order that He might confirm the promises belonging to the fathers [9]and that the Gentiles on behalf of [His] mercy might glorify God even as it stands written,

> Because of this I shall praise you [s] among the Gentiles and to your [s] name I shall sing.

[10]And again it is saying,

204

Rejoice, O Gentiles, with His people.

[11]And again,

> Continue praising the Lord, all you [pl] Gentiles,
> And let all the peoples praise Him.

[12]And again Isaiah is saying,

> The root of Jesse will exist,
> And He who is rising up to be ruling over [the]
> Gentiles;
> On Him will [the] Gentiles hope.

[13]And may the God of hope fill you with all joy and peace while you are believing, in order that that you may continue increasing in hope by [the] power of the Holy Spirit.

15:14-21   Paul's explanation of his task

[14]And I myself also stand persuaded concerning you [pl], my brothers, that you yourselves also are full of goodness, having been filled with all knowledge, being able also to continue admonishing one another. [15]But the more boldly I have written to you [pl] in part, as one reminding you [pl] again because of the grace which has been given to me from God, [16]in order that I may be a minister of Christ Jesus unto the Gentiles, continuing to serve the gospel of God as a priest, in order that the offering of the Gentiles may become acceptable because it has been sanctified by [the] Holy Spirit. [17]Therefore, I am having [my] boast in Christ Jesus in reference to the things pertaining to God; [18]for I will not dare to speak of any thing [except] those which Christ accomplished by means of me for [the] obedience of [the] Gentiles, by word and deed, [19]by [the] power of signs and wonders, by [the] power of [the] Spirit; so that I have from Jerusalem and roundabout to Illyricum caused the gospel of Christ to be fully known. [20]And thus [I am] earnestly striving to continue preaching the gospel

where Christ has not been named, lest upon another's foundation I continue building; [21]but just as it stands written,

> They will see to whom it was not announced concerning Him,
> And the ones who have not heard will understand.

15:22-29   Paul's explanation of his personal plans

[22]Wherefore also I was repeatedly hindered these many times from coming to you [pl] [23]but now, because I am no longer having place in these regions and because I have been having a longing to come to you [pl] for many years, [24]as soon I am going to Spain, [I shall come]. For I am hoping, while I am passing by, to see you [pl] and by you [pl] to be helped on my journey there, if from you [pl] [i.e., from your company] first of all in some measure I may be satisfied; [25]but now I am going to Jerusalem in order to be ministering to the saints; [26]for Macedonia and Achaia resolved a certain contribution to make for the poor ones of the saints which are in Jerusalem. [27]For they resolved and they are their debtors; for if [1st] in their spiritual things the Gentiles fellowshipped, they ought also in fleshly things to minister to them. [28]Therefore, after I have accomplished this, and after I have sealed for them this fruit, I shall go away through you [pl] [i.e., through your city], to Spain; [29]and I know that, while I am coming to you [pl], in the fullness of the blessing of Christ I shall come.

15:30-33   Paul's exhortation to prayer for his mission

[30]But I am beseeching you [pl], brothers, by means of our Lord Jesus Christ and by means of the love of the Spirit, to strive together with me in [your] prayers on behalf of me to God [31]in order that I may be delivered from those who are not believing in Judea and [in order that] my ministry for Jerusalem may become acceptable to the saints, [32]in order

that, with joy having come to you [pl] through the will of God, I may find rest in company with you [pl]. [33]May the God of peace [be] with all of you [pl]. Amen.

ROMANS 16

16:1-16   Paul's expression of greetings

[1]And I am commending to you Phoebe, our sister, who is also a servant of the church which is in Cenchrea, [2]in order that you may welcome her in [the] Lord worthily of the saints and you may assist her in whatever matter she may be having need of you [pl], for she herself also a helper of many became and of me myself [also].

[3]Greet Priscilla and Aquila, my fellow-workers in Christ Jesus, [4]who on behalf of my life their own necks [s] laid down for whom not only I myself am giving thanks but also all the churches of the Gentiles, [5]and [greet] the church in their house. Greet Epaenetus, my beloved, who is the first fruits of Asia for Christ. [6]Greet Mary, who labored much for you [pl]. [7]Greet Andronicus and Junias, my fellow-countrymen and fellow-prisoners, who are of note among the apostles, who also before me have become in Christ. [8]Greet Ampliatus, my beloved, in [the] Lord. [9]Greet Urbanus, our fellow-worker in Christ, and Stachys, my beloved. [10]Greet Apelles, the approved one in Christ. Greet those [of the household] of Aristobulus. [11]Greet Herodion, my kinsman. Greet those [of the household] of Narcissus, who are being in the Lord. Greet Tryphaena and Tryphosa, who have labored in [the] Lord. [12]Greet Persis, the beloved, who labored much in [the] Lord. [13]Greet Rufus, the elect one in [the] Lord, and his mother and mine. [14]Greet Asyncritus, Phlegon, Hermes, Patrobas, Hermas, and the brothers together with them. [15]Greet Philologus and Julia, Nereus and his sister, and Olympas and all the saints together with them. [16]Greet one another with a holy kiss. All the churches of Christ continue to greet you.

16:17-20a   Paul's evaluation of closing warnings

[17]I continue begging you, brothers, to continue looking out for those causing divisions and occasions for stumbling contrary to the teaching which you yourselves learned, and continue turning away from them; [18]for such ones are not serving our Lord Jesus Christ but their own belly, and by means of smooth and fair speech they are deceiving the hearts of the innocent. [19]For your [pl] obedience has come to [the knowledge of] all; over you, therefore, I continue rejoicing, but I continue desiring you to be wise with reference to goodness and innocent with reference to evil. [20a]And the God of peace will crush Satan under your [pl] feet shortly.

16:20b   Paul's extending another benediction

[20b]May the grace of our Lord Jesus [be] with you [pl].

16:21-23   Paul's expression of greetings from his fellow-workers

[21]Timothy, my fellow-worker, is greeting you, and Lucius and Jason and Sosipater, my fellow-countrymen. [22]I myself, Tertius, who has written the epistle, am greeting you in [the] Lord. [23]Gaius, my host and [host] of the whole church, is greeting you. Erastus, the treasurer of the city, is greeting you, and Quartos, the brother. (Verse 24 is missing in our best Greek manuscripts.)

16:25-27   Paul's ending of the epistle

[25]Now to the One who is being able to establish you according to my gospel and the message concerning Jesus Christ, according to [the] revelation of [the] mystery which for eternal times has been concealed [26]but now which has been manifested and which by means of [the] prophetic writings according to the commandment of the eternal God, has been made known for the obedience [stemming]

from faith among all the Gentiles, [27]to the only wise God, by means of Jesus Christ, be the glory unto the ages of the ages. Amen.

Review Assignments Over the Epistle to the Romans

Introduction
1. Read the entire epistle at one sitting.
2. Summarize the contents of each chapter in a phrase or two. Using only main points, work out an outline of the epistle. (Do not use any sources other than the New Testament and any notes you may have jotted down in your reading of the epistle. Watch for the words righteous, righteousness, sin, and law.)

Romans 1:1-7
1. List all of the things which Paul tells about himself in these verses; about Christ; about the Roman Christians; and about the Gospel.
2. What is an apostle? How does an apostle differ from a disciple?
3. List some reasons why this introduction is necessary to the whole Roman epistle.
4. Is sainthood an achievement or a gift? Explain this answer. Be sure to use Romans 1:1-7 for whatever help they may be in answering this question.

Romans 1:8-17
1. List the various things Paul says concerning himself in these verses and then what he says concerning the Gospel.
2. List the phrases in these verses which show Paul's sincere interest in the Roman Christians and their church. (Do not copy entire verses.)
3. Memorize the key verses of Romans 1:16-17.
4. What is meant by "the righteous ones by faith shall live" as Paul uses the expression here?

Romans 1:18-32
1. List the various sins of the Gentile world as they are found in these verses. Describe each briefly in a single phrase, telling exactly what it is. (At least 25)
2. Does a man need to hear of Christ to be saved? Give reasons for your answer. If he does, how can a heathen man who never hears of Christ be held inexcusable for his lost condition? See Romans 1:19,20. If he does not need to hear of Christ, then how do you explain such verses as Acts 4:12, Rom. 10:13,14, etc.?

Unto what three things does God give these sinners up in Romans 1:24, 26, 28. Define specifically what each of these items means.

Romans 2:1-16

1. List the various characteristics of divine judgment as seen here. In other words, in what manner is God going to judge mankind? Give a verse reference with each entry.
2. When will the judgment described here occur and what people will it affect? Give reasons for your answer.
3. Briefly summarize in your own words what Paul is saying in 2:12-15.
4. How would you answer someone who said Paul is teaching "justification by obedience to the law" here in Romans 2:10, 13 and is therefore contradicting his teaching of justification by faith which he teaches elsewhere?

Romans 2:17-3:8

1. List the things which Paul says in these verses characterize the Jew. Give the verse reference with each entry.
2. What claim made by the Jew is implicit in the argument beginning with 2:25?
3. How does Paul re-define the principle of circumcision in this section?
4. According to Paul in Romans 2, is it possible to be a "true Jew" today? Give reasons for your answer.
5. Divide a sheet of paper into three columns. Using Romans 3:1-9, in   column one, place the question Paul asks of his readers; in column two,   give the answer which he gives to the question; and in column three, state   the relation of the answer in column two to the question in column one. Be   sure you understand each question, its own answer, and how the answer   relates to the question. (Note: Some of Paul's answers do not seem to fit   their questions. Your job is to show how they do answer the questions asked.) To help you, the five questions for column one are as follows:
    a. What therefore is the advantage of the Jew, or what is the profit of circumcision? (These are really the same question.) 3:1
    b. What if certain ones were not faithful (to their part of the covenant), their unfaithfulness will not render inoperative the faithfulness of God, will it? 3:3

c. But if our unrighteousness continues enhancing the righteousness of God, what shall we say? God, the One who is going to inflict wrath, is not unrighteous, is He? 3:5

   d. But if the truthfulness of God by my lie is made supremely great for His glory, why am I also still being judged as a sinner? 3:7

   e. What therefore? Are we (Jews) in a worse position than they (the Gentiles)? 3:9

Romans 3:9-20

1 Using Romans 3:9-20, list the universal expressions which Paul uses to indicate that everyone is under the condemnation of God and apart from God's grace discussed in Rom. 3:21 and following.

2. According to the quotations Paul uses from the Old Testament, what parts of the body are involved in this sin problem? Is there any significance relative to these particular parts of the body? What is it, if any?

3. What point is Paul emphasizing here in 3:9-20?

4. In your own words briefly, what does it mean "to be justified"?

5. How does 3:9-20 relate to Romans 1:18-3:8? How does it prepare for 3:21-31?

Romans 3:21-31

1. What are the characteristics of the righteousness from God which is presented in 3:21-31? List at least 10 (nouns, please).

2. Define the following expressions: redemption (3:24); propitiation (3:25); sins done aforetime (3:25); this present season (3:26).

3. How can God be just and also the Justifier of sinners like we are? (Compare 3:10.)

4. In what way does this "justification by faith" establish the law, as Paul asserts in 3:31?

5. Define the following terms and discuss briefly their relation to each other:
   justification, righteousness, and imputation. Use all three of them in one sentence.

Romans 4:1-17a

1. Why does Paul introduce Abraham and David at this point? List several possible reasons.

2. What is the relationship between justification and good works as seen in these examples? Between justification and circumcision?
3. What promises is Paul speaking about in Romans 4:13 and following?
4. Read James 2:14-26. How would you answer someone who asserted that Paul, in Romans 4:1 and following contradicts the plain teaching of James 2:21-24 regarding Abraham's justification? List the points you would make.

Romans 4:17b-25
1. Reviewing the life of Abraham in Genesis, list the times of testing for his faith as recorded there. Upon which of these does Paul major in Romans 4:17b-25?
2. What characteristics of faith as a virtue can be seen here in Paul's discussion of Abraham's faith?
3. What is meant by "many nations" in v. 18?
4. In what specific way is chapter 4 related to 3:21-31?

Romans 5:1-11
1. List the blessings of anyone who is justified by faith as seen in these verses. In a phrase, explain what is meant by each one.
2. List the names of Deity used in these verses. What significance is there in the use of the divine names here?
3. In your own words, what is the thought development in verses 7 and 8?
4. What relation does 5:1-11 have with 1:18-3:20? with 3:21-4:25?

Romans 5:12-21
1. Identify and describe four interpretations of the following phrase from 5:12, all sinned.
2. List the individual contrasts between the first Adam and the last Adam, Christ, as seen in Romans 5:12-21.
3. Define the following words: to impute (5:13); figure (5:14); and trespass (5:15 and others).
4. In your own words, discuss the argument of 5:12-21 in a brief paragraph.
5. In what ways do 5:12-21 link up with 5:1-11?
6. How would you answer someone who held to a universalistic doctrine of salvation (that ultimately all will be saved) on the basis of this passage and especially 5:17,19? This doctrine is that all die because all sinned in Adam; likewise all will

be saved and live eternally because of Christ's obedience reckoned to the account of all. (See also I Corinthians 15:21,22.)

7. What is meant by the phrase in 5:20, "And the law came in alongside"?
8. What answer would you give a person who said he did not like Paul's teaching here because he did not like the idea of God's condemning us for someone else's sin, namely Adam's?
9. What is the relationship between 1:18-4:25 and the whole of chapter 5?

Romans 6:1-14

1. How does the problem of 6:1 arise from the discussion of 5:12-21?
2. How does Paul use the analogy of baptism to answer the problem raised in 6:1?
3. What is meant by the following: our old man (6:6) and the body of sin (6:6)?
4. When did the crucifixion of "our old man" take place according to the text?
5. What is the solution to a defeated Christian life according to 6:11-14?
6. How do these verses teach the necessity of a spiritual crisis in the life of most believers subsequent to salvation? What happens at such a crisis?

Romans 6:15-7:6

1. How does the problem of 6:15 grow out of Paul's previous discussion in 6:1-14?
2. What further analogy does Paul introduce to answer the problem raised in 6:15? How does he use it?
3. Define "sanctification."
4. How does the problem of 7:1 grow out of the previous discussion?
5. What is the third analogy used by Paul here to answer this? List the members of the analogy and specify to what each refers in the relationship between the believer and Christ. What is awkward about the analogy as Paul develops it here?
6. What is meant by service in newness of the spirit and not in oldness of the letter?

Romans 7:7-25

1. What declaration in 7:1-6 gives rise to the question in 7:7?
2. Read Romans 7:7-25 five times, listing four or five key words as indicated by their being repeated.

214

3. How does this passage answer the question of 7:7? List the characteristics of the law which Paul gives here. List also the functions which he says it performs.
4. Why does 7:25b follow the declaration of 7:25a?
5. What is the main teaching of this particular section of Romans?
6. How would you relate it to 6:1-7:6?
7. List the points you would make in favor of this experience of Rom. 7:7-25 being that of a Christian, not a non-Christian. Compare Romans 7:14 and I Corinthians 3:1.

Romans 8:1-11
1. What does it mean to be walking according to the Spirit?
2. List the names for Deity used in these verses and indicate which one is emphasized.
3. What is the significance of 8:9 for every Christian? How do you relate the idea of 8:9 to the experience of being filled with the Spirit?
4. Discuss the following statement in the light of these verses: They that are Christ's either have or will have the Spirit.

Romans 8:12-37
1. Using Romans 8:1-37, list all of the ministries of the Holy Spirit for the Christian to be found in Romans 8.
2. List the verbs in 8:29,30 relating to God's action with reference to the believer. Define each. What significance is there in the order in which they appear?
3. What is Paul stressing in 8:37-39? Do these verses teach "eternal security" for a sinning believer, that is, one living according to the flesh. Give reasons for your answer.

Romans 9:1-33
1. How is Romans 9 related to what has preceded it?
2. What does Paul mean by saying in 9:6 that it is not as though the word of God has come to naught? What in the context might make it look as though God's word has come to nothing?
3. What does Paul mean by saying, For they are not all Israel who are of Israel? How is this developed in the following verses? How does this answer the problem posed in 9:6a?
4. Study again Romans 9:6-29 and list all of the phrases or clauses which stress the sovereignty of God in human affairs, together with the reference for each.

Romans 10:1-21

1. List the things which characterize the Jew according to Romans 10:2 and following (nouns, please).
2. Why are the two conditions for salvation stated in 10:9 so difficult for a Jew?
3. Show how each question in 10:14,15 serves to build a climactic argument. Reword these questions to make positive statements out of them.
4. List the results of the preaching of the glad tidings to Israel. To answer this, study Romans 10:16-21.
5. How do we know that the sovereignty of God does not (although it could, since He is omnipotent) violate the free will of man in his living on the earth? In answering this, cite phrases and clauses from Romans 10 which indicate that man has a free will. Give a verse reference with each.

Romans 11:1-36

1. What suggested the question Paul asks in 11:1 and how does Paul answer it?
2. Summarize in single statements the truths which Paul is setting forth in Romans 11:1-12. List these statements in 1,2,3 order.
3. Identify the following from the olive tree analogy here: the root, the natural branches, the wild olive branches, the original branches broken off, the cutting off, and the grafting.
4. What warnings does Paul give to his Gentile readers 11:20-22? List them.
5. List several possible meanings for the following: and so all Israel will be saved when the Redeemer comes out of Zion.
6. Re-read the entire chapter at this point, listing in one column those virtues which are commended there (e.g., prayer v. 2), listing in the second column those vices which are condemned (e.g., murder v. 3), and listing in the third column the attributes of God which are described (e.g., faithfulness to His promises v. 1; foreknowledge v. 2). Give the Scripture verse with each entry. Be very complete.

Romans 12:1, 2

1. What is the therefore in 12:1 there for? To what does it refer?
2. What is the relationship between the section introduced by Romans 12:1,2 and Romans 1:18-ch. 11?
3. Why does Paul exhort Christian people to present their bodies when these same bodies already belong to God? See I Cor. 6:19,20; and Rom. 6:12-14,19.

4. List several ways in which the sacrifice of 12:1 differs from the sacrifices of Old Testament times.
5. If these two verses were all you had of the Word of God on the will of God, what would you know about the will of God? Begin each statement with the words "The will of God...."

Romans 12:3-21
1. List the things which Paul says here should characterize the Christian's relation to fellow members of the body of Christ, (verses 3-8)
2. List several ways in which the physical body is a good analogy of the Church, the Body of Christ. (They do not all need to be found here. See also I Corinthians 12.
3. In 12:9-21, Paul presents those things which should characterize the Christian's relationships with others. List at least 20 of them. (nouns, please.)
4. What is meant by the expression, heaping coals of fire upon the heads of one's enemies? Is this commanded? Give reasons for your answers.

Romans 13:1-7
1. List the God-ordained purposes of government rulers according to 13:1-7.
2. List the God-ordained obligations which the Christian has in relation to the government according to these verses. List other obligations of a contemporary sort which Christians should fulfill in relation to their   government officials.
3. Is obedience to one's government an absolute entity or one dependent upon the character of the government and/ or the kind of demands it makes on the individual citizen? Support your answer from Romans 13:1-7 and other Scripture references.
4. What does Paul mean by saying that the government has a right to bear the sword? How does this teaching line up with Matt. 5:39-48 and love for enemies?
5. What is the relation between this passage and the question of pacifism and the conscientious objector?

Romans 13:8-14
1. What is to be the Christian's relation to the law of God according to this   passage?
2. Are the ten commandments as such relevant for the Christian today? If so, give several reasons why you feel they are. If not, list several reasons why you think they are not.

3. List the things which characterize this present age according to Romans 13:11-14. Define each (nouns, please).
4. What is to be the Christian's relationship to this present age according to these verses? (Compare Romans 12:2 with this passage.)
5. What is the solution with regard to any trouble the Christian might have with this present age according to 13:14? How will this help him? Put this solution into your own words.

Romans 14:1-15:4
1. List the reasons Paul gives for showing love to a Christian brother, be he strong or weak. Give verses which support your reasons.
2. Identify what Paul means by the terminology, "a weak Christian" and "a strong Christian."
3. State several principles drawn from this section with which you think Paul would answer a Christian who asserts that he is going to live the Christian life as he himself pleases with no consideration for any other Christians' opinions.
4. Explain the last clause of chapter 14, for whatever is not out of faith is sin.
5. Is the following principle biblical? Explain your answer. "Certain actions may be right for a Christian under certain circumstances and wrong under other circumstances."

Romans 15:5-33
1. List the things which Paul tells the Roman Christians about himself in this section.
2. Discuss his immediate plans as stated; his remote plans.
3. What evidence is there in this section concerning misgivings on his part about his reception in Jerusalem?
4. Outline the steps in the life of Paul following this trip to Jerusalem. After some research, what points are there in favor of the fact that Paul "finished his course" and did succeed in preaching in Spain?

Romans 16:1-27
1. List several reasons why this long list of names of Roman Christians may have been added to this particular epistle.
2. With the use of Romans 16 and a Bible dictionary or encyclopedia, list all of the things known about Phoebe.
3. With a Bible dictionary as your source, list the things known about Priscilla and Aquila.

Conclusion

1. Summarize the argument of Romans in a paragraph of not more than 750 words. What is asked for here is the development of Paul's thought throughout the Roman epistle.
2. What about this study of Romans seems to indicate the necessity for a spiritual crisis experience subsequent to regeneration for most believers?
3. According to Paul in Romans, what plan does God have for you as a believer in Christ AFTER He saves you? Give chapters and verses to support your points.

About the Author

Dr. Wesley Gerig taught for 51 years at Fort Wayne Bible College, Summit Christian College and now Taylor University Fort Wayne (TUFW), retiring from full-time teaching in June 2008. Dr. Wes, as he was known around the campus, was Professor of Bible, Theology, and Biblical Languages. While teaching over just about every book of the Bible, Paul's Epistle to the Romans was one that Dr. Wes held close to his heart. For many of his teaching years, Romans was a class that every Fort Wayne Bible College graduate had to take and pass in order to receive their degree.

Besides teaching, Dr. Wes has also served many churches as interim pastor, offering biblical teaching and counsel during times of pastoral transition. He has also traveled the world, leading three trips to the Middle East, as well as lecturing in the Dominican Republic, Ecuador, Greece, Jamaica, Japan, the Philippines, Russia and Taiwan.

Dr. Wes and his late wife, Mary Carolyn served the Lord together for over 55 years and have four grown children and 12 grandchildren.

Acknowledgements–Second Printing

Dr. Wes has touched many lives with his study and teaching, yet we are also grateful for Mary Carolyn and her behind the scenes role she played. This book would not have been printed without Rev. Jeff and Jean Gerig, Dr. Wes and Mary Carolyn's son and daughter-in-law, pioneering this project with their encouragement and by typesetting the original manuscript.

Aimee Betsui, former employee of TUFW spent countless hours reviewing for typos and Lucinda Neff designed the cover in coordination with Dr. Wes. Thanks also go to several members of the Gerig family, Dr. Jay Platte, who prepared the manuscript for the second printing, and to Sherri Harter from Taylor University, who allocated funds for the initial printing costs.

Lastly, we thank those who purchased all of Romans from the first printing. We pray reading this book will bring back many precious memories, but more importantly that it will help you in your faith journey! Ultimately, we want to give thanks to God for what He has done through Jesus and His Word!

December, 2013
Michael D. Mortensen
Director of FW Alumni & Friend Relations
Fort Wayne Alumni & Friends Resource Center

CPSIA information can be obtained
at www.ICGtesting.com
Printed in the USA
LVHW080233130720
660499LV00018B/727